THE WESTERN SKETCH-BOOK.

BY

REV. JAMES GALLAHER.

BOSTON:
PUBLISHED BY CROCKER AND BREWSTER.
NEW YORK: M. W. DODD.
PHILADELPHIA: WILLIAM L. MARTIEN.
1850.

STEREOTYPED AT THE

BOSTON STEREOTYPE FOUNDRY.

PREFACE.

THE articles in the Western Sketch Book are mostly on religious subjects. It was not intended, however, that they should be exclusively so: some of the anecdotes are merely historical; yet it is hoped that they will convey to the reader valuable information.

In the sketches here furnished of "men and things," great regard has been had to accuracy and truth. The facts stated may be relied on as of the most authentic character. It was the settled purpose of the author, that as an historical record, this publication should occupy the highest ground. There are a few articles of an allegorical cast, given as professed extracts from ancient books which have long since been lost — "the Book of Ahijah the Shilonite," "the Book of Nathan the Prophet," "the Book of the Visions of Iddo the Seer," &c. The reader will, of course, understand that the giving of these articles as "extracts," is merely a part of that allegorical or figurative mode of representation which the author has chosen to employ.

The views on the subject of revivals of religion, which pervade this volume, are such as the author believes he has received from the Bible, and has had confirmed by an experience in the ministry of more than thirty-four years.

When describing scenes in which I myself have been concerned, I have used the pronoun in the first person singular. On this subject I fully agree with Dr. Dwight, former president of Yale College.

"Dr. Dwight," said an inquirer, "is it not better for a minister, when speaking of himself, to say 'we,' rather than 'I?'

"I think not," answered the doctor.

"But it avoids the appearance of *egotism.*"

"Ah, well," said Dr. Dwight, "I would rather have egotism than *wegotism.*"

CONTENTS.

1 *

THE WESTERN SKETCH-BOOK.

INTRODUCTION.

I STOOD on the bank of the Mississippi, and gazed upon the rush of its mighty stream. Wave pressed on wave; and the broad tide, with a force that no earthly power could withstand, swept onward to the ocean. "Great river!" I exclaimed, "hast thou rolled on thus from age to age? Hast thou maintained this majestic march through the lapse of more than fifty centuries? Then what is the history of this immense country on thy borders? What people gazed upon thy stream three thousand years ago? Were there then intellectual beings here, to adore that mighty God who dug thy deep channel, and spread out at thy side these broad, fertile plains, and covered thee with the bright blue heaven?" Such were the questions that arose in my mind; but there was none to answer. I looked back on the past history of the west. But, beyond the period of sixty or seventy years, there sets in a thick, impenetrable darkness — "even darkness which may be felt;" and all is, to us, buried in the gulf of hopeless oblivion. Events that transpired then, however interesting they may have been, are irrecoverably lost: no effort of ours can call them back, or secure for them a record on the pages of memory.

Another question arose: Will the man who stands

where I stand now, a hundred or a thousand years hence, experience the same desire to know the early history of the mighty west, of which I now am conscious? The answer is clear: He will. Then I am resolved to "gather up the fragments," not already lost, of the history of the west, and preserve them, —

> "That ages yet unborn may read,
> And trust and praise the Lord."

The west is, as yet, only an infant. But this infant possesses the elements of a fearful and stupendous growth. Ere long, the inhabitants of the world will open their eyes, and with astonishment behold a giant standing here. His height will be terrible, and his power such, that earth's foundations will bend beneath his footsteps; and at the lifting of his hand distant nations will tremble.

Yes, the teeming millions of a crowded population will soon spread over this wide and wonderful region. The banks of these long rivers will be studded with "cloud-capt towers and gorgeous palaces;" and religion, and education, and science, and cultivated society will be here, to an extent that earth has not witnessed in ages that are gone. In that day, the mighty population of the west will eagerly inquire after the early history of their country.

I have determined, therefore, to gather up the facts within the period of my own memory, and arrange them, and dedicate the record to the generations following. A larger work, entitled "The Early Religious History of the West," which the author has for years been preparing, is more particularly referred to, than the mere sketches contained in the present volume.

THE HONEY-BEE.

How strong is the propensity in man to honor the prophet that is dead, while he rejects the prophet that is living! Scribes, Pharisees, and Jewish rulers would build the sepulchres of Samuel, Isaiah, and Zachariah; but when Jesus Christ, the living Prophet, appeared, preaching the same truths, they cried out, "Away with him from the earth! Crucify him! crucify him!"

Men admire and eulogize those very attributes in the dead prophet which they cannot bear in the prophet that is living. Go to any revival-fighting Presbyterian minister in the west or south. He will expatiate with much enthusiasm on the preaching of John Knox, when such multitudes, in one generation, were turned from darkness to light. He will hastily search his library for a printed account of that remarkable sermon of Livingston, in Scotland, on the Monday of a sacramental meeting, under which five hundred souls were converted to God. He will speak, with great interest and earnestness, of the blessed results that followed the preaching of Samuel Davies in Virginia, and James Waddell, afterwards known far and wide as the *Blind Preacher* mentioned by Wirt in his "British Spy." These preachers and their hearers are gone from earth.

"Their hatred and their love is lost,
Their envy buried in the dust;
They have no share in all that's done
Beneath the circuit of the sun."

But speak to this same man of a revival in the present age. "Ah, there were sad indiscretions!" "animal excitement!" "spasmodic movements!" &c. That is it: build the sepulchre of the prophet that is dead, and scowl at the prophet that is living. Eulogize Elisha and Daniel, but stone Stephen to death, and crucify his Lord and Master.

In like manner, we are ready to acknowledge a providence of God toward those who are dead and gone, which we are slow to admit in reference to those now living. We can believe that God sent against Pharaoh "swarms of flies," armies of frogs, and legions of locusts. These were judgments from God. His hand was made bare. We see it at once, and confess it without difficulty; for these things took place above three thousand years ago. We can believe that God brought the quails around the camp of the Israelites as they journeyed through the wilderness, and that he sent hornets before them to drive out the Canaanite, the Hittite, and the Hivite, (Ex. xxiii. 28,) for these things, also, were done in a remote age of the world. But are we willing to believe that there are, at this hour, around the church and around the individual saint, the same careful, constant, almighty guardianship and direction that there were in the days of Moses, of Joseph, and of Abraham? Are we willing to believe that now the sparrow does not fall to the ground without the hand of God? and that the very hairs of our heads are all numbered? To such questions, many will give the practical answer, "*No!*"

This infidelity concerning the presence and providence of God in our own day, is the crying sin of the present age. The High and Holy One is the same from everlasting to everlasting. With him there is no "variableness, or shadow of turning." And had we an inspired account of what God is doing now in behalf of his redeemed people, we should find that for the good of each believer the hand of the Lord is stretched out still, and that his providence has all the divine minuteness and particularity, at this moment, which it possessed when Noah, Daniel, and Job stood before him.

Modern unbelief will scarcely scruple to admit that God may have controlled the affairs of this world long, long ago; but *now*, in this enlightened age, it is fanaticism to believe in a particular, all-directing providence. *Now*, all events are the sport of blind chance, contingency, accident.

I am about to state a well-authenticated fact in the early history of the western country. The honey-bee, with strict, constant, and invariable uniformity, goes in front of the Christian population, as the wave of emigration rolls westward. No one fact is more unquestionably established than this, in the experience and observation of frontier western men. Ten, twenty, thirty miles in advance of the white settlements, the honey-bee swarms in every forest, filling with delicious honey the hollows in the trees, and often the caverns, crevices, and openings in the rocks. Long has it been the custom, with those near our western border, to take their wagons, in the latter part of the summer, and go a few miles in advance of the population, and load them with honey. But go two hundred miles into the Indian country, and there has not been a honey-bee there in two thousand years—never, within the memory of the present race of Indians. The Indians regard the bee as the certain forerunner of the white men. The moment they find that the bee has penetrated their country, they begin to lament and wail — "The white man is coming! We must give up the country!"

I will state another fact. The quail follows the white man. Quails, by hundreds and by thousands, come flocking around the tent, the camp, or the cabin of the white man as he journeys west. But go one hundred miles into the Indian territory, no quail has ever been seen there since the red man occupied the country. How do you account for these facts? Let me ask, how do you account for the hornets going before the camp of Israel, to drive out the Canaanite, the Hittite, and the Hivite? How do you account for the quails coming round the camp of Israel in such quantities? In both cases we see the hand of God. "The church" was with Israel "in the wilderness," (Acts vii. 38,) and it was for the sake of the church those wonders were done. God now has a church among our western population. The ark of his covenant is there, and still his hand does wonders for Zion's sake.

As the above facts may appear strange to some of my readers, I wish here, somewhat at large, to "speak what I know, and testify what I have seen." My father lived, from my earliest recollection, within a few miles of the Tennessee River. South of this river, within the bounds of the state of Tennessee, was the Indian territory. It was a lovely and inviting country, but the Indians positively refused to sell it to the white people on any conditions. In this obstinate refusal they persisted for more than twenty years; and the wave of American emigration in that direction was checked, and stood, like the tide of Jordan in the days of Joshua, as if held back by an arm divine. At length the forerunner of the white man passed the barrier, and spread among the red people consternation far and wide. I remember the morning well, when my father's brother called at our dwelling and made the announcement, "The bees have crossed the Tennessee, and are spreading among the Indians, who are greatly alarmed, and believe that they must now give up their country." Few records have been preserved in the west of the events of that early day. I cannot, therefore, be exact as to dates. But this I remember well — that, shortly after the above announcement, the Indians left the country, and the beautiful land which they had held so long was covered with a numerous and enterprising white population.

Many years ago, I was informed, by what I then considered good authority, that when the bees first crossed the Ohio River, in the neighborhood of where Shawneetown now stands, the old Indian chiefs went through the woods wailing and lamenting, "The white man is coming! We must leave the place of our birth, the graves of our fathers, and go to the west! The white man is coming!"

I distinctly remember the narrative given at my father's fireside, by Andrew Jackson, while acting as one of the judges of our state, and some time before his election to the office of major-general of the militia of Tennessee. He told of that memorable mustering of the bees at Nashville, which has since been so carefully recorded in Hon. Judge Haywood's "History of Tennessee." The period was about the year 1800 or 1801. Nashville was then a very small village, just struggling into existence. On a certain day, swarms of bees began to collect in the garden of Judge McNary. Five swarms were there at once — presently, ten, twenty, thirty, forty, fifty. They clustered together on every shrub in the garden, then on the fence that surrounded it, banked up on each side of the fence, until barrels, hogsheads, and wagon-loads were there. The population became greatly excited. They apprehended that this phenomenon must be ominous, and multitudes came from far to witness it. But, so far as I know, it has remained without explanation, unless, indeed, the opinion prevalent among the pioneer population be taken as such; to wit, that this was the mustering of the armies of the honey-bee, preparatory to their sallying forth to take possession of the mighty plains of the great west; for as yet the white man had only taken possession of portions of Tennessee, Kentucky, and Ohio.

When the news reached the settlements of the Creole French, in Southern Missouri, that the honey-bee had appeared at Kaskaskia, in Illinois, a lady inquired of her neighbor, "Could we not send over and get a *pair of them*, and raise bees?"

An American female had reached St. Genevieve, on the west bank of the Mississippi, somewhat in advance of the emigrating multitude. She discovered a honey-bee dancing at the window of a house occupied by a family of Creole French. "Why, there's a bee," said she to the lady of the house. "Ah!" said the lady, "is that the thing that makes the honey? Well, could we not catch it, and tame it, and keep it?"

It was stated to me by an old citizen of Missouri, that when the first swarm of bees came to St. Louis, and settled, in a large mass, on some object in the town, several of the primitive population ran to procure straw and fire to burn them up, thinking that they were wasps, or hornets, or something in that line. But an American was providentially there, who remonstrated against giving to the strangers a reception so rude and inhospitable. He explained something of their nature and usefulness, and prevailed on some one to construct a hive, and allow the new comers a home in the then young metropolis of the mighty west.

About the month of August, in the year 1840, at Plattville, in Wisconsin, I met a Methodist missionary, named Cavanaugh, who had been for years employed among the Indians up near the mouth of the St. Peter's. He told me that the progress of the bees, moving as a "pillar of cloud" in front of the white settlements, was then an object of troubled apprehension and dread among the Indians where he labored. "Old Indian chiefs," said he, "will now ask, with trembling anxiety, 'How far have the bees got up the Mississippi?'" In the month of February, 1849, at Columbus, in Indiana, I met again this same brother Cavanaugh, and inquired, "How is it now with your Indians and the bees?" "Ah," said he, "the bees have reached those Indians now, and the white emigrant is close upon their trail."

The following passage is found in the "Report of the Exploring Expedition to the Rocky Mountains in the Year 1842, by Captain J. C. Fremont," p. 69: "Here, on the summit, where the stillness was absolute, unbroken by any sound, and the solitude complete, we thought ourselves beyond the regions of animated life; but while we were sitting on the rock, a solitary bee came winging his flight from the eastern valley and lit on the knee of one of the men. We pleased ourselves with the idea that he was the first of his species to cross the mountain barrier — a solitary pioneer to foretell the advance of civilization."

Gregg in his "Commerce of the Prairies," p. 178, vol. i., says, "The honey-bee appears to have emigrated exclusively from the east, as its march has been observed westward. But none have yet reached this portion of the western dominion." And at p. 206, vol. ii., he says, "The bee, among western pioneers, is the proverbial precursor of the Anglo-American population. In fact, the aborigines of the frontier have generally corroborated this notion, for they used to say they knew the white man was not far behind when the bees appeared among them."

Many other interesting specifications might be given, but my design is not to extend this article beyond a reasonable limit. Enough has been said to show that this notable fact in the history of western emigration is a clear manifestation of the hand of God. And not only so, but it is a dispensation of great kindness to his people, many of whom are found among the frontier emigrants. I have seen very pious people sending out their children to collect this honey and the honeycomb. The comb yielded the beeswax, a valuable commodity. The honey also was an important article in the commerce of the country. The western rivers bore these articles to New Orleans, where they were sold or exchanged for the benefit of the families in the frontier settlements. Many households were thus made comfortable, who, without such a provision in divine providence, must have felt the pinchings of want. Often has the western minister expatiated on these themes. Often has he reminded the people that Jehovah is a covenant-keeping God, that he "keepeth covenant and mercy with them that love him, to a thousand generations;" that the temporal as well as the spiritual wants of his people are the objects of his care. And as he scattered the manna over the face of the wilderness before his ancient church, so now he is mindful of his covenant. He giveth bread to the hungry, and the redeemed of the Lord have abundant reason to say that his mercy endureth forever.

There are persons now living in Illinois, in Missouri, in Iowa, and in Wisconsin, who arrived there before there was a quail in all that country. But soon after the Anglo-Americans had pitched their tents in the land, the quails came around them by thousands and by tens of thousands. Why is this? From whence do they originate? It is the hand of God. I will mention one great purpose that is answered by the quail. It strikes dumb the lips of pride. He who wishes not to see the hand of God, will say the bees that go before the wave of American population proceed from domesticated bees among the settlers, although the vastness of their multitude, and notable facts like that at Nashville, utterly refute the theory. But where the sceptic can find even the shadow of an argument against the hand of God, he will, like Pharaoh of old, harden his heart. But ask him, "From whence come the quails? From domesticated quails? He is dumb. The fact is, you cannot tame a quail. At least, I have known some very thorough experiments, which resulted in total failure, and believe that the quail is generally regarded as incapable of domestication. Should any one say the quails feed on the farmer's grain, — his corn and his wheat, — and therefore they follow the American emigrants, I answer, that this does not touch the mystery; because the prairie hen, or American grouse, the wild goose, and the crane, are just as fond of corn as the quails — perhaps more so. But these birds are all over the face of the wilderness, and live independent of the cultivated fields of the white man. Yet when the farmer comes near their wild abode, and ploughs up the earth, and produces his crop of corn, you will see the prairie hen, the wild goose, the crane, clustering around the corn stacks, and manifesting far more greediness for grain than you ever see exhibited by the quail. The mystery is not touched. Whence comes the quail?

Ascertain from whence the hornets came, that went before the standard of Israel; ascertain from whence the quails came, that fell around their camp; and then you will have no difficulty in understanding the phenomena that now precede and accompany the standard of Zion, as she lengthens her cords and enlarges her boundaries. God's church is in that moving multitude which is pressing westward. The ark of his covenant is there. And now, as in ancient times, his church is "engraven on the palms of his hands." You can account for the above-mentioned facts, just as you account for the sea giving up its dead at the sound of the last trumpet. It is the hand of God.

THE GREAT WESTERN REVIVAL

OF 1800.

WHOEVER has carefully examined the history of Israel, as detailed in the sacred oracles, may have remarked, that very often the prophets endeavored to recall to the minds of that people the period and the scenes of their first espousal to God. Indeed, there is no narrative more calculated to wake up in our own heart the living emotions of religion, than the story of our first saving acquaintance with Christ. It is profitable to the individual, to the family, and to the church at large, that these manifestations of God's power and mercy should be told to children, and to children's children.

In relation to this matter, I have often thought that the church of God in the *west* has reason to adopt the language of the Psalmist, "Come and hear, all ye that fear God, and I will declare what he hath done for my soul." "He brought me up out of a horrible pit, out of the miry clay, and set my feet upon a rock, and established my goings. And he hath put a new song in my mouth, even praise unto our God: many shall see it and fear, and shall trust in the Lord."

It is now my purpose to sketch some of the scenes in the early history of the church of God in the west. Before the close of the revolutionary war, large bodies of emigrants had settled in Tennessee and in Kentucky.

Many of them were from Virginia, many were from Pennsylvania, and many also were from North and South Carolina. Quite a large number of these were religious men. Extensive and powerful revivals of religion had been granted to the American churches, while we were yet colonies of Great Britain. In New England, Edwards, Bellamy, and their fellows, were the favored instruments. In New Jersey, Gilbert and William Tennant, and their contemporaries, were greatly blessed. In Virginia, Samuel Davies, whose sermons have since been so widely circulated, and James Waddell, labored with immense success. Among my earliest recollections are the glowing descriptions which old persons, then living in my father's neighborhood, would give of the preaching of this James Waddell. There was a kindling animation in the aged countenance, and their eyes would fill with tears, at the mention of his name. He is the Blind Preacher so eloquently described by Hon. William Wirt in his "British Spy." When Wirt saw him, he was old, and frail, and blind; yet evidently the wreck of a superior man. Long before this period, he had been a messenger of mercy to multitudes of the perishing; and the gospel, through his instrumentality, had been to many glad tidings of great joy. It should be mentioned further, that in the Carolinas also, and in Georgia, the gospel, at this time, had made great progress. Georgia was one of the first points in America where George Whitefield preached; and from thence to the most northern colony he found the fields white to the harvest. Indeed, there were such religious prospects in our country before the revolution, that Jonathan Edwards entertained and published the opinion that the millennium, or latter day glory, would first shed its light on the souls of men in America.

Now, such was the condition of the American church, when that wave of population, which had risen on the sea-shore, and rolled abroad over the Atlantic regions, began to ripple over the comb of the Alleghany, and rush down and spread itself over the fertile plains of the west. Many of the first emigrants from Pennsylvania, Virginia, and the Carolinas, carried their religion with them. And it seems that, at that early period, religion could better "bear transportation," than at a later day.

War has almost invariably a demoralizing tendency; and the war of our revolution, however necessary and important in its connection, was not exempt from this unhappy concomitant. But, perhaps, in no other part of our country were the sad results of war realized, at that time, to the same extent as in the new settlements of the west. There the supply of Bibles and pastors was limited. Religious privileges were few. And many of the population were as sheep having no shepherd. There was less, therefore, to counteract the evils incident to war than in other sections of our land.

Above all this, it must be observed, that when peace was concluded with Great Britain in the year 1783, and other citizens could return to the pursuits of peaceful life, and the enjoyment of gospel ordinances, the frontier population of the west were embroiled with hostile Indians for the space of half a generation. During this period of fierce conflict between the white and the red man, those Indian tribes that hung around our western border produced not a few "men of renown."

Headed by some of these daring chiefs, a strong band of Indians would make a sudden incursion into the white settlements, and murder, burn, rob, and perpetrate cruelty in the most frightful and barbarous forms. The scalping-knife was red with the blood of the mother, the tomahawk was buried in the brain of the helpless child! Until, terrified with the apprehension of the vengeance they had provoked, the Indians would fly with the utmost precipitation. Then, for ten or fifteen miles around, the white population was aroused, and the Indians were pursued not only with retaliating, but with exterminating vengeance. Who will wonder, that, when seventeen years of such life as this came right in after the seven years of the revolutionary war, the Sabbath and sacred things were in a great measure forgotten or trodden down? A generation sprang up, in which dexterity and prowess in Indian warfare were the great objects of ambition, and, indeed, the high road to fame. And in the mean while, the light of religion, carried to the west at the time of its first settlement, surrounded long by adverse influences, shone but faintly, while iniquity abounded and waxed bold.

It is necessary here to pause and notice the state of things in Europe at this period. Our country, when young, was far more influenced by Europe than she is now. The year 1728 is memorable as the great era of infidelity in Europe. Voltaire formed, about this period, his great plan for destroying the Christian religion. I quote the language of Dr. Dwight, of Yale College. This eminent writer observes that Voltaire, for the purpose of blotting out Christianity, "engaged, at several succeeding periods, a number of men, distinguished for power, talents, reputation, and influence —

all deadly enemies to the gospel, atheists, men of profligate principles and profligate lives. This design he pursued with unabated zeal fifty years; and was seconded by his associates with an ardor and industry scarcely inferior to his own. In consequence of their united labors, and of the labors of others, from time to time combined with them, they ultimately spread the design throughout a great part of Europe; and embarked in it individuals, at little distances, over almost the whole of that continent. Their adherents inserted themselves into every place, office, and employment, in which their agency might become efficacious, and which furnished an opportunity of spreading their corruptions. They were found in every literary institution, from the abecedarian school to the academy of sciences; and in every civil office, from that of the bailiff to that of the monarch. They swarmed in the palace; they haunted the church. Wherever mischief could be done, they were found; and wherever they were found, mischief was extensively done. Of books they controlled the publication, the sale, and the character. An immense number they formed; an immense number they forged; prefixed to them the names of reputable writers, and sent them into the world, to be sold for a song; and when that could not be done, to be given away. Within a period shorter than could have been imagined, they possessed themselves, to a great extent, of a control, nearly absolute, of the literary, religious, and political state of Europe.

"With these advantages in their hands, it will easily be believed, that they left no instrument unemployed, and no measure untried, to accomplish their own malignant purposes. With a diligence, courage, constancy, activity, and perseverance, which might rival the efforts of demons themselves, they penetrated into every corner of human society. Scarcely a man, woman, or child was left unassailed, wherever there was a single hope that the attack might be successful. Books were written and published, in innumerable multitudes, in which infidelity was brought down to the level of peasants, and even of children, and poured with immense assiduity into the cottage and the school. Others, of a superior kind, crept into the shop and the farm-house; and others, of a still higher class, found their way to the drawing-room, the university, and the palace. The business of all men who were of any importance, and the education of the children of all such men, were, as far as possible, engrossed, or at least influenced, by these banditti of the moral world; and the hearts of those who had no importance but in their numbers and physical strength. A sensual, profligate nobility, and princes, if possible, still more sensual and profligate, easily yielded themselves and their children into the hands of these minions of corruption. Too ignorant, too enervated, or too indolent, to understand, or even to inquire that they might understand, the tendency of all these efforts, they marched quietly on to the gulf of ruin, which was already open to receive them. With these was combined a priesthood, which, in all its dignified ranks, was still more putrid; and which eagerly yielded up the surplice and the lawn, the desk and the altar, to destroy that Bible which they had vowed to defend as well as to preach, and to renew the crucifixion of that Redeemer whom they had sworn to worship. By these agents, and these efforts, the plague was spread with rapidity, and to an extent which astonished heaven and earth; and life went out, not in solitary cases, but by a universal extinction.

"While these measures were thus going on, with a success scarcely interrupted, Dr. Adam Weishaupt, professor of the canon law in the university of Ingoldstadt, a city of Bavaria, a man of no contemptible talents, but of immense turpitude, and a Jesuit, established the society of Illuminees. Into this establishment he brought all the systematized iniquity of his brotherhood — distinguished beyond every other class of men for cunning, mischief, an absolute destitution of conscience, an absolute disregard of all the interests of man, and a torpid insensibility to moral obligation. No fraternity, for so long a time, or to so great an extent, united within its pale such a mass of talents, or employed in its service such a succession of vigorous efforts. The serpentine system of this order Weishaupt perfectly understood. The great design of the Jesuits had always been to engross the power and influence of Europe, and to regulate all its important affairs. The system of measures which they had adopted for this end, was superior to every preceding scheme of human policy. To this design Weishaupt, who was more absolutely an atheist than Voltaire, and as cordially wished for the ruin of Christianity, superadded a general intention of destroying the moral character of man. The system of policy adopted by the Jesuits was, therefore, exactly fitted to his purpose; for the design, with this superaddition, was exactly the same.

"With these advantageous preparations, he boldly undertook this work of destruction, and laid the axe at the root of all moral principle, and the sense of all moral obligation, by establishing a few fundamental doctrines, which were amply sufficient for this purpose. These were, that God is nothing; that government is a curse, and authority a usurpation; that civil society is the only apostasy of man; that the possession of property is robbery; that chastity and natural affection are mere prejudices; and that adultery, assassination, poisoning, and other crimes of a similar nature, are lawful, and even virtuous. Under these circumstances were founded the societies of Illuminism. They spread, of course, with a rapidity which nothing but fact could have induced any sober mind to believe. Before the year 1786, they were established in great numbers throughout Germany, in Sweden, Russia, Poland, Austria, Holland, France, Switzerland, Italy, England, Scotland, and even in America. In all these was taught the grand and sweeping principle of corruption, that the end sanctions the means — a principle which, if every where adopted, would overturn the universe.

"The design of the founder and his coadjutors was nothing less than to engross the empire of the world, and to place mankind beneath the feet of himself and his successors.

"Voltaire died in the year following the establishment of Illuminism. His disciples, with one heart and one voice, united in its interests, and, finding a more absolute system of corruption than themselves had been able to form, entered eagerly into all its plans and purposes. Thenceforward, therefore, all the legions of infidelity are to be considered as embarked in a single bottom; and as cruising together against order, peace, and virtue, on a voyage of rapine and blood.

"The French revolution burst upon mankind at this moment. Here was opened an ample field for the labors of these abandoned men in the work of pollution and death. There is no small reason to believe, that every individual Illuminee, and almost, if not quite, every infidel, on the continent of Europe, lent his labors when he could—and his wishes when he could not—for the advancement of the sins and the miseries which attended this unexampled corruption. Had not God taken the wise in their own craftiness, and caused the wicked to fall into the pit which they digged, and into the snares which their hands had set, it is impossible to conjecture the extent to which they would have carried their devastation of human happiness. But, like the profligate rulers of Israel, those who succeeded regularly destroyed their predecessors.

"Between ninety and one hundred of those who were leaders in this mighty work of destruction, fell by the hand of violence. Enemies to all men, they were, of course, enemies to each other. Butchers of the human race, they soon whetted the knife for each other's throats; and the tremendous Being who rules the universe, whose existence they had denied in a solemn act of legislation, whose perfections they had made the butt of public scorn and private insult, whose Son they had crucified afresh, and whose word they had burnt by the hands of the common hangman, swept them all, by the hand of violence, into an untimely grave. The tale made every ear which heard it tingle, and every heart chill with horror. It was, in the language of Ossian, "the song of death." It was like the reign of the plague in a populous city. Knell tolled upon knell; hearse followed hearse; and coffin rumbled after coffin; without a mourner to shed a tear upon the corpse, or a solitary attendant to mark the place of the grave. From one new moon to another, and from one Sabbath to another, the world went forth, and looked after the carcasses of the men who transgressed against God; and they were an abhorring unto all flesh."

Our revolutionary war closed about the time when this French infidelity was at its height, and before its frightful results had been fully disclosed.

The government of France had taken part with us in our struggle against England. The noble-hearted Lafayette had embarked in our cause with a generous enthusiasm that deeply affected the American people. Other distinguished Frenchmen had been our friends. Now, it was at this juncture, when we were disposed to give the warmest welcome to whatever came from France, that a deep, dark tide of that horrible infidelity ploughed its way, like the Gulf Stream through the Atlantic, and heaved its huge surges on the American shore. The valleys were flooded; the swelling waves rose and buried the hills; upward the awful deluge prevailed, and rolled its black billows above the tops of the tallest mountains. In the new settlements of the west the desolation was dreadful. There were few that escaped the deadly inundation. So rare were religious privileges, that it was extremely difficult to find materials sufficient to construct an ark, in which one entire family might be saved. It was proclaimed over all the land, that France — enlightened, scientific, fashionable France — had renounced the gospel, had burned the Bible in the streets of Paris by the hands of the common hangman, and had inscribed in broad characters, over the entrance into the common burying-ground, that "death is an eternal sleep."

And moreover it was confidently asserted, by those who had opportunity to know, that Thomas Jefferson, regarded in the west as a great political luminary, had rejected the gospel, and adopted the infidelity of France; that most of our enlightened statesmen were following his example. Jefferson, as a politician, had, at that period, immense popularity; and the influence of his name, when in unison with the downward current of depravity, was mighty.

Such was the attitude of the west, in relation to religion and religious privileges, from the year 1783 till 1800 — harassed by almost incessant Indian wars, impelled in the broad road by the folly and wickedness bound up in its own heart, and bewitched and bewildered by the abominable example of those whose names possessed fascination, because they were inscribed on the rolls of fame.

In the midst of this period of spiritual darkness, Paine's "Age of Reason" came forth. Paine was favorably known to the American people as a political writer during the conflict of the revolution. His works entitled "Common Sense," and "The Rights of Man," had secured for him a wide-spread reputation. And in the minds of the multitude, he was closely identified with the cause of American freedom. Rarely, in his assaults on the church of God, has that "arch-angel ruined," whose name is called Apollyon, been able to occupy such vantage-ground. The appeal to the American people was this: "You have thrown off allegiance to the British king; now throw off the yoke of superstition, and be freemen indeed." Paine scoffed at all that was sacred in religion — profanely mocked and blasphemed the ordinances of God. O, it was a tremendous eruption of the bottomless pit! The shock had well nigh thrown down the hope of the church. The smoke that ascended filled all the air with blackness, and eclipsed the sun; while ashes, cinders, and lava came down, threatening to bury every vestige of good that yet remained in society.

In a letter to the editors of "The New York Magazine," the venerable Gideon Blackburn says, "About the years '98 and '99, the darkness was thick, like that in Egypt, — a darkness which might 'be felt.' The few pious in the land were ready to cry out, 'Has God forgotten to be gracious? Are his mercies clean gone? Will he be favorable no more?'"

About this period, pious men in the west began to call on the name of the Lord with that earnestness and importunity which takes no denial. In Logan county, Kentucky, Rev. James McGready and some Christian people appointed seasons of special prayer. They also set apart days of fasting and humiliation before God.

The great revival of 1800, like that granted to the disciples on the day of Pentecost, was preceded by a season of deep humiliation and earnest prayer to God.

THE REVIVAL.

The first conclusive proofs that the Lord had heard prayer, and visited his people, were received in Logan county, Kentucky. The work began "at the house of God." It was according to the prayer of the Psalmist: "Restore unto me the joys of thy salvation, and uphold me with thy free spirit; *then* will I teach transgressors thy ways, and sinners shall be converted unto thee." The people of God were brought near to him. The preaching of the gospel and the ordinances of the Lord's house were to them the bread and the water of life. And while they admired the freeness, the fulness, and the firmness of God's covenant mercy, the very dust and ruins of Zion were precious in their eyes, and believing prayer in her behalf went up as a "cloud of incense" before God. Presently an awful solemnity took hold of the public mind. Persons hitherto careless flocked, in great numbers, to the place of worship. The power of preaching was greatly increased. God was "fearful in his praises." And in prayer, Christians were enabled to "come boldly to a throne of grace."

I design to give, presently, Dr. Baxter's account of these seasons, written at the time; but first I wish to lay before the reader some particulars which are imprinted on my own memory, and have remained most distinct and clear, through all the years that have intervened. The "little cloud" which had begun to pour out its blessing on the churches in Logan county, Kentucky, soon spread, like that in Elijah's day, until it covered the face of heaven. My father's residence was then in East Tennessee, some two hundred and fifty miles distant from the point where the revival first appeared; but brief was the time that elapsed until it was in the midst of our population.

1. A deep solemnity pervaded the entire community, filling the minds of old and young with awe and reverence in view of God and his holy gospel. I remember, with a distinctness that is marvellous to myself, the unparalleled impression in our neighbor-

hood. We had assembled in the house of worship. Each man and woman seemed to realize the sentiment of the patriarch, "Surely the Lord is in this place." Rev. Mr. Dobbins, then of North Carolina, afterwards well known in Ohio, preached a sermon. The attention was profound. During the sermon, two young men of respectable families, well known in the congregation, began to tremble in their seats; they were perfectly silent, but their trembling was visible to all that were in the house; the people felt that the great Master of assemblies was among them. They knew that this was that mighty power of God, of which they had heard among the churches in Kentucky. How much a young mind may have erred in its estimate, I cannot say. But it then seemed to me, that the appearance of the forerunner of the final Judge, approaching our earth with the trump of God, could scarcely have added to the awfulness of the solemnity. Stout, stubborn sinners, who before had blasphemed God and scoffed at sacred things, were struck down as literally as Saul of Tarsus, on his way to Damascus. But this brings me to another branch of the subject; that is, —

2. The FALLING DOWN. This was one of the forms of that *bodily exercise*, as it was then called, which accompanied this remarkable work. It must be borne in mind that the country had been overrun by a bold, blaspheming infidelity, which scowled at sacred things, and attempted to browbeat and bear down all that was called by the name of the Lord Jesus. Thomas Moffit, Esq., now of Springfield, Illinois, assured me, that in the part of Kentucky where his people then lived, "it was believed that, at the commencement of

the year 1800, at least one half of the men and women were the avowed disciples of Thomas Paine." I mentioned this statement to the aged and venerable Abraham McElroy, of Northern Missouri. His reply was this: "Say not one half; say *nine tenths;* for thus it was in the region of Lebanon, Kentucky, where I then resided; and I myself was among the number."

Such is a sample of western society at the commencement of that revival. The awful solemnity which now arrested the public mind was accompanied with bodily affections as notable and singular as those of Saul on his way to Damascus. Bold, brazen-fronted blasphemers were literally cut down by the "sword of the Spirit." "The word of God was quick and powerful, and sharper than any two-edged sword, piercing even to the dividing asunder of the soul and spirit, and of the joints and marrow." Under the preaching of the gospel, men would drop to the ground, as suddenly as if they had been smitten by the lightning of heaven. Among these were many persons in the prime of life — strong men; business men; men whom no human being ever thought of charging with enthusiasm. Here was the avowed infidel, prostrate on the ground, confessing and lamenting his folly before God. There was the notorious profligate, crying for mercy. Here was the celebrated frontier warrior, famous for his dexterity and prowess during the Indian troubles; and now, "behold, he prayeth!" And there was the humbled politician, seeking an inheritance more durable than earthly fame. The language employed at that time, by the plain western people, in describing the results of these meetings, was, that so many "fell." At one meeting, "fifty fell;" at another, "seventy-five;" again, at another, "one hundred and twenty fell." Dr. Baxter speaks of a meeting, at which many thousands attended, where "three hundred fell." He mentions another at which "five hundred fell." At the great meeting at "Cane-ridge," which continued for six days, and at which it was believed there were twenty thousand people, it was said that not less than "one thousand fell." Those who fell would generally lie perfectly quiet for a considerable time; in some instances, an hour; in some, much longer; in others, not so long. There were cases, though of comparatively rare occurrence, in which persons lay for the space of twelve or twenty-four hours.

From their own statements, I learned that those who lay in that quiet state were entirely sensible of all that was passing around them, while, at the same time, their views on divine subjects were wonderfully clear and impressive. Their minds were directed to the holiness and grandeur of God; the purity and sacredness of his law; the guilt and hatefulness of sin; the great love of God in giving his Son to redeem lost man; the beauty and glory of Christ as Mediator; the worth of the soul; the preciousness of the gospel; the value of time; the brevity of life; the solemnity of death, of judgment, and of eternity.

Christ, the divine Savior, was exalted and extolled in the preaching, the praying, and the praising of the church, in that day. Perhaps I cannot better present this feature of that work, than by inserting a popular hymn, then in very general use, which was a favorite with many thousands. O, the multitude of voices, now silent in death, which once sent up these strains to the praise of the blessed God!

"Thy mercy, my God, is the theme of my song,
The joy of my heart, and the boast of my tongue:
Thy free grace alone, from the first to the last,
Hath won my affection, and bound my soul fast.

"Without thy sweet mercy, I could not live here;
Sin soon would reduce me to utter despair;
But through thy free goodness my spirits revive,
And He that first made me still keeps me alive.

"Thy mercy is more than a match for my heart,
Which wonders to feel its own hardness depart.
Dissolved by thy goodness, I fall to the ground,
And weep to the praise of the mercy I've found.

"The door of thy mercy stands open all day
To the poor and the needy, who knock by the way;
No sinner shall ever be empty sent back,
Who comes seeking mercy for Jesus's sake.

"Thy mercy in Jesus exempts me from hell;
Its glories I'll sing, and its wonders I'll tell:
'Twas Jesus, my Friend, when he hung on the tree,
Who opened the channel of mercy for me.

"Great Father of mercies, thy goodness I own,
And the covenant love of thy crucified Son:
All praise to the Spirit, whose witness divine
Seals mercy, and pardon, and righteousness mine."

3. A spirit of prayer was granted to these converts that was truly marvellous. Men who had never before prayed in public, and from the careless tenor of whose lives it might be fairly inferred that they had rarely, if ever, prayed in secret, would now pour forth their supplications with a liberty and a propriety of expression that utterly astonished their former acquaintances.

They would quote Scripture, in their addresses to the Deity, with a pertinence and an accuracy that could only be accounted for on the principle that "their hearts were lifted up in the ways of the Lord," and that all the powers of their mind were quickened by the divine Spirit. The compass of their petitions, and the force of their language, were wonderful. This extraordinary gift in prayer evidently accompanied that bodily exercise. Even children but five or six years old had this power in prayer, and those clear, affecting views of divine truth, when they were the subjects of that singular dispensation. A worthy Presbyterian elder, now a citizen, of Springfield, mentioned to me the case of a little girl, at the meeting at Caneridge: her exact age he did not know, but she was so small that her father carried her about in his arms. She spoke of Christ in a manner that melted down all who heard her. She talked of his everlasting love, that brought him to earth to save lost men; the deep sorrows he bore for our sakes. She spoke of the scenes in Gethsemane and on Calvary, the grave in which Christ was laid, his resurrection, his ascension, his intercession, and the solemnities of his second coming. Careless and hard-hearted sinners gathered around, some of them old in sin, some who had been avowed unbelievers; but all within the hearing of her voice were overcome and brought to tears by the affecting truths which she uttered.

I wish to record another fact. Of the professors of religion who were in the country when this revival began, perhaps one half became the subjects of this bodily exercise; that is, they either fell, or were affected in some other way. These were invariably ***baptized*** *with that spirit* of prayer. In many cases, the bodily exercise did not continue long. But that marvellous power of prayer was lasting as life. I could mention names in abundance to substantiate this fact. I commenced preaching on the 15th of December, 1815. I lived and labored in the ministry until 1830, on the ground where this work had prevailed with power and great glory. The meridian splendor of this revival was from the year 1800 to 1805, though it continued, in many places, for several years longer. Now, I can name men, with whom I was well acquainted during the first fifteen years of my ministry, — which reaches a period thirty years distant from the commencement of this wonderful work of God, — men of humble pretensions, ordinary capacity and acquirements, who had been church members before, but were now blessed in this revival, who, when they engaged in prayer, would at once rise above and beyond themselves; yes, above and beyond all that I ever heard, whether elder, deacon, or minister, who had not been baptized with the spirit and power of that memorable divine visitation. And I state this, while I tell the reader that I was not myself a subject of that great work. My father, my mother, and my eldest sister were; but I never had any hope of conversion during that season of mercy. Yet its leading facts are indelibly imprinted on the tablet of my memory; and when I speak of it, "I speak what I know, and testify what I have seen." One fact more. This extraordinary power in prayer continued with those persons through their life. Many of them are now gone. Some, however, continue to this day. And the man who has been acquainted with that *strain* or *manner of prayer*, will know it in a moment, whenever or wherever he may have the opportunity to hear it again.

The God of the Bible is the God of providence. And there is often an affecting analogy between facts which we now observe, and notable facts in the early history of the church, as recorded in the sacred book. When Moses came down from Mount Sinai, after that wonderful interview with God, his face shined in a manner that was marvellous, and it continued thus to shine till the day of his death. I have thought of this, when meditating on the unquestionable fact, that those who were brought so near to God in this great revival of 1800, and had granted to them such clear vision of Jehovah's holy character, and of that Mediator whose name is "Wonderful," and whose death purchased redemption for men, had a striking peculiarity instamped on their prayers, which continued through all the remaining part of their earthly pilgrimage.

The following letter from Dr. Baxter, written at that day, is exceedingly valuable. I give it to the reader, as it contains a picture of the times drawn by the hand of a master. Through the entire prime of his life, the writer ranked among the very first ministers in the Presbyterian church. For many years, he was president of Washington College, at Lexington; and at the time of his death, he was professor of theology in the Union Theological Seminary, Virginia.

Letter from the Rev. George Baxter to the Rev. A. Alexander, dated Washington Academy, Virginia, January 1, 1802.

"Rev. and Dear Sir, —

"I now sit down, agreeably to promise, to give you some account of the revival of religion in the state of Kentucky. You have, no doubt, heard already of the Green River and Cumberland revivals. I will just observe, that the last summer is the fourth since the revival commenced in those places; and that it has been more remarkable than any of the preceding, not only for lively and fervent devotion among Christians, but also for awakenings and conversions among the careless; and it is worthy of notice, that very few instances of apostasy have hitherto appeared. As I was not myself in the Cumberland country, all I can say about it is from the testimony of others; but I was uniformly told by those who had been there, that their religious assemblies were more solemn, and the appearance of the work much greater, than what had been in Kentucky: any enthusiastic symptoms which might at first have attended the revival had greatly subsided, whilst the serious concern and engagedness of the people were visibly increased.

"In the older settlement of Kentucky, the revival made its first appearance among the Presbyterians, last spring. The whole of that country, about a year before, was remarkable for vice and dissipation; and I have been credibly informed that a decided majority of the people were professed infidels.

"During the last winter, appearances were favorable among Baptists, and great numbers were added to their churches. Early in the spring, the ministrations of the Presbyterian clergy began to be better attended than they had been for many years before; their worshipping assemblies became more solemn; and the people, after they were dismissed, showed a strange reluctance at leaving the place: they generally continued some time in the meeting-houses, in singing or in religious conversation.

"Perhaps about the last of May or the first of June, the awakening became general, in some congregations, and spread through the country in every direction, with amazing rapidity. I left that country about the first of November, at which time this revival, in connection with the one in Cumberland, had covered the whole state, excepting a small settlement which borders on the waters of Green River, in which no Presbyterian ministers are settled, and I believe very few of any denomination. The power with which this revival has spread, and its influence in moralizing the people, are difficult for you to conceive, and more difficult for me to describe. I had heard many accounts, and seen many letters, respecting it, before I went to that country; but my expectations, though greatly raised, were much below the reality of the work.

"The congregations, when engaged in worship, presented scenes of solemnity superior to what I had ever seen before; and in private houses it was no uncommon thing to hear parents relate to strangers the wonderful things which God had done in their neighborhoods, whilst a large circle of young people would be in tears. On my way to Kentucky, I was told by settlers on the road, that the character of Kentucky travellers was entirely changed, and that they were now as distinguished for sobriety as they had formerly been for dissoluteness; and, indeed, I found Kentucky the most moral place I had ever been in: a profane expression was hardly heard, a religious one seemed to pervade the country, and some deistical characters had confessed that, from whatever cause the revival might originate, it certainly made the people better.

"Its influence was not less visible in promoting a

friendly temper: nothing could appear more amiable than that undissembled benevolence which governs the subjects of this work. I have often wished that the mere politician or Deist could observe with impartiality their peaceful and amicable spirit. He would certainly see that nothing could equal the religion of Jesus for promoting even the temporal happiness of society. Some neighborhoods, visited by the revival, had been formerly notorious for private animosities; and many petty lawsuits had commenced on that ground. When the parties in these quarrels were impressed with religion, the first thing was to send for their antagonists; and it was often very affecting to see their meeting: both had seen their faults, and both contended that they ought to make concessions; till at last they were obliged to request each other to forbear all mention of the past, and to act as friends and brothers for the future.

"Now, sir, let modern philosophists talk of reforming the world by banishing Christianity, and introducing their licentious systems; the blessed gospel of our God and Savior is showing what it can do. Some circumstances have concurred to distinguish the Kentucky revival from most others of which we have had any account; I mean the largeness of the assemblies on sacramental occasions, the length of time they continued on the ground in devotional exercises, and the great numbers who have fallen down under religious impressions. On each of these particulars I shall make some remarks.

"With respect to the largeness of the assemblies: It is generally supposed that at many places there were not fewer than eight, ten, or twelve thousand people.

4 *

At a place called Caneridge meeting-house, many were of opinion there were, at least, twenty thousand: there were one hundred and forty wagons which came loaded with people, besides other wheel carriages: some persons had come two hundred miles; the largeness of these assemblies was an inconvenience; they were too numerous to be addressed by one speaker; it therefore became necessary for several ministers to officiate at different stands: this afforded an opportunity to those who were but slightly impressed with religion to wander to and fro between the different places of worship, which created an appearance of confusion, and gave ground to such as were unfriendly to the work to charge it with disorder. Another cause, also, conduced to the same effect. About this time, the people began to fall down in great numbers under serious impressions; this was a new thing among Presbyterians: it excited universal astonishment, and created a curiosity which could not be restrained. When people fell, even during the most solemn part of divine service, those who stood near were so extremely anxious to see how they were affected, that they often crowded about them so as to disturb the worship. But these causes of disorder were soon removed; different sacraments were appointed on the same Sabbath, which divided the people; and the falling down became so familiar as to excite no disturbance. In October, I attended three sacraments: at each there were supposed to be between four and five thousand people, and every thing was conducted with strict propriety. When persons fell, those who were near them took care of them, and every one continued quiet until the worship was concluded.

"The length of time that people continue at the places of worship, is another important circumstance of the Kentucky revival. At Caneridge, they met on Friday, and continued till Wednesday evening, night and day, without intermission, either in the public or private exercises of devotion; and with such earnestness that heavy showers of rain were not sufficient to disperse them. On other sacramental occasions, they generally continued on the ground until Monday or Tuesday evening; and had not the preachers been exhausted and obliged to retire, or had they chosen to prolong the worship, they might have kept the people any length of time they pleased; and all this was, or might have been done, in a country where, less than twelve months before, the clergy found it difficult to detain the people during the usual exercises of the Sabbath. The practice of encamping on the ground was introduced, partly by necessity, and partly by inclination. The assemblies were generally too large to be received by any common neighborhood. Every thing, indeed, was done, which hospitality and brotherly kindness could do, to accommodate the people. Public and private houses were opened, and free invitations given to all persons who wished to retire. Farmers gave up their meadows, before they were mown, to supply the horses. Yet, notwithstanding all this liberality, it would have been impossible, in many cases, to accommodate the whole assemblies with private lodgings. But besides, the people were unwilling to suffer any interruptions in their devotions, and they formed an attachment to the place where they were continually seeing so many careless sinners receiving their first impressions, and so many Deists constrained to call on the formerly despised name of *Jesus;* they conceived a sentiment like what Jacob felt at Bethel — 'Surely the *Lord* is in this place; this is none other but the house of *God*, and this is the gate of heaven.' The number of persons who have fallen down under serious impressions, in this revival, is another matter worthy of attention; and on this I shall be more particular, as it seems to be the principal cause why this work should be more suspected of enthusiasm than some other revivals. At Caneridge sacrament, it is generally supposed not less than one thousand persons fell prostrate to the ground, among whom were many infidels. At one sacrament which I attended, the number that fell was thought to be more than three hundred. Persons who fall are generally such as have manifested symptoms of the deepest impressions for some time previous to that event. Immediately before they become totally powerless, they are seized with a general tremor, and sometimes, though not often, they utter one or two piercing shrieks in the moment of falling. Persons in this situation are affected in different degrees: sometimes, when unable to stand or sit, they have the use of their hands, and can converse with perfect composure. In other cases, they are unable to speak; the pulse becomes weak, and they draw a difficult breath about once in a minute. In some instances, their extremities become cold, and pulsation, breathing, and all the signs of life, forsake them for nearly an hour. Persons who have been in this situation have uniformly avowed that they felt no bodily pain; that they had the entire use of their reason and reflection; and when recovered, they would relate every thing that had been said or done near them, or which could possibly fall within their observation. From this it appears that their falling is neither a common fainting, nor a nervous affection. Indeed, this strange phenomenon appears to have taken every possible turn to baffle the conjecture of those who are not willing to consider it a supernatural power. Persons have sometimes fallen on their way from public worship, and sometimes after they had arrived at home; in some cases, when they were pursuing their common business on their farms, or when retired for secret devotion.

"It was observed, generally, that persons were seriously affected for some time previous to their falling. In many cases, however, it is otherwise; numbers of thoughtless sinners have fallen as suddenly as if struck with lightning. Many professed infidels and other vicious characters have been arrested in this way, and sometimes at the very moment when they were uttering blasphemies against the work. At the beginning of the revival in Shelby county, the appearances, as related to me by eye-witnesses, were very surprising indeed. The revival had before this spread, with irresistible power, through the adjacent countries; and many of the pious had attended distant sacraments with great benefit. These were much engaged, and felt unusual freedom in their addresses at the throne of grace, for the outpouring of the divine Spirit, at the approaching sacrament in Shelby.

"The sacrament came on in September. The people, as usual, met on Friday; but all were languid, and the exercises went on heavily. On Saturday and Sunday morning, it was no better. At length, the communion commenced; every thing was still lifeless. While the minister of the place was speaking at one of the tables, without any unusual animation, suddenly there were several shrieks from different parts of the assembly; instantly persons fell in every direction, the feelings of the pious were suddenly revived, and the work progressed with extraordinary power till the conclusion of the solemnity.

"This phenomenon of falling is common to all ages, sexes, and characters; and when they fall, they are differently exercised. Some pious people have fallen under a sense of ingratitude and hardness of heart, and others under affecting manifestations of the love and goodness of God; many thoughtless persons under legal convictions, who have obtained comfort before they arose. But perhaps the most numerous class consists of those who fall under distressing views of their guilt, who arise under the same fearful apprehensions, and continue in that state for some days, perhaps weeks, before they receive comfort. I have conversed with many who fell under the influence of comfortable feelings; and the account they gave of their exercises while they lay entranced was very surprising. I know not how to give you a better idea of them, than by saying that in many cases they appear to surpass the dying exercises of Dr. Finley; their minds appeared wholly swallowed up in contemplating the perfections of the Deity, as illustrated in the plan of salvation; and whilst they lay apparently senseless and almost lifeless, their minds were more vigorous, and their memories more retentive and accurate, than they had ever been before. I have heard men of respectability assert that their manifestations of gospel truth were so clear as to require some caution, when they began to speak, lest they should use language which might induce their hearers to think they had seen those things with bodily eyes; but at the same time, they had seen no image nor sensible representation, nor indeed any thing beside the old truths contained in the Bible. Among those whose minds were filled with the most delightful communications of divine love, I but seldom observed any thing ecstatic. Their expressions were just and rational; they conversed with calmness and composure; and on their first recovering their speech, they appeared like persons recovering from a violent disease, which had left them on the borders of the grave. I have sometimes been present when those who fell under the influence of convictions obtained relief before they arose. In these cases, it was impossible not to observe how strongly the change in their minds was depicted in their countenances. Instead of a face of horror and despair, they assume one open, luminous, and serene, and expressive of all the comfortable feelings of religion. As to those who fall down under legal convictions, and continue in that state, they were not different from those who receive convictions in other revivals, excepting that their distress is more severe. Indeed, extraordinary power is the leading characteristic of this revival; both saints and sinners have more striking discoveries of the realities of another world, than I have ever known on any occasion.

"I trust I have said enough on this subject to enable you to judge how the charge of enthusiasm is applicable to it. Lord Lyttleton, in his letter on the conversion of St. Paul, observes, (I think justly,) that enthusiasm is a vain, self-righteous spirit, swelled with self-sufficiency, and disposed to glory in its religious attainments. If this be a good definition, there has been, perhaps, as little enthusiasm in the Kentucky revival as in any other. Never have I seen more genuine marks of that humility which disclaims the merit of its own duties, and looks to the Lord Jesus Christ as the only way of acceptance with God. I was, indeed, highly pleased to find that Christ was all and all, in their religion as well as in the religion of the gospel. Christians, in their highest attainments, seemed more sensible of their entire dependence on divine grace; and it was truly affecting to hear with what agonizing anxiety awakened sinners inquired for Christ as the only physician who could give them any help. Those who call these things enthusiasm ought to tell us what they understand by the spirit of Christianity. In fact, sir, this revival operates as our Savior promised the Holy Spirit should, when sent into the world: it convinces of sin, of righteousness, and of judgment — a strong confirmation, to my mind, both that the promise is divine, and that this is a remarkable fulfilment of it. It would be of little avail to object to all this, that probably the professions of many were counterfeited. Such an objection would rather establish what it meant to destroy; for where there is no reality, there can be no counterfeit; and besides, where the general tenor of a work is such, as to dispose the more insincere professors to counterfeit what is right, the work itself must be genuine. But as an eye-witness in the case, I may be permitted to declare that the professions of those under religious convictions were generally marked with such a degree of engagedness and feeling as wilful hypocrisy could hardly assume. The language of the heart, when deeply impressed, is very distinguishable from the language of affectation. Upon the whole, sir, I think the revival in Kentucky among the most extraordinary that have ever visited the church of Christ, and, all things considered, peculiarly adapted to the circumstances of that country. Infidelity was triumphant, and religion on the point of expiring: something of an extraordinary nature seemed necessary to arrest the attention of giddy people, who were ready to conclude that Christianity was a fable, and futurity a dream. This revival has done it; it has confounded infidelity, awed vice into silence, and brought numbers beyond calculation under serious impression. While the blessed Savior was calling his people, and building up his church in this remarkable way, opposition could not be silent. At this I hinted above; but it is proper to observe, that the clamorous opposition which assailed the work at its commencement, has been in a great measure borne down before it; a large proportion of those who have fallen were first opposers, and their example has taught others to be cautious, if it has not taught them to be wise.

"I have written on this subject to a greater length than I first intended; but if this account should give you any satisfaction, and be of any benefit to the common cause, I shall be fully gratified.

"Yours, with the highest esteem,

"G. BAXTER.

"The Rev. A. Alexander."

I now close this article with a very few remarks.

1. Were there not many disorders and irregularities connected with this great work of God? The reader has seen Dr. Baxter's opinion; and he was regarded through life as a man of clear and sound judgment,

whose decisions were entitled to much regard. But I ask the question again, because there has been much mistake on this point. There has been much written and published in the east concerning the irregularities and disorders of that day, for which there was just about as much foundation as there has been for the lugubrious effusions of certain English tourists in America, in view of the semi-barbarian condition of the American people. As most persons are prone to regard themselves as very highly civilized, so we are all ready to look upon ourselves as peculiarly "discreet" and "judicious." There is often in the church much difficulty in finding persons who are willing to labor for the conversion of sinners; who are ready to "go out into the highways and hedges, and compel them to come in, that God's house may be filled." But who ever saw any lack of persons who were eager to do "the judicious," "the prudent," "the circumspect," "the fault-finding," which the good of the church demanded? There is no supererogation to which we are more prone, than that of indulging painful apprehensions lest all the "prudence," "sound judgment," and "descretion," should have been allotted to ourselves. Thoughtful, anxious man! vex not in vain thy righteous soul. There is not the least danger that fretting, fault-finding, or any of the virtues belonging to that amiable constellation, will die with thee! How slow are men to learn the lesson taught by the death of Uzzah! He supposed it was necessary for him to take hold of the ark, in order to keep it steady. He had no right to touch it. "And God smote him there for his error; and there he died by the ark of God." (2 Sam. vi. 6, 7.)

Two of the ministers who labored in that revival, with whom I was afterwards well acquainted, were graduates of Princeton College, during the presidency of Dr. Witherspoon. Rev. Samuel Doak, D. D. and Rev. Edward Crawford were "burning and shining lights," at that period, among the churches of the west. Dr. Doak was, for more than twenty years, occasionally the subject of the "bodily exercise." Indeed, from its appearance in 1800, until his death in 1830, he was often affected by it. He was a powerful man in both mind and body; an excellent scholar, such as Princeton graduates at that day generally were; and a thorough Calvinist, of the Scotch Presbyterian school. He was among the very early settlers in the west; emigrated there from Virginia near the close of the revolutionary war; and, through a long life, glorified God, and preached the gospel of peace and good will to men. He was the president of the college at which Gideon Blackburn, Dr. Nelson, and many of our western ministers were educated. With Rev. Edward Crawford I spent a number of months, while I was a student of theology. My impression is, that he was never in person affected by the bodily exercise; but he labored abundantly in the churches where it prevailed. I have heard him speak of it often. He believed that similar bodily affections had frequently taken place in the experience of Bible saints. He would quote the text where Abraham fell on his face before God "and laughed." (Gen. xvii. 17.) He would point to the soldiers of King Saul, and the case of Saul himself, (1 Sam. xix. 18—24,) and to David dancing and shouting before the ark of the Lord. (2 Sam. vi. 14, 15.) He would refer also to the scenes described Neh. viii. 9—11, where it required all the authority of Nehemiah, Ezra, and the Levites, to "still the people." So overwhelming were their emotions when they "understood the words of the law." He would repeat the language of Christ, (Luke vi. 23,) "Rejoice ye in that day, and leap for joy; for behold, your reward is great in heaven." How would a venerable apostle appear in our eyes at the present day, should we see him, wrapped in his plain mantle, his long white beard reaching down to the waist, leaping for joy, in view of his reward in heaven? Mr. Crawford would illustrate and confirm his opinion of the bodily agitations which attended that revival, by reference to the scenes on the day of Pentecost, the conversion of Saul of Tarsus, and the bodily prostration of both Daniel and St. John, when blessed with visions of God. It would have been thought "passing strange" by the good people among whom these venerable fathers lived and labored, had any one charged them with "lack of judgment," "want of discretion," or asserted that their views of the revival were not entitled to high respect. Gideon Blackburn was in the prime of life during this precious season of divine mercy. He was then, and long afterwards, extensively known to the American churches as an effective and indefatigable minister of the New Testament. Dr. Anderson, of Tennessee, who labored much with Blackburn, has often expressed the opinion, that, in all likelihood, the disclosures of the judgment day will show that the seal of God, in the form of "souls renewed," was set to the ministry of Blackburn, to an extent rarely equalled, since the days of inspiration, among ambassadors of the cross.

Blackburn's opinion of the great revival will be seen

by the following extract of a letter to a friend in Philadelphia, dated

"MARYVILLE, TENN., *January* 20, 1804.

"Rev. and Dear Sir, —

"The wonderful appearances attendant on the revival in the state of Tennessee, has arrested the attention of both the friends and enemies of religion. The bodily exercise has assumed such a variety of shapes as to render it a truly Herculean task to give an intelligible statement of it to any person who has never seen it. However, I do not hesitate to say, that it is evidently the Lord's work, though marvellous in our eyes.

"Since my return to the state of Tennessee, I have attended eight sacraments; and these in different parts of the country. From one thousand to thirty-five hundred have been assembled together — of course, collected from considerable distances. I have conversed particularly with upwards of eight hundred persons on their exercises, views, feelings, &c., and I am constrained to say, that I have discovered far less extravagance, disorder, and irregularity, than could have possibly been expected in so extraordinary an awakening, especially when part of it took place among persons settled in the back parts, and entirely destitute of the means of grace. If crowded audiences, earnest praying, practical preaching, and animated singing, may be considered irregular, there is a great deal of irregularity. If crying out for mercy, if shouting glory to God for salvation, are disorderly, then there is some disorder; but, I presume, not more than there was at the day of Pentecost.

"The only thing with us, which can be construed into disorder or extravagance, is the motions of the body under the exercise. In most of the cases, when the paroxysm begins to go off, the subject feels the strongest desire for prayer, and frequently expresses himself in the most pathetic, fluent, and pertinent manner I ever heard. Children of five or six, and persons who before appeared grossly ignorant, express themselves in such a manner, form their petitions so judiciously, and introduce Scripture so pertinently, that I question if the greatest doctor of divinity in America would not blush in the view of his own inferiority.

"The subjects of those exercises are found in all classes, ranks, and degrees — the person of eighty and the child of four; the master in affluence, and the slave in bondage; the clergy in the pulpit, and the laity in the pews; the man of long religious standing, those of a recent date, and many who have no religion at all. It is universally agreed that there is no religion in the bodily exercise; yet it is thought to be a very solemn, external call, is well calculated to impress the mind, and ought to be improved.

"In short, I have not only heard of it, and seen it, but have *felt* it, and am persuaded that it is only to be effected by the immediate finger of God. There are some impostors, there are some extravagances; but these make no characteristic feature of the work, and are held in absolute abhorrence by the pious. The best evidence of a revival is the fruit produced. To this we shall attend: a full enumeration of this would swell my long letter to a volume. The infidel of many years' standing is often seen laying down his weapons at the foot of the cross, and heard crying out, "There is a Savior. I enjoy more sweetness in a moment, than I have done for years,' &c. *These things I have seen and heard.* They have also declared, that men and books could never have so effectually convinced them of the truth, as the bodily exercise has done. Those of the same class, who are not convinced, are completely silenced. The ball room, tippling shops, and taverns, have, in a number of instances, been thrown open to the pious, and converted into places of prayer and praise in social exercise. The most profane settlements, where religion was not known, or the name of God mentioned only in blasphemy, are regularly formed into societies, and meet weekly for social prayer. The very caves of the mountains, where a few of the more indifferent had crowded, are now sounding with praise to God. Praying societies may be attended every day or every night in the week, by a ride of a few miles. In these, boys of twelve or fifteen will cheerfully take their part, when called upon. In all these societies, there is one appointed to preside, who reads the Scriptures, chooses and points out the hymns, and calls on persons to pray, as he chooses; and thus all is conducted with decency and order. It is not uncommon on Sabbath evenings, and frequently in the week, to find twenty or more children associated in a silent grove, none of them more than twelve years old, and engaged in the most solemn prayer.

"I have drawn near them, and seen and heard wonders indescribable — some crying to Jesus for mercy; some shouting, 'Glory to God for salvation;' others praying for their own souls — their brothers, sisters, fathers, mothers, friends, ministers — praying for the church — the heathen — yea, for the world at large. O, sir, nothing but the hosannas of the children on the entry of Christ into Jerusalem, could equal the praises of these infants. Nor is this a hasty flash, but continues, while they are evidently become both more dutiful and docile. Their desire, as soon as they take the bodily exercise, for instruction and for the means of grace, is past conception. The poor black slaves are much reformed; they are more dutiful, faithful, and upright; and many of their nights, after days of fatigue, are spent in social prayer. In a word, the Christian is animated, the hypocrite alarmed, and sinners tremble. The doctrines of the cross are thirsted after, and more fully understood, than they would have been, in a common way, in ten years' regular attention. Total depravity, free grace, inexcusable rebellion, and infinite mercy, are favorite topics. The great object appears to be, to despise self, and exalt the Redeemer. The sinner ceases to make terms with his Creator, and surrenders in entire, unconditional submission. The love of Christians for each other has increased at least tenfold, especially with those who have been the subjects of the bodily exercise, (for it is to be remarked, that all Christians are not the subjects of it,) and the zeal for the interest of Zion has had a proportionate increase. Prayer, praise, and religious conversation, are clearly the order of the day; and this practice, passing through the common circles of society, has bettered their state and sweetened the relations of life.

"These are some of the effects produced; and while such is the fruit of the moral tree, I shall consider the root good, and the cause producing it divine. I ought to have remarked, that the bodily exercise is not the effect of the weakness of the nervous system, for the weak, hysterical female will often remain unmoved, while the stout and sturdy veteran will sink and fall by her side. As soon as any person who has been the subject of the exercise has been attacked by sickness, the exercise leaves him entirely, until he again recovers strength, when it returns with force proportionate to his returning strength. After all I have said, you will not be able to form an accurate judgment of the thing without being a spectator yourself; nor can it be fully described by any man on earth. I have simply stated facts so far as I have gone, not any by hearsay, but what I have seen myself. Should the bodily exercise produce as good fruits in Philadelphia as it has done here, I should sincerely wish to hear of it making its appearance in that city. When persons are under the bodily exercise, they can think and express themselves beyond their common level very considerably; and of this I am convinced by experience.

"I am, &c.

"GIDEON BLACKBURN."

2. But were there not alarming errors in doctrines that sprang up in the west during that revival? Did not Arianism and Socinianism come in like a flood? Did not Shakerism appear and make many converts? I answer, Arianism and Socinianism, in their various forms, were making great progress at that time in Germany, in England, in the province of Ulster, Ireland, and in portions of our Atlantic states. And it is true, that while the public mind was waked up on the great subject of religion in the west, Arianism and Socinianism appeared in some parts of the country: there were

some cases, among both ministers and people, where these forms of error were embraced, which occasioned deep regret in the church. It is further true, that three Shaker missionaries, from Lebanon, in New York, I believe, came to the west, and succeeded in forming two small societies in Kentucky, and one in Ohio. This is about the extent to which Shakerism obtained any permanent foothold in the west. The revival prevailed over large districts of Western Pennsylvania. The region round about Pittsburg was greatly blessed. It prevailed extensively in Western and South-western Virginia. It literally covered most of the settled portions of Ohio, Kentucky, and Tennessee, and visited extensive regions in North and South Carolina and Georgia. Through this entire range of country, the Baptist church, the Methodist church, and the Presbyterian church, were blessed and prospered greatly; and yet, because Socinianism and Arianism made a limited impression in portions of Kentucky and Ohio, while they were marching in triumph through some of the Atlantic regions and through large districts of Europe, and because Shakerism was imported from the east, and planted at two points in Kentucky, and one in Ohio, the devil has labored hard to send abroad the proclamation, that the great western revival resulted in little else than disorders — Arianism and Shakerism. In a conversation which I once had with Dr. Nelson, concerning this outpouring of the Spirit of God, by which the overspreading tide of infidelity was arrested, and the west transformed into a Christian land, he expressed much regret that this richest blessing, bestowed by a bountiful God, in our early history, should have been so egregiously misrepresented and misunderstood in other parts of the Union. I asked him this question —

"Do you not think, doctor, that the devil must have immense talent?"

"Sir," said he, "my respect for his talent is rising regularly, the more I see of his management."

When God has been pleased graciously to visit a people with the quickening power of his Spirit, and many have been turned from sin to holiness, and from Satan to God, is it not marvellous that good men can be so deluded by the wiles of the great adversary as to become evidently eager to impute all the wrong things that may appear in that community, for ten or twenty years afterwards, to the influence of the revival? With as much propriety, you might charge the apostasy of Judas to the ministry of Jesus Christ.

Inspiration tells us, that in order to accomplish his base designs, the devil assumes various disguises. At one time he is a serpent — "that old serpent." Again, "he goeth about as a roaring lion." And again, he appears as a "great red dragon." Now, I venture to surmise, that had we an inspired history of the stratagems of the devil at this day, we should find, that he resorts to another disguise, in order to deceive, to wit, that of a turkey-buzzard; and he will flutter and flap his foul wings over a fragment of his favorite carrion, and, if possible, raise dust enough to prevent you from discerning all the beauty that is visible among "the cattle upon a thousand hills."

Why should Arianism, Socinianism, or Shakerism be brought up to dishonor the western revival of 1800, when all these "isms," originated elsewhere, were but imported into the west, and never prevailed there as they have prevailed in regions where that revival was unknown? Certain it is that no men more regretted any departures from sound doctrine than did those good men whose labors were so abundantly blessed in that dispensation of the Holy Spirit, by which the west, in its infancy, was consecrated to the service of God.

Nor do I believe that now, after the lapse of near fifty years, there is any part of the Christian world, where, in proportion to their numbers, there is in the several evangelical denominations more of that religion which God approves, than in the region visited by the revival of 1800.

I will here mention one district, one denomination, and one family.

The *district* is that included within the bounds of the Presbyterian synod of Tennessee, that is, East Tennessee, and a portion of South-western Virginia. This region was powerfully visited with the Spirit of God during the great revival. And in fact, the revival continued there when it had ceased at many other points. Fifteen years after the commencement of this glorious work, I entered the ministry in that country, and labored there until 1830. I was extensively acquainted with churches and families through much of that region. It was then called the "Switzerland of America," in reference to the mountainous features of the country, and the prevalence of pure, Protestant religion. If, at that period, there was any considerable number of Arians and Socinians, or even one Shaker family, in all that range of country, I know not where they were to be found. An accurate and extensive knowledge of the Bible, in connection with a consecration of the soul to God in Christ, existed among that people to a degree that is rare in this fallen world. This was the fruit of God's Spirit in that memorable revival.

The *denomination* to which I refer is that of the Cumberland Presbyterians. This body of Christian people began their organized existence during that great divine visitation. They now have a membership numbering, as I am informed, some hundred and twenty or thirty thousand. I say nothing of the shades of opinion, in which they may vary from other Presbyterian bodies. They preach salvation through the atonement of a divine Redeemer, and the renewing power of the Holy Spirit. There are among them very many strong men — "workmen that need not to be ashamed." And their blessed Master has been with them in every part of that wide field where they have labored, and has made his gospel "the power of God unto salvation" to many thousands of believing souls. From my inmost soul I honor these men, and I will speak of it in the presence of the church of my God. For without patronage or prospect of adequate worldly support, they "did put their life in their hand," and met difficulties and dangers that were formidable and many, and by their instrumentality "the Lord wrought a great salvation." Zion's friends have seen it, and rejoice.

I have no hesitation in declaring my belief, that during the last forty years, no body of Christian ministers in America, or even in the world, have *preached so much good, effective preaching*, and *received so little worldly compensation*, as the ministers of the Cumberland Presbyterian church. That church now stands before earth and heaven a monument of God's great work in the revival of 1800.

The *family* I wished to mention is that of my grandfather. I am confident that there is no impropriety in this. My aim is that Zion's God may be glorified, and the work of God's Spirit may be seen in its bearing on a single house.

My grandfather, with a family of seven sons and two daughters, emigrated from the state of Pennsylvania to East Tennessee very soon after the treaty of peace with Great Britain, in 1783. Both the parents died within a few years after their removal, leaving this large family of young persons, amid the trials and dangers of a new country, distracted with Indian hostilities. One of the brothers went to a distant part of the country at an early day. The conclusion of his earthly history I never knew. But the six brothers and the two sisters, all now married and blessed with families, were living comparatively near to each other at the commencement of the great revival. Thus far they had all lived "without God and without hope in the world." In that wonderful visitation of divine mercy, these six brothers and their wives, these two sisters and their husbands, were all made the happy subjects of renewing grace. O, I have heard these brothers, and these sisters, after they had entered on their march for the city of God, singing the honors of their Redeemer in such lines as these: —

"Amazing grace! how sweet the sound!
That saved a wretch like me.
I once was lost, but now am found;
Was blind, but now I see.

" 'Twas grace that taught my heart to fear,
And grace my fear relieved.
How precious did that grace appear,
The hour I first believed!

" Through many dangers, toils, and snares,
I have already come;
'Tis grace has brought me safe thus far,
And grace will lead me home.

" The Lord has promised good to me;
His word my hope secures;
He will my shield and portion be,
As long as life endures.

" Yes, when this flesh and heart shall fail,
And mortal life shall cease,
I shall possess, within the veil,
A life of joy and peace.

" The earth shall soon dissolve like snow,
The sun forbear to shine;
But God, who called me here below,
Will be forever mine."

These brothers and sisters are now gone to "the heavenly Jerusalem, and to an innumerable company of angels." From most of their families I have been separated for many years. But I have received the joyful intelligence that among them the mercy of the Lord has gone down to children, and to children's children. Of the family of one of these brothers, however, I can speak more particularly. In that family, both of the parents lived and "walked with God" more than forty years from the period when they first entered into his holy covenant. They then died in faith, and in hope of a glorious immortality. Ten of their children attained the years of maturity: all of these consecrated themselves to God early, in the morning of life. Six of their number have already crossed the cold stream, and gone up "to the general assembly and church of the first born, which are written in heaven." Of the surviving four, three are sons, who have long labored in the west as ministers of the gospel in the Presbyterian church. Two of them, at this date, (November, 1849,) have been preaching about twenty-five years. Their ministry has been owned of God, and blessed to the souls of many. The other son, however unworthy of the privilege, has preached the gospel of Christ almost thirty-four years. In his family, the six eldest children have dedicated themselves to God while very young; one at the age of nine years, and all the others before their years had numbered twelve.

These humble statistics are recorded, in the "Western Sketch-Book," to the glory of the great name of Zion's King, and that honest inquirers, who are desirous of knowing the truth, may have facts before them from which to judge of the fruits and results of the "western revival of 1800."

The facts given here, however, are but a "handful to the harvest." But, O, "the Lord shall count, when he writeth up the people, that this and that man was born there." And distant generations will rise up and give hallelujahs to his name, that he baptized our beloved western country, in its early infancy, by this memorable outpouring of his Holy Spirit.

There is here another instance of that beautiful analogy, before mentioned, between the ancient and modern dispensations of God's providence and grace. "When the day of Pentecost had fully come, there were dwelling at Jerusalem" — that is, they were collected to celebrate the feast of Pentecost — "Jews, devout men, out of every nation under heaven." God's grace came down on them, and three thousand were converted in one day, and five thousand in another, and great multitudes were thus added to the infant church. Now, mark, when this pentecostal season was concluded, and all these converts returned to their homes, they carried the elements of Christianity with them into almost every part of the heathen world. When the apostles afterwards went abroad among the nations to preach the gospel and organize churches, in almost every province, in almost every city, in almost every nook and corner of the Gentile world, they found more or less of these early converts, to hold up their hands, to join with them in prayer, to assist them by their counsel, and, in fact, to furnish a nucleus around which churches might be gathered; and the apostles rejoiced, while they marvelled, at the depth, and height, and perfection of the counsels of God.

Now, for more than thirty years, communities at a distance have been emptying their population into the great valley. Not only have the streams poured in from the older states of our happy Union, but European nations have sent over their thousands and their hundreds of thousands. With the alien character of our foreign population, and the proneness of the American emigrant to forget his religion when he goes to the west, we know not what the results might have been, had no other element been thrown in by divine Providence. But God had interposed. He had imbued the strong, resolute western man with supreme love to Christ and his church. He had, by his Holy

6 *

Spirit, made this fearless, decided western man *a Christian* and *a Protestant.* And the minister who for more than thirty years has travelled in the west, preaching and organizing churches, has found this firm, determined western man standing up at every point for the honor and for the church of his divine Master. And he, with great frequency, is the nucleus around which young churches are formed in the wide west to the glory of our Redeemer.

Other agencies have come into the field since, and they have done well. But "render unto Cesar the things that are Cesar's, and unto God the things that are God's." Be it known, therefore, unto thee, "O earth! earth! earth!" that the mighty west is a *Christian* and *Protestant* land, because the God of glory appeared there at an early day, and poured the abundance of his salvation upon her people. Ah, she will carry down to far distant ages the decided impression and fixed character instamped upon her childhood by the seal of the Holy Spirit.

RECOLLECTIONS OF GENERAL JACKSON.

Colonel Samuel M. Grant, of Northern Missouri, first waked up my mind to the importance of recording and preserving the testimony of General Jackson on the subject of the truth and value of the Christian religion. Said he, "I was in Palmyra at the time the news was received of General Jackson's public profession of faith in Jesus Christ. A gentleman, whom I had long known as a professed rejecter of the gospel, hailed me at the door of his office, and desired me to come in. I entered, and he held up a newspaper, and said, 'I have just been reading the account of General Jackson making a profession of the religion of Jesus Christ. It is long since my eyes have known a tear; but now I have been weeping freely in view of that venerable old man standing up in the church and confessing Christ as his Savior.'" Such was Colonel Grant's account of this incident in Palmyra, which, he said, affected his heart much, as he had long known this gentleman, and had regarded him as hopelessly sunk in the vortex of infidelity; and now he was surprised and gratified to find him startled and roused to such an extent by the public religious stand taken by General Jackson. Colonel Grant then proceeded to remark, "In my early days, the palpable and notorious infidelity of Thomas Jefferson spread a desolation that was mournful over the entire face of the western country. Jefferson was distinguished as a politician. His fame was every where as the draughtsman of the Declaration of Independence. And when it was blown abroad that Thomas Jefferson had imbibed the French infidelity, and rejected the gospel, it was like 'the destruction that wasteth at noonday.' The enemies of religion took courage, put on airs of immense consequence, boasted, plumed themselves, and threw up their blasphemy in the face of Heaven. Ah! it was reputable, it was literary, it was scientific, to scowl at the gospel, and pour forth 'great swelling words' against all that is sacred. But now," continued Colonel Grant, "here is a man, raised up by the hand of God to the possession of an influence far beyond all that Jefferson ever possessed; for Jefferson never was able to wield public opinion, in this great nation, as General Jackson has done. And yet this man publicly prostrates himself before the cross, and calls on the crucified Redeemer as his Lord and his God. The American church should not suffer this important testimony of General Jackson to be overlooked or forgotten." Such were the remarks of Colonel Samuel M. Grant. I felt their appropriateness and their power. I had known General Jackson personally from early childhood. My father's house was one of his occasional resting-places, while he officiated as judge in the state of Tennessee, long before he was elected general. I remembered his conversation in the family. I remembered that when the infidelity of Voltaire, Volney, and Thomas Paine were fashionable, rampant, and considered as almost essential to the standing of a gentleman, Judge Jackson freely and frequently averred his full and unwavering confidence in the divine authority of the Bible, and the truth of the gospel declaration that Jesus Christ is the only Savior of lost men, and that we must repent of sin, and obey the gospel of Christ, or our souls cannot be saved. I often thought of the importance of recording General Jackson's testimony in relation to the gospel; but his name was so identified with the politics of the country, that it was difficult to say any thing concerning him, without touching some political chord, which I wished not to agitate.

But now the old general is gone. The political ambition which his name so often awakened, has almost wholly died away. The generation with which he was identified is rapidly passing into eternity. And soon the language of the poet, in its fullest extent, will be applicable to him in his earthly history: —

"He suffered, but his pangs are o'er;
Enjoyed, but his delights are fled;
Had friends — his friends are now no more;
And foes — his foes are dead."

Andrew Jackson was the son of an eminently pious mother, who died when he was about fourteen years of age. By this mother he was early taught the Holy Scriptures, and his young mind deeply imbued with the knowledge of the great doctrines of the gospel. With the Catechism of the Westminster Assembly he was familiar before his mother's death. The Christian counsel, the prayers, the pious example of that mother, attended him through all the meanderings of his eventful life, and had a controlling agency in moulding and guiding the thoughts and sentiments of his powerful mind.

He emigrated from South Carolina, his native state, to Tennessee, when infidelity flooded all the land. With that infidelity Andrew Jackson would have no communion. He was not then a church member; but *he honored God in word* by the frank, full, and often-repeated declaration of his absolute confidence in the truth of the Holy Scriptures, and man's need of the great salvation therein revealed. It was, indeed, a rare and affecting spectacle — a young lawyer of acknowledged talents, great promise, and brilliant worldly prospects, standing up the fearless advocate of the religion of the Bible; breasting, with undaunted fortitude, a perverted and polluted public sentiment, and amidst the scoffs and sneers of popular sceptics around, unmoved as the rock that breaks the billows which in vain attempt to shake it.

The elements of true greatness were already conspicuous in the character of the youthful Jackson. Those extraordinary attributes of mind already stood forth, which in after life enabled him to sway and direct public opinion in one of the greatest nations on the earth — attributes of mind which so lifted him up, that, in fact, he will be to posterity the most notable landmark of the age in which he lived. For this reason his testimony to the divinity of the gospel had great weight. General Jackson was not at this period a professor of religion. Nor can it be said that he avoided the fashionable amusements of the day. But *he honored God in word.* And when the faithful minister of the gospel publicly rebuked sin, Jackson honored the messenger of God, and acknowledged the righteousness of the message.

An instance of this occurred in the ministerial labors of Rev. Robert Henderson. This venerable man was a zealous and powerful preacher, who labored abundantly among the plain, frontier population of the west. In those primitive days, the minister of the gospel considered it his duty to rebuke sin, in whatever circle of society it might lift up its deformed head. Henderson had a courageous heart, fervent piety, and descriptive powers of a very high order. Perhaps the reader would be pleased with a specimen of the style of Henderson in reproving sin. If so, he shall be gratified. Among the popular vices then in vogue, horse-racing and cock-fighting were preëminent. The latter fashionable sport, as it was then called, had many admirers among western gentlemen. Of this number General Jackson was one. The consequence was, that game chickens were in high repute, and were objects of much attention. There had been a large collection of gentlemen at one of our western villages, and General Jackson was among them. The day had been spent in their favorite sport. It was Saturday; and, as the evening drew on, Rev. Robert Henderson rode into town, stopped at the principal hotel, and announced that he would preach in the court-house on the next day. The tidings went abroad on the wings of the wind, for Henderson was well known, and it was generally expected that, when he appeared, popular and fashionable vices would meet with rough handling.

The morning came. The congregation assembled. The sermon commenced. "Lo, this only have I found, that God hath made man upright; but they have sought out many inventions." (Eccl. vii. 29.) The preacher spoke in elevated terms of the exalted and noble existence which the great God bestowed on man at his creation. He was created rational and immortal. He was endued with capacity for receiving the knowledge and enjoying the fellowship of the Most High. He was made but a little lower than the angels. He was created in the image of God; and when man, perfect in body and soul, was stationed in Eden, the spectacle was so interesting, that enraptured throngs of celestial beings fastened their fixed gaze upon him. Angelic multitudes came from far to behold this new specimen of the wonderful workmanship of the Most High. And while they saw, in holy, happy man, rich disclosures of the wisdom, the goodness, and the glory of the Eternal One, 'the morning stars sang together, and all the sons of God shouted for joy.'

"But, O, 'how are the mighty fallen! How has the fine gold become dim!' Paradise is lost, and man is

"Fallen, fallen, fallen, fallen,
Fallen from his high estate!"

The trail of the serpent degrades and pollutes the earth on which we tread. The energies of Adam's sons are now exhausted in pursuit of bubbles and vanity. 'They sow the wind, and they reap the whirlwind.' I will give you an example. On my arrival at this place on last evening, I was happy to learn that quite a number of distinguished gentlemen were in town — colonels, and generals, and judges; men whom their fellow-citizens have delighted to honor, and to whom God has given endowments calculated to bless and adorn society. I anticipated an intellectual feast. I was glad of the opportunity of spending an evening in such an enlightened circle. I congratulated myself in prospect of an entertainment so rich both in pleasure and in profit.

"And now, friends, what do you suppose was the great theme of discussion in this assembly of superior men? Some may, perhaps, conjecture that they discoursed of international law — those measures of enlightened policy which are calculated, on the largest scale, to benefit the human race. But no; such was not their theme. Others may suppose that the attention of this select body of men was occupied by some new discovery in astronomy. As our glasses are improved, remoter fields of creation come to view. But no; this was not their subject. Or, do you imagine that their eyes were directed to the wonders of redemption, which drew down celestial armies to Bethlehem, and caused them to sing heavenly anthems in the hearing of men? No, friends; such was not their topic. The whole burden of conversation for the evening — I blush while I repeat it, but the duty is imperative — the whole burden of conversation was, 'game chickens! game chickens! — their long pedigrees, their rare qualities, their bloody battles!' Tell it not in Gath! publish it not in the streets of Askalon! O, when will our influential men learn and regard the divine maxim, that 'righteousness exalteth a nation, but sin is a reproach to any people'!"

An inferior mind would have taken offence at the plain dealing of this resolute ambassador of God. Not so did General Jackson. Early the next morning, he called at the minister's room, and, in a manner the most frank and cordial, thanked him for his faithfulness in rebuking sin, and his efforts for the best interests of society. He declared his full conviction of the truth of the gospel, and that obedience to it was essential to salvation. And from that period, General Jackson was the firm, unwavering supporter of this minister, until Robert Henderson was called to go the way of all the earth.

It was said, that General Jackson *honored God in word*, long before he became a member of the church. I wish to dwell a little on this point. For a number of years, facts have been coming before my mind, which have fastened upon it this conviction, that the amount of guilt brought on the soul of man by *evil words*, is very great. There is a wretched and wide-spread delusion on the public mind in reference to this matter. Many think that words are but breath, — mere empty air, — and that there is but little crime in the use of light and idle words on the subject of religion. Hence many, whose conscience would cry out against a sinful act, will indulge in light and jocular words on serious things. I will mention one or two facts that have deeply affected my own mind. In the year 1840, I saw, in Northern Illinois, an old man, of steady and regular habits, who kept aloof from the church, while his wife, and daughter, and son-in-law, and other members of the family, turned to the Lord. At length, I asked him, in the presence of his family, if he was not willing to turn to the Lord. He replied, "There is no hope for me, I have *said so much* against the Lord." I was not sure that I correctly understood him, and therefore asked again, what it was that he had remarked. "There is no hope for me," replied the old man, "*I have spoken so much against the Lord.*" It was the first time in my life, that I had heard a person single out the guilt contracted by sins of the tongue, as pressing with awful weight on the troubled soul; and for a moment I was silent. His daughter was sitting by. She was a woman, perhaps, twenty-seven years of age. Said she, "Why, father, I don't remember to have heard you speak against Christ and his religion." "My child, it was before you were born." His wife was present. They had been married more than thirty-three years. "Why, husband," said she, "I don't remember to have heard you speak against the religion of Christ." "My dear, it was before you were acquainted with me. When I was a young man, I joined myself to a club of infidels. Our aim was to bring religion into contempt by ridicule; and, O, I have said so much against the Lord, that there is now no hope for me." Here was an old man, quailing under the terrible load of guilt brought upon his soul by evil words uttered some thirty-five or forty years before. Take another instance. A man, whose head was white with the frost of seventy winters, called upon me when alone in my room in Missouri, and said, "What can I do? My heart is cold and dead. I fear I have grieved away the Spirit of God. When I was young, I courted infidelity. I thought it was evidence of a superior mind to scowl at the gospel, and make light of sacred things. I did so, till the habit was formed and fixed; and now for a long time I have been trying to get rid of it. But my heart seems dead to the gospel, and the ghost of that infidelity which I courted when young, follows me wherever I go. It has been haunting me for years; and I shudder at the apprehension that it will haunt me into the grave."

One of the most successful politicians of his day, in the western country, had allowed himself to profane the language of God's word by introducing it on light and trivial occasions. He would point a joke with a quotation from the Holy Scriptures. When jesting and indulging in playful remarks, the word of God was in his mouth with painful frequency. He became habitually addicted to an irreverent, profane, and shocking familiarity with the words of eternal truth. Many were amused and made merry with his supposed wit. But every good man, that heard him sporting with the solemn language of God, was grieved. At length, a sad change came over him. He lost all interest for political life. He lost all relish for the society of his friends. He lost all regard for his own family. His heart withered, life became a burden, heavy, horrible, insupportable. And while occupying the governor's chair, he took a loaded rifle, and put a violent end to his earthly existence. It was thought that, by light and vain words, he had grieved away the favor of God. And woe to that man from whom God departs.

Addison's hymn entitled "Gratitude" is very beautiful; but perhaps the very finest stanza in that hymn is this: —

"Ten thousand thousand precious gifts
My daily thanks employ;
Nor is the least *a cheerful heart*,
That tastes those gifts with joy."

It is the smile of God that enables us to rise in the morning with cheerfulness, and address ourselves with good heart to the cares and toils of the day. But woe to that man from whom the smile of God is taken away.

Wicked words have an awful tendency to banish the soul from the favor of God. Enoch, the seventh from Adam, predicts that one leading object of the final Judge, in the great day, is to execute judgment on sinners for the "hard speeches" which they have spoken against him. Two of the ten commandments are employed to guard men against sins of *the tongue.* And it is a sin of the tongue — blasphemy against the Holy Ghost — that "shall never be forgiven, neither in this world, neither in the world to come."

I visited General Jackson twice, in the month of September, 1843. He was then very frail, and had the appearance of extreme old age; but he was reposing with calmness and confidence on the promise and covenant of God. He had now been a member of the church for several years. And when I witnessed his serenity and his unclouded hope, I thought of the manner in which he had *honored God in word*, when the cause of religion was very unpopular, and when a deluge of infidelity threatened to desolate the whole land.

It is to be regretted that most of our political men, — presidents, governors, and those high in authority, — when they speak on the subject of religion, use language so guarded and equivocal, that a Turk, a Jew, or an enlightened heathen could adopt it. They will speak of the "Supreme Being," "the great Disposer of all events," "the source of national prosperity," &c., &c. But General Jackson's language was that of a decided Christian. He spoke of the divine Redeemer; his wonderful union with the nature of man; his vicarious death in the room of sinners; pardon through his blood; and eternal glory in heaven, bestowed on believers for his righteousness' sake.

There was a little company of Christian friends present in the Hermitage. After expressing the warmest interest in the church of Christ, and his hope that she would yet prosper and bless the world, General Jackson turned to me, and said, "There is a beautiful hymn on the subject of the exceeding great and precious promises of God to his people. It was a favorite hymn with my dear wife till the day of her death. It has been very precious to me. It commences thus: 'How firm a foundation, ye saints of the Lord.' I wish you would sing it now." So the little company in the Hermitage, at his request, sung the following hymn: —

"How firm a foundation, ye saints of the Lord,
Is laid for your faith in the excellent word!
What more can he say than to you he hath said,
You who unto Jesus for refuge have fled?

"In every condition, in sickness, in health,
In poverty's vale or abounding in wealth,
At home and abroad, on the land, on the sea,
As thy days may demand shall thy strength ever be.

"Fear not; I am with thee; O, be not dismayed;
I, I am thy God, and will still give thee aid;
I'll strengthen thee, help thee, and cause thee to stand,
Upheld by my righteous, omnipotent hand.

"When through the deep waters I call thee to go,
The rivers of woe shall not thee overflow,
For I will be with thee, thy troubles to bless,
And sanctify to thee thy deepest distress.

"When through fiery trials thy pathway shall lie,
My grace, all-sufficient, shall be thy supply:
The flame shall not hurt thee; I only design
Thy dross to consume, and thy gold to refine.

"E'en down to old age, all my people shall prove
My sovereign, eternal, unchangeable love;
And when hoary hairs shall their temples adorn,
Like lambs they shall still in my bosom be borne.

"The soul that on Jesus hath leaned for repose,
I will not, I will not desert to his foes;
That soul, though all hell should endeavor to shake,
I'll never, no, never, no, never forsake."

The sublime and glorious doctrine embodied in this hymn was the food of his spirit, the joy and the rejoicing of his heart. When I looked upon him, now desolate, in extreme old age; his early friends almost entirely gone; his beloved wife in the grave; his own health failing amidst accumulating infirmities, yet reposing, with absolute satisfaction and serenity, on the free, the firm, the everlasting gospel, — I was forcibly reminded of that rich, unparalleled paragraph, near the close of Christ's Sermon on the Mount: "Therefore whosoever heareth these sayings of mine, and doeth them, I will liken him unto a wise man, which built his house upon a rock: And the rain descended, and the floods came, and the winds blew, and beat upon that house; and it fell not: for it was founded upon a rock." I walked into his garden, and there was the grave of his wife, covered with a plain marble slab, with the inscription, "RACHEL JACKSON," with the date of her birth, and her death, and beside it his own grave, all prepared and ready for the reception of his body, when death should call him home.

I learned, that when the weather was good, he spent a portion of every day at this grave, in meditation and prayer; and that he believed he was there blessed with the presence of Him who has taken the sting from death, and the victory from the grave. I returned to the house. My parents had long been his particular friends, but they are now departed. He met me in the hall, and said, "Your father and your mother are gone!" I silently assented; my emotions forbade me to speak. "Well," said he, "they lived to *a good old age.*" It is impossible for any one, who never heard General Jackson speak, to understand all the interest that he threw into this brief Bible quotation. His attitude, his tones, the whole manner of the venerable man impressed me with a sense of new beauties in that precious promise, (Gen. xv. 15,) "Thou shalt go to thy fathers in peace: thou shalt be buried in a good old age."

The Christian character of General Jackson is seen in his reply to Commodore Elliott concerning the sarcophagus, or marble tomb, which had once been prepared for an eastern king or emperor. Commodore Elliott had brought from Asia this sarcophagus, and presented it to the National Institute at Washington, that through the National Institute it might be presented to General Jackson. The officer who presented it to the Institute, remarked, "It is believed to have once held the remains of ALEXANDER SEVERUS, and it is a fit resting-place for all that is mortal of ANDREW JACKSON."

Commodore Elliott wrote to General Jackson, and the following is his reply:—

"HERMITAGE, *March* 27, 1845."

"Dear Sir,—

"Your letter of the 18th instant, together with the copy of the proceedings of the National Institute, furnished me by their corresponding secretary, on the presentation, by you, of the sarcophagus for their acceptance, on condition it shall be preserved, and in honor of my memory, have been received, and are now before me.

"Although laboring under great debility and affliction from a severe attack, from which I may not recover, I raise my pen and endeavor to reply. The steadiness of my nerves may, perhaps, lead you to conclude my prostration of strength is not so great as here expressed. Strange as it may appear, my nerves are as steady as they were forty years gone by; whilst, from debility and affliction, I am gasping for breath.

"I have read the whole proceedings of the presentation, by you, of the sarcophagus, and the resolutions passed by the board of directors, so honorable to my fame, with sensations and feelings more easily to be conjectured than by me expressed. The whole proceedings call for my most grateful thanks, which are hereby tendered to you, and through you to the president and directors of the National Institute. But with the warmest sensations that can inspire a grateful heart, I must decline accepting the honor intended to be bestowed. I cannot consent that my mortal body shall be laid in a repository prepared for an emperor or a king. My republican feelings and principles forbid it; the simplicity of our system of government forbids it. Every monument erected to perpetuate the memory of our heroes and statesmen ought to bear evidence of the economy and simplicity of our republican institutions, and the plainness of our republican citizens, who are the sovereigns of our glorious Union, and whose virtue is to perpetuate it. True virtue cannot exist where pomp and parade are the governing passions; it can only dwell with the people — the great laboring and producing classes, that form the bone and sinew of our confederacy.

"For these reasons I cannot accept the honor you,

and the president and directors of the National Institute, intended to bestow. I cannot permit my remains to be the first in these United States to be deposited in a sarcophagus made for an emperor or a king. I again repeat, please accept for yourself, and convey to the president and directors of the National Institute, my most profound respects for the honor you and they intended to bestow. I have prepared an humble depository for my mortal body beside that wherein lies my beloved wife, where, without any pomp or parade, I have requested, when my God calls me to sleep with my fathers, to be laid — for both of us there to remain until the last trumpet sounds to call the dead to judgment, when we, I hope, shall rise together, clothed with that heavenly body promised to all who believe in our glorious Redeemer, who died for us, that we might live, and by whose atonement I hope for a blessed immortality.

"I am, with great respect,

"Your friend and fellow-citizen,

"ANDREW JACKSON.

"To Com. J. D. Elliott, *United States Navy*."

This letter is among the last productions of his pen. His death soon followed. I hope yet to see the above letter beautifully printed, on fine material, handsomely framed, and kept in some conspicuous place in the house of American families, for the instruction of children and children's children.

Christian people of America! bless the name of God, that he has given you a president who was not ashamed to speak of "our glorious Redeemer, who died for us, that we might live;" "the sounding of the last trump, to call the dead to judgment;" and his "atonement," through whom we "hope for a blessed immortality."

The death of the worthy old general furnished a fine illustration of the sustaining power of the gospel when earthly comforts wither and die. "Henry," said he to a highly-valued young friend who was attending in his room — "Henry, when we have lived as long as we can be useful to others, and as long as we can enjoy life ourselves, we should be willing to go at our heavenly Father's call. That is now my condition. I have lived long; but, now the frailties of age are upon me, I can no more be useful to my friends. Indeed, I can only be a burden to them. I can no longer be useful to the church of God. The pains of disease are upon me. I can no longer enjoy the bounties of Providence in life. What then? It is time to die. My heavenly Father calls, and I trust I am ready to go."

The physician who attended General Jackson on his death-bed, wrote a very instructive and powerful letter, describing the last parting scene in the Hermitage. The chamber of death seemed very near "the gate of heaven." The soul of the dying man was full of the hope of immortality, while he took an affectionate farewell of the members of his family, the children, the servants, all who belonged to the household. He commended them to God in Christ — spoke with unwavering confidence of life in heaven for the followers of the Redeemer. He then entered the cold stream of death, and was seen no more.

"As some tall rock, that lifts his awful form,
Swells from the vale, and midway leaves the storm,
Though round its breast the rolling clouds are spread,
Eternal sunshine settles on its head."

With a few additional remarks I shall close this article.

1. General Jackson, in theology, was a decided and thorough Calvinist. That sublime system of divinity, so clearly taught in the Holy Scriptures, and so accurately epitomized in the Shorter Catechism of the Westminster Assembly, was the joy and the rejoicing of his heart. His ordinary conversation abounded with references to the hand and counsel of God. When rehearsing facts that had occurred in his military or political life, he would repeatedly pause and say, "It was the hand of God." "Divine Providence ordered it so." "Such an officer was cut down; he was a noble man. I felt his loss much, but it was the hand and counsel of God." This continual reference to divine Providence, in all the events of life, was a strongly-marked feature of his conversation. I must here give an anecdote. An able jurist, born and educated at the east, had emigrated to the west; and, by diligence and fidelity in his profession, he had become prosperous and popular. He was now a candidate for an important office, in a district where the popularity of General Jackson was absolutely overwhelming. It was well known that the candidate, whose friendship for Jackson was in the subjunctive mood, would most certainly be elected "to stay at home." It was indispensable to success that the voters should know before the election that the candidate was the friend and admirer of Jackson. Our jurist was very hostile to the doctrines of Calvinism. Indeed, I fear his hostility went further; for I had been told how he worried some young preachers, with sceptical objections to the Bible. I was thrown into his society not long before

the election day. After a few moments' conversation, said he, "Calvinism degrades the human mind. I say, it degrades the human mind!"

"Yes, sir," was my reply — "yes, sir, Calvinism degraded your New England man Jonathan Edwards, as all Europe and all America confess, into the most distinguished theological writer who has ever put pen to paper in the English language. Both hemispheres maintain that Jonathan Edwards is unequalled among English theological writers. How Calvinism degraded him! Again, Calvinism has degraded General Jackson, as you maintain in all your public addresses, throughout your electioneering canvass, into the most eminent military and political man which the world has produced in the present age. How degrading is the influence of Calvinism!"

2. General Jackson, in his intercourse with his neighbors and with society, was "the good man" and the perfect gentleman. It is to be regretted that heated politicians and crazy fanatics should be so successful in misrepresenting men and things, as to keep worthy citizens in one section of our country under injurious mistakes relative to their fellow-citizens in another section. Christianity, common sense, love to God, and benevolence to man, are the same, east and west, go where you will, throughout our great country.

A few years ago, I had the privilege of sitting for a number of successive days in the senate chamber at Washington. I looked on Webster from Massachusetts, Wright from New York, Calhoun from South Carolina, Burges from Rhode Island, Preston, a native of Virginia, Clay from Kentucky, Judge White from Tennessee, and all their fellow-senators; and I said,

"Be you Whigs or be you Democrats, be you from the east or from the west, from the north or from the south, any country on earth might be proud to call you her citizens. And I will rejoice that the beloved land where I was born, nurses in her bosom such a body of men."

3. Let me close with repeating, that General Jackson, from *early life*, was characterized by reverence for sacred things. He spoke reverently of the word of God, the house of God, the ordinances of God. He *honored God in word.* And God blessed him while he lived, and blessed him when he died.

THE EAGLE AND THE GNAT.

THE following article was prepared for a highly practical purpose. In the region where the author lived, that scriptural and sublime system of Christian doctrine, denominated "Calvinism," was most bitterly assailed, and that too, in many instances, by persons who had taken no pains to have their minds expanded by searching the word of God. There is a curious fact here. The man who has never looked into a law book, knows that he is ignorant of law. The man who has never read a medical work, knows that he is ignorant of medicine. But the man who has neglected to read the Bible, is not equally conscious of his ignorance on divine subjects. Tell that man of the "sovereignty of God," the "doctrine of election," or any kindred doctrine, and his heart will rebel against it at once. And he will be "wiser in his own conceit than seven men that can render a reason." The fact is, men are born with hearts opposed to the sovereignty of God, and the *system of doctrine* that maintains it. In this controversy, the depraved *heart* decides, and not the understanding. Now, when I have encountered persons who were eager for argument, while they evidently "loved darkness" and "hated the light,"—persons who would "glory in their shame," while they were "willingly ignorant" of God's word and the sublime *system of eternal truth* unfolded there, — I have sometimes rehearsed to them the story of "The Eagle and the Gnat;" and the result, generally, if it has not been conviction, has certainly been silence.

The reader, if he chooses, may consider the ensuing story as an extract from "The Book of Nathan the Prophet," mentioned 2 Chron. ix. 29, detailing "the acts of Solomon first and last." A very valuable volume, containing an authentic and instructive history of the times, but not being divinely inspired, it has been lost amid "the war of elements and the wreck of matter," which have intervened between the age Solomon and the present day. The following extract alone has come down to our time — a mere fragment, still floating on the waves, the only remaining memorial of the noble vessel that has perished forever.

EXTRACT FROM THE BOOK OF NATHAN THE PROPHET.

"When Solomon had completed that greatest work of his life, the building of the temple of God, on Mount Moriah, it excited much interest through a wide extent of country. Persons who had a highly cultivated taste for architecture — those who were fond of beholding fine specimens of the building art — came from far, and feasted their eyes on this beautiful house. And while they gazed, they spoke one to another of the immense blocks of white marble that appeared in the wall, the tall pillars that rose in front of the building, the symmetry and the splendor of Solomon's Porch, and, indeed, the grandeur, the consummate proportions, and the unparalleled perfection of the entire edifice.

"But the fame of this wonderful house not only

spread among the children of men into distant lands, — it attracted also the admiring gaze of other orders of creation, as will appear from the following narrative.

"A broad-winged eagle, a mighty prince among the feathered nations, had taken an extensive excursion through the regions of the air, and chanced, in his flight, to pass over the Mountains of Judea. Turning his eye to survey the city of the great king, he beheld the newly erected temple, adorning the topmost height of the Hill of David. Captivated with the surpassing beauty of the building, he at once paused in his rapid flight, steadied and balanced himself on his wide-spread wings, and resolved to take a full and satisfactory survey of this majestic temple. That part of the building which fronted the south was now directly before him, and the clear, comprehensive eye of the delighted eagle could take in the whole structure 'from turret to foundation stone.' The grandeur of its noble outline, the perfect proportion and exquisite finish of each and every part, together with the matchless symmetry of the whole, excited the highest admiration. He then moved slowly round to the east, and then paused a while and viewed the temple from thence. He then viewed it from the north, and then again from the west. Having at length feasted his eye with a survey of the temple on every side, the monarch of birds resumed his lofty flight, and while indulging in vast, exalted conceptions of the wisdom of Solomon, the projector and the builder of this marvellous house, he directed his course to the summit of the tallest cliff of Mount Carmel.

"No sooner had he arrived there, than the birds, ever glad of an opportunity to cheer and honor their king, began to cluster in musical circles around him. But the eagle appeared reserved, thoughtful, and wrapped up in the meditations of his own mind. But as the smaller birds, who were very anxious, and indeed impatient, to receive his notice, kept perpetually

> Giggling, ogling, bridling,
> Turning short round and sidling,

the eagle at length, with mingled gravity and affection, addressed them thus : —

" 'My children, think it not strange, that, since my return, I have been less prompt than usual to sympathize with you in your amusements and your joys. I have just returned from beholding a spectacle that has strangely engrossed all my thoughts, and in the contemplation of which I have experienced, in an unusual measure, astonishment and delight. I allude to the splendid, majestic temple, which the wise king of Israel has just completed on the Mountain of Moriah, to the honor of the name of the great God. I have travelled through the length and breadth of Egypt, acknowledged among all the nations as the "cradle of the arts." I have seen her towers, her temples, and her pyramids. I have visited also Nineveh and Babylon, now at the zenith of their glory ; I have beheld their cloud-capped towers and gorgeous palaces. Yet nothing erected by the hand of man has ever come before my eye that will compare, in perfection of beauty, with the temple which King Solomon has built at Jerusalem for the worship of the God of his father.'

" The eagle ceased. There was something in his tone and manner that effectually silenced, for the time, the throng of feathered warblers by whom he was surrounded.

"A great oak was standing near, and in the rough bark which formed its outer covering was sticking a *small* snail-shell. The original inhabitant had left it fastened by a little slime to the bark of the oak. It was empty, smooth, transparent, and *exceedingly small.* A little gnat, distressingly inflated with self-conceit, had found this untenanted mansion, and, in the vagaries of his diminutive mind, had determined to pitch upon the deserted snail-shell for his own habitation. He admired its glassy smoothness, its twirling fashion, and its many adaptations to his convenience and comfort; and, when snugly housed there, he regarded himself as one of the most prominent and important citizens that could be found in all the lofty ranges of Mount Carmel. This little gnat, puffed up with inordinate self-esteem and vain glory, was sitting near the entrance of his cell, and heard the description given by the eagle of the magnificent temple of Solomon. Having unbounded confidence in his own superior capacity as a judge of architecture, while he entertained serious doubts as to the capacity of the eagle, he at once determined to go to Mount Moriah, and examine the building for himself. Having made every necessary arrangement, he set off on his momentous mission, singing along as his little wings fanned the air. And although neither bird nor beast took any notice of his movements, or had the slightest idea that he was gone, yet such were his vast conceptions of his own dignity and weight in the community at large, that he doubted not but that his departure on this journey would be chronicled among the memorable events in the history of the hill country.

"After a most fatiguing flight, the little gnat, dilated

with immense imaginations concerning his great critical powers, arrived at the far-famed temple. But, alas! when he attempted to scan and survey the mighty structure, his little eye had no capacity to perform the task. The vast building rose before him in its length, its breadth, its height, and all its majestic proportions, while the diminutive gnat, so contracted were his organs of vision, could only view a single point of the stupendous edifice. Undaunted, however, and swollen with self-esteem, he set forward in his work of examination.

"'What huge, misshapen mass is this?' exclaimed the indignant gnat, as he crawled over an immense block of white marble, in the west wall of the temple, on which the eagle, a little before, had gazed with astonishment and delight. 'It must be entirely out of proportion. One cannot find its termination in any direction. What a shapeless, unwieldy mass it must be!' Then moving on a little farther, he encountered a pimple near the size of a pin's head: this, of course, had been unnoticed in the comprehensive survey of the eagle. But here the agitated gnat started back with a gesture of horror. 'Most uncouth irregularity! The back of my hand to the wisdom of Solomon, and his masonry, too, if this is a specimen of his proficiency in the art of building!' A little farther on, and he found a joint where two great blocks of marble came together: a very fine hair could not have entered the crack; but to the tiny eye of the puffed-up gnat it seemed a mighty opening. 'Heyday!' he exclaimed; 'what a frightful chasm is here! yawning caverns! yawning caverns!' Thus the conceited and self-important gnat went on, discerning none of the higher beauties of the temple, because of his total incapacity to take an enlarged view, but stumbling on numberless objections, the existence of which were entirely owing to the pitiful contraction of his own powers of vision. Presently he declared 'that his taste was outraged and his patience exhausted; that the whole building was unworthy of criticism; and that he should leave it in disgust.'

"On his return to Mount Carmel, he alleged positively, that the statements of the eagle were false and deceptive; that he himself had given the whole matter a thorough examination, in the conducting of which he had drawn extensively on the resources of his intellect and the treasures of his learning, and that the grand results of his investigation were the following: —

"1. That fame, which has gone forth into all lands, pronouncing the temple an unparalleled building, is a liar.

"2. That the claim of Solomon, and his coadjutors, Hiram the widow's son, and Hiram king of Tyre, to be regarded as great master builders, is all humbug.

"3. That the Queen of Sheba, and her very great train, 'with camels that bore spices, and very much gold, and precious stones,' came from the uttermost parts of the earth on a fool's errand.

"4. And finally, that the little, glassy snail-shell, in which he, the selfsame illustrious and memorable gnat, had taken up his abode, is a structure incomparably superior to the far-famed, consecrated house, which Israel's king had built on the Mountain of Moriah."

ELIJAH AND THE CARMELITE;

OR,

THE EVILS OF RAIN.

The following article was written and published in the year 1835. It first appeared in "The Cincinnati Journal and Luminary," then edited by Rev. Thomas Brainard, now pastor of the Third Presbyterian Church, in the city of Philadelphia. The history of its origin is the following: From the year 1825 till the year 1832, the God of grace had blessed portions of his church in the United States with precious revivals of religion: perhaps from '28 till '31, they were most extensive and powerful. Near this latter date, "Letters on Revivals" were published, in which "cautions," "indiscretions," and "evils," were marvellously conspicuous. If any thing was said in favor of revivals, it seemed to be only in order to prepare the way for a doleful enumeration of "excesses," "extravagances," "mischievous disorders," of which the venerable brother doubtless had either heard or dreamed. Now, the church is sufficiently prone to "leave her first love," and become cold and dull in the cause of God; but when this sad tendency is aided and aggravated by letters or lectures from respectable ministers, the results are distressing.

Alas for a drowsy church, when subjected to an undiluted dispensation of the nightmare!

Most of us can remember, when we were children, how close we would cluster around a kitchen fire, while a superstitious old nurse told her favorite ghost stories — "rawhead and bloody bones;" "sheeted spectres, taller than life, walking by moonlight through the lonesome graveyard;" "murdered men, seen at midnight, moving in solemn procession, each one carrying his head under his arm," &c., &c. I have seen children shuddering while they listened to such stories, until each one was afraid to look over his shoulder, and yet more afraid to go into a distant room to bed. And, after all, the poor old superstitious granny had never seen a ghost in all her life. Now, in like manner, — if small things may be employed to illustrate things that are great, — I have seen the church terrified with "ghost stories" about revivals, until she was almost afraid to move in any good enterprise; and the narrator in the latter case had seen just about as many "spectres" as in the former.

That man whose ministry God has never honored with revivals, may be a useful and important man in the church. He may render services that are valuable in other departments of ministerial effort. But he should publish neither "letters" nor "lectures" on revivals; because that, in this as in other matters, *experience* teaches many things, of which the *inexperienced* are necessarily ignorant.

I cannot set this subject in a stronger light than by giving the following anecdote of Dr. Nelson: He had been laboring in the west, with great earnestness, to convert men to God. He would select a solemn passage of Scripture, and prepare a sermon, and then go and preach that sermon, expecting, through the presence and power of the Holy Spirit, to convert sinners to God, as certainly as the strong axe-man who goes to work with a sharp axe, and is conscious of his dependence on God, expects to cut down the forest-trees. In the midst of these arduous and delightful labors, Nelson was grieved to see a series of "letters on revivals," issuing from the study of a professor who had long been mewed up in the seclusion of a seminary. The author was a worthy man, qualified to give instructions on a subject which he understood, but an entire stranger to revivals of religion, so far as his own ministry was concerned, and likely to remain so; while, in the kingdom of God's grace, *appropriate* causes are necessary in order to produce certain effects.

But the "letters on revivals!" Lackaday! They abounded in proof of the position of John Bunyan, that the old prince of darkness, in warring against man's soul, surrounded the town with an army of twenty thousand "doubters"! And they *doubted* at ear gate, and *doubted* at eye gate, and *doubted* at every gate, till finally they *doubted* the gates open, and *doubted* the whole town into the possession of the great adversary of God and man.

Dr. Nelson's heart was filled with sorrow that such disastrous influences should emanate from such a quarter. But what can a plain, western man do, when a cold, blighting stream of "east wind" comes sweeping over the garden of the Lord, chilling and nipping the tender plants, and freezing all before it? Alas for the churches in the west, when "the star in the east" is overspread with mist and darkness!

Such was the attitude of things when Nelson made a visit to the east. He was walking along a street in one of the principal cities, when he discovered an extensive bookstore. At one side of the door, on a broad sheet, was an advertisement in large letters, "Dr. —— on Revivals, for sale here." At the other side of the door hung a similar advertisement, "Dr. —— on Revivals, for sale here." Nelson paused, surveyed the broad sheets for a moment, then stepped into the store, and, addressing the bookseller, said, "Have you got here the Treatise of the Emperor Nicholas of Russia on the proper method of cultivating *Cotton* and *Sugar-Cane?*"

"Why n–no," said the bookseller, drawling out the answer; "we have not got it, and I should think that Nicholas, out in the far north, among the snows of Russia, would be likely to know very little on the subject, as, most certainly, he has never seen a plant of either cotton or sugar-cane."

"Well," continued Nelson, "have you got the Dissertation of President Boyer of Hayti on the Proper Method of building *Ice-Houses?*" "No," replied the bookseller; "and there again, I should think that Boyer, in the West Indies, having never seen ice, would be a most unsuitable person to attempt to write a dissertation on the subject."

"Ah!" said Nelson, turning towards the door, "I see that you have "Dr. —— on Revivals," and I did not know but that you might have those other works. Good morning, sir."

The reader now will readily understand the position of things in the church, which called forth the dialogue between "Elijah and the Carmelite." The article has gone through many newspaper editions. It is now presented to the public in a permanent form.

The reader will perceive that the great drought, in Elijah's day, most probably took place long after the close of the earthly pilgrimage of "Iddo the seer." But if the prophet Daniel saw, in vision, the great contest between the Persian Ram and the rough Macedonian Goat, which occurred ages after the good prophet had slept with his fathers, who will object to a similar privilege being granted to the author of "The Visions of Iddo"? This article, at its first publication, was introduced by the following note: —

"Brother Brainerd, —

"Many of our wise and worthy men have labored much to put our church on her guard against the *evils* that have attended revivals of religion; and many of our talented and substantial ministers have become so watchful and prudent in guarding against these evils, that in large sections of the church, revivals have ceased altogether. Now, I am not going to debate with those who act on the principle, that the best way to guard against going wrong, is *not to move at all*, and that the surest mark of being *sound* in the faith, is to be *sound asleep*. But I think it would be well for the *friends* of revivals — and those writers are careful to tell us they are such — to take some pains to count over the *blessings*, as well as the evils, that attend them. I think also that good might be done if some of the fathers would write a series of letters on the *evils* of universal stupidity and spiritual death in the church of the living God.

"The following article your readers may, if they

choose, regard as an extract from the book of 'The Visions of Iddo the Seer.' It is not long since we had from the east the announcement that the long-lost book of Jasher has been found. Now, if we in the west have recovered from oblivion the book of the Visions of Iddo, it is but another proof of the progress of discovery and improvement of the present age.

J. G.

EXTRACT FROM THE BOOK OF "THE VISIONS OF IDDO THE SEER."

"The sins of Israel had found them out. The terrible scourge foretold by Moses was upon them — 'Thy heaven that is over thy head shall be brass, and the earth that is under thee shall be iron. The Lord shall make the rain of thy land powder and dust.' The brooks were dried up, and the streams of the rivers had failed: for three years and six months there had been no rain upon the earth. The fowls of heaven and the flocks and herds of the field were crowding, in meagre and famishing multitudes, along the dry channel, in search of water, or, panting and reeling over the dusty plain, were dying under the action of intolerable thirst. In the city, the moan of the starving mother was answered by the scream of starving children: there was no water, there was no bread. The green earth was faded; the flowers were withered and gone. The fields, once beautiful with rising corn, now appeared scorched and desolate; and even the tall forest trees, on the sides and summit of Mount Carmel, stood leafless and dreary, as the prophet of God went up from the place of sacrifice to the top of the mountain to pray for rain. He cast himself down upon the earth, and cried to the Lord God of Israel to have mercy on his people, and send them the showers of heaven, that they might live and not die. He felt deeply for those that were perishing. He knew that none but God could help, and he prayed with that earnestness and importunity that takes no denial.

" While Elijah was thus engaged, he was approached by one who had long dwelt in a cave in the side of Mount Carmel. He was a tall, lean, hard-featured figure, whose visage was strongly marked with expressions of fretfulness and fault-finding — one of those 'murmurers and complainers' who habitually overlook the *good* in the kingdom of nature and the kingdom of grace, and fix their minds only on what they consider the *evils*. Inefficient and worthless himself, as to any useful enterprise, the labors of his life had been to decry and hinder the usefulness of others. He had evidently been a sufferer during the long and destructive famine, for he appeared shrivelled and shrunken in both soul and body; but his sufferings had not produced in his heart self-abasement toward God, nor had they awakened emotions of kindness and compassion for wretched, dying men. As Elijah now paused in his prayer, and bade his servant 'go up to a lofty peak of the mountain, that rose to a great height, and look towards the sea,' if there were any evidences of a cloud rising, he was thus addressed by the old Carmelite : —

" 'Prophet of God, I find you are praying earnestly for rain.. Now, I am a *friend of rain.* I approve of rain; that is, when rain comes as it ought to come, and as it might come. But I have known many sore evils connected with rain in this country; yes, *evils* at the very thought of which my heart is in agony. And you, prophet, should be very cautious and prudent how you pray for rain, lest these distressing evils should again befall us.'

"*Elijah.* The evils of rain! certainly your fears have taken a strange direction; you had better be deprecating the *evils of drought.* Don't you see how the earth is scorched with intense heat? Every green thing is burned up, the animals dead and dying, while Famine is stalking, ghastly and grim, from house to house, and from city to city. Nothing but the mercy of God, speedily granting the showers of heaven, can arrest the desolation, and prevent the universal extinction of life; and yet you are harrowing up your mind with horrible apprehensions of the *evils of rain.*

"Here Elijah turned away from the old man in anguish of spirit, and threw himself prostrate before the Lord; and his urgent prayer that the awful judgment might be turned away from Israel was continued, till his servant came back from looking towards the sea, and said, 'There is nothing.' 'Go again,' said Elijah. The servant went, and the old Carmelite resumed his discourse.

"'Prophet of God, I wish you to understand me. I am decidedly *in favor of rain.* I think highly of it. In fact, I wish we might have more rain than we have; that is, rain of the *right kind;* such, for example, as they had in the good old days of our fathers, when rains were of a much better description than they have been of late. Indeed, in the early part of my own lifetime, I have seen rains that were far preferable to the rains we have had during the last fifteen or twenty years. And, prophet, this is a subject on which I have a right to be heard, for I have been persecuted by the people of the land. While I have been warning them against the evils of rain, they have taken up an opinion that I am opposed to rain altogether. This I consider downright persecution.'

"*Elijah.* Warning them against the evils of rain! Surely you have not been thus engaged during the last three years and six months.

"*Carmelite.* Surely I have. Why, prophet, there were so many deploring the prevalence of drought, and expressing anxiety for rain, that I saw there was danger of their not being sufficiently cautious and prudent; and while I heartily approve of genuine rains, — those, I mean, that are under proper regulations, and rightly conducted, — I wish to put the people on their guard against rains that are spurious, and do more harm than good. I have turned my attention, therefore, with particular interest, to the evils with which the rains in Israel for some years back have been attended.

"*Elijah.* Well, you are a curiosity, beyond a doubt. There has not been a single drop of rain in all the land for three years and six months; we are wading to the knees in dust, starving for water and for bread, and the awful drought threatens to make the whole land a desolation; and yet you are fuming and fretting, and raving round the country, warning the population to guard against the evils of rain. You strongly remind me of an absurdity that I have often seen among a certain class of prophets, who have greatly troubled Israel. I have seen one of these prophets go to a people that were sunk in stupidity and spiritual death, and preach and expatiate on the *evils of excitement.* There is great absurdity in warning a people who are benumbed and torpid, and three fourths dead, against the dangers of excitement. I felt constrained to rebuke one of these but a day or two since. His people were as cold as the cliffs of Mount Carmel. He was declaiming on the 'evils of excitement!' Said I, 'Infatuated man! do you not see that your people are chilled to the heart, by *your freezing ministry?* Both you and they are colder than the clods of the valley: why, then, declaim against excitement? There is no danger from that quarter while *you* are their instructor. You had far better exert yourself to warn them against being *spiritually frost-bitten!* There is the real danger!'

"*Carmelite.* Prophet, I wish you to understand me. Uh! uh! (coughing.) I have been lecturing — uh! uh! — lecturing and laboring — uh! uh! uh! — amidst trials and difficulties — uh! uh! — almost choked with the dust — uh! uh! uh! — that seems to be flying in all directions — uh! uh! uh! — trying to impress the people with a sense of the vast importance of guarding against the "evils of rain."

"*Elijah.* Yes, the whole atmosphere is burdened, almost to groaning, with dense clouds of dust, produced by this dreadful drought; and you yourself are choked to the very verge of suffocation; and moreover you are withered, shrivelled, and shrunken into the likeness of a mere skeleton, by that frightful monster famine, that is scattering desolation round the land; and yet such is the wretched perversion of your mind, that instead of realizing the true cause of all this distress, you are boggling and boisterous about the 'evils of rain.'

"'Wonderful infatuation! Carmelite, interrupt me no more.' So saying, he turned and addressed his cry to the God of Abraham, Isaac, and Jacob, that he would remember his covenant, and have mercy on his people. Here his servant returned the second time from looking toward the sea, and said, 'There is nothing.' 'Go again,' said Elijah, and continued his fervent prayer.

"The old Carmelite, finding that the prophet would consume no more time in listening to his murmuring and complaining, addressed himself to the servant of Elijah, whom he followed back and forth, as he went, now to look toward the sea, and then to report to his master the result of his observation.

"'Servant of Elijah, while your master is praying for rain, and you are looking out for evidences of its coming, it is my duty to warn you of the evils you are likely to bring on the house of Israel. Not that I am opposed to rain, for I think well of it; that is, *real* rain, such as Israel had in days of old. Ah, if we could have such rains now as they had in the days of Moses, and Joshua, and Samuel, I should be among the first to welcome and rejoice in them. Those were blessed rains, and blessed days to Israel. O, if Elijah would only pray for such rain as they had then, how heartily would I unite with him, and hold up his hands! But these transient modern rains that he is praying for, the fact is, I cannot abide them.'

"*Servant.* And is not rain essentially the same thing now that it was in the days of Moses, and Joshua, and Samuel? I must caution you in my turn: beware of that spirit which eulogizes the prophet that is dead, and persecutes the prophet that is living. Think not to exalt Moses while you scowl at Elijah; for one spirit animated them both.

"*Carmelite.* Not at all, not at all: the rains in the time of Moses and the fathers were widely different from what they are of late. I can enumerate a dozen evils connected with modern rains.

" *Servant.* Ah, that is a small business. The merest cobweb-man can find fault, raise objections, and make himself troublesome. A man may excel in that line, and yet be himself utterly worthless, indeed 'worse than worthless.' But, Carmelite, can't you join with the prophet Elijah in his prayer? Here is a perishing population all around you — millions of people at the very door of death. We must have help from Heaven very soon, or it will be too late. Come, join with the prophet, and wrestle in prayer for the showers of heaven, that the many ten thousands of Israel may live and praise the Lord.

" *Carmelite.* I doubt the 'discretion' of Elijah.

" *Servant.* How! What is that you say? *You* doubt the discretion of Elijah?

" *Carmelite.* That is precisely what I said. Now you shall hear my reasons. Very shortly before Elijah passed the door of my cave, on his way up the mountain, I was told that he had very recently been engaged in some singular innovations.

" *Servant.* Ah! What innovations? Give the particulars.

" *Carmelite.* Why, it was reported that he had built an altar of twelve stones, and that he made a trench about the altar. And then he put the wood in order, and cut a bullock in pieces, and laid him on the wood, and said, Fill four barrels with water, and pour it on the burnt sacrifice and on the wood. 'And he said, Do it the second time. And they did it the second time. And he said, Do it the third time. And they did it the third time. And the water ran about the altar; and he filled the trench with water.' Is this true?

" *Servant.* True, every word true.

" *Carmelite.* Well, it was further reported that he then prayed earnestly to the God of Israel. 'And then the fire of the Lord fell, and consumed the burnt sacrifice, and the wood, and the stones, and the dust, and licked up the water that was in the trench.' And when all the people saw it, they were so powerfully affected, that they fell on their faces; and they said, 'The Lord he is the God! The Lord he is the God!' Now, is this report true?

" *Servant.* True to the letter.

" *Carmelite.* There must have been great danger of 'excitement' among the people, in view of such scenes. But it is further reported that Elijah said unto them, 'Take the prophets of Baal; let not one of them escape. And they took them; and Elijah brought them down to the brook Kishon, and slew them there.'

" *Servant.* That history is also true.

" *Carmelite.* The prophet Elijah must then be willing to agitate the people and produce 'excitements.' I have no confidence in his 'discretion.' But you have interrupted me, and broken the thread of my discourse. I wished to speak of some of the 'evils of rain.'

" *Servant.* Well, then, go on, in your own way.

" *Carmelite.* Well, in the first place, rain, in modern times, does not come as it ought to come; it ought to come as a *blessing.* The face of heaven should be mild and smiling, and calculated to inspire the hearts of men with cheerfulness and joy; then all would welcome the rain with perfect unanimity, and the serenity and harmony of families and neighborhoods would not be interrupted by it. Instead of this, I have seen the black cloud roll up its pitchy volumes in the north-west, and throw its terrible shadow across the heavens: earth was shrouded in darkness, its pale inhabitants quaked with terror, and many have been driven to absolute distraction. Yes, these evils I have seen in connection with modern rains.

"2. When the rain descended, it did not come in soft and gentle distillations, so as gradually to water the earth to make it bring forth and bud; but I have seen it violently poured down from the rent cloud in foaming cataracts, so as to tear up the earth, wash off the soil, and do great injury.

"3. Many modern rains have brought from the clouds such an immense discharge of water, that the streams were swollen above their banks, the plains were overflowed, fences, stacks of corn, flocks and herds have been swept away and destroyed: it was all done by rain. Such calamities never were known to happen in dry weather.

"4. I have also known, along with modern rains, gusts of wind that unroofed the buildings, prostrated the fruit trees, and strewed the face of the country with havoc and devastation. Can any one deny that these are great evils?

"5. It is also well known, that in connection with modern rains, there have been flashes of lightning and peals of thunder of awful character — the tall oak and the majestic cedar have been shivered to atoms; the barn and the mansion house have been set on fire and burned to the ground, and in many cases human life has been destroyed in a moment. Who would not prefer perpetual drought to rains attended with such immense evils? Nor is this all; for,

"6. I have known modern rains come quite out of season, and the ripe harvest was greatly injured, and the mown grass was totally destroyed by excessive and unseasonable rains; and further,

"7. I have observed, with an accuracy that could not be mistaken, that rains, after all that has been said in their favor, actually nourish rank and noxious weeds. Yes, thorns, thistles, briers, brambles, and innumerable pernicious plants, are unquestionably nourished by rain. In proof of this, see how clean the fields are now — not a hurtful weed to be seen within the whole enclosure. Ah, it is because we have had no rain for three years and a half to make such weeds grow and thrive. That is the true reason.

"*Servant.* But the wheat is all burned up, too. The scorching drought, that has destroyed the weeds, has also consumed every vegetable that is valuable.

"*Carmelite.* Well, well; I am not talking of wheat. I am speaking of the noxious weeds that rain produces. But as you mention wheat, I will tell you what I have observed on that subject, and this will be *evil* number

"8. The rain, if it makes the wheat grow, makes the *chaff grow too.* I have noticed, in seasons when we had rain, that in close connection with the wheat, there were quantities of chaff; not a grain of wheat could you find, but there was chaff on the very same stalk. Let the advocates of rain deny this, if they can. And further,

"9. Modern rains are very transient in their influence. I have seen the ground become as *dry* a few weeks or months after the rain, as it was before it fell. I tell you, that is one of my strongest objections to modern rains: they are *transient;* the ground will actually get dry after it has been moistened by them.

" *Servant.* Then you need another shower.

" *Carmelite.* Ah, there is where you are wrong. If we had the *right kind* of rain, its influence would not pass away so soon. Rain did not dry up thus in the days of Moses and the fathers.

" *Servant.* I have read the history of Moses, and if you will compare Ex. xv. 1—18, with the 24th verse of the same chapter, and the 3d and 4th verses of chapter xvi., you will find there were some sudden droughts then, as well as in later days.

" *Carmelite.* But I have a tenth objection. I have known the health of many worthy citizens ruined by rain. In fact, many diseases, such as rheumatisms, coughs, consumptions, &c., are promoted by rain. O, if men could be persuaded to dwell on the top of Giboa, where there is no rain, neither any dew, what delightful health they might enjoy!

" *Servant.* Stop, Carmelite! stop, I beseech you!

They had now just reached the top of this lofty peak, for the seventh time, that looked out toward the sea. The servant, in a sudden transport of joy, seized the Carmelite by the arm, and pointed eagerly to the south-western horizon. 'Behold, Carmelite, behold, on the distant verge of heaven, don't you see a little object rising there, like " a man's hand " '? The Carmelite looked for a moment in the direction the servant pointed. Presently unwonted paleness overspread his long, lean, leathern visage. His frame began to tremble, and his knees to smite one against another. 'That looks very much like a cloud!' he exclaimed in accents of troubled agitation. 'Ah, yes, I see. It is spreading alarmingly! It throws its volumes abroad in all directions! We are threatened with rain! My cave! My cave! My only chance for shelter is in my cave!' And suiting the action to the word, he hurried down the mountain, and darted into his cave. There, in its deep and gloomy recesses, he brooded over the awful condition of the country, and wrung his hands, and exclaimed, 'Alas! alas! how imminent is the danger! The day is darkened! The sun is eclipsed! The black clouds are over the entire face of heaven! Just what I apprehended and dreaded! But the prophet Elijah was so self-willed and obstinate that he would listen to no reason, no remonstrance! There! there!' he cried out, as he heard the roaring of 'a great and strong wind that rent the mountains, and brake in pieces the rocks,' 'There! there! my worst forebodings are realized! I said there would be wind! How wide the desolation will spread! But an indiscreet prophet can't be managed. There's no making him "judicious." Eh! Eh!' he suddenly shrieked, in a sharp, shrill outcry, as a bright blaze of lightning kindled up all the mountain side, and glared into the cave of the Carmelite, so as to make every object, for a moment, distinctly visible. 'There's the lightning! there's the lightning! and next we shall have the thunder peal that will make the mountain tremble. And the rain has already begun. Yes, I hear it, I hear it. It's pouring down! It's pouring down! There goes a foaming torrent, dashing impetuously and raving by the very door of my cave. I warned Elijah faithfully of all this, but he was deaf to counsel. It was all in vain! It was all in vain!'

"Thus the old Carmelite continued to writhe, wring

his hands, and pour forth lamentations during all the while that there was the sound of an abundance of rain.' He remained close in his cave for a number of days, brooding over the horrors of the alarming visitation that had come upon the country in answer to the prayer of Elijah. The *evils*, the *evils* of rain! When, at length, he ventured forth, vegetation was every where springing up; the fields were clothed in living green; all nature was rejoicing,—

'For the queen of the spring, as she passed o'er the vale,
Left her robe on the trees, and her breath on the gale.'

The lambs were leaping for joy, the tuneful birds filled the groves with melody. Happy families were sending presents and congratulations one to another. Age smoothed its care-worn brow to bless the Lord, while children clapped their little hands, and sung, 'Hosanna.'

"But as for the Carmelite, none of those things moved him. The *evils of rain* was the theme of his meditation, and burden of his tongue. He passed from farm to farm, inquiring whose field had been injured by the washing rain, whose roof had leaked, who had been caught out in the shower, who had taken cold, or had a cough, or rheumatic pain aggravated; and from the facts he collected, he was greatly strengthened in his notion about the *evils of rain*, and could declaim on the subject more eloquently than ever."

STAGE-COACH DISCUSSION.

In the month of October, 1838, a company of travellers were passing in a stage-coach from Vicksburg to Clinton, in the state of Mississippi. Among the passengers was a minister of the gospel, and a gentleman who was then a member of the legislature of that state; a senator, I believe. And now, for a number of years past, he has been a senator from Mississippi, in the congress of the United States.

The free and desultory conversation in the stage turned at length on the subject of religion. When the following dialogue, in substance, took place: —

Senator. I understand that you are a minister of the gospel.

Minister. Yes, sir.

Senator. There are some things in the Bible which to me appear difficult of comprehension. I should be pleased to hear your explanation, if you have no objections.

Minister. None at all. But let me ask, have you studied the Bible?

Senator. Well — why — perhaps not so much as I should have done.

Minister. Are you not then unreasonable? That book relates to eternity. It treats of subjects of immeasurable importance. You have given it but little attention, and yet wonder that you do not comprehend all that it contains. You act not thus in other matters. Here is a man who never spent one half week of his life in attempting to acquire a knowledge of mathematics. He takes up a volume of Euclid ; he looks into it for a little time, and then objects,—" Here are points, lines, angles, circles, triangles, &c. I cannot comprehend their meaning." You would say to him, " Sir, you have not given that book the attention which its importance demands. It is not strange, therefore, that you do not comprehend its contents. If you will turn your thoughts to it, and bestow upon it the proper amount of study and of time, you will behold truth, beauty, grandeur, in those very figures that now appear unmeaning and mysterious."

" But, perhaps," said the minister to the senator, " you were going to specify the particular difficulty that you have encountered in the Bible."

Senator. I was about to mention the passage in the book of Joshua, where Joshua commands the sun and moon to stand still.

Minister. And what is the particular difficulty there ?

Senator. To speak of the sun standing still, is not good philosophy ; for we know it is the diurnal revolution of the earth that gives to the sun, and the moon, and the stars, their apparent motions.

Minister. Certainly, sir ; and Sir Isaac Newton understood that altogether as well as we ; and yet he would speak of the sun rising, and the sun setting, the moon rising, and the moon going down ; and all philosophers talk thus when they wish to be understood. The Bible uses the language common to man.

It was designed to be understood. Allow me to say, sir, that you do yourself injustice in bringing forward an objection like this. It is not worthy of a philosopher. On the same ground, you would reject every almanac published in Europe and America. For all these almanacs not only speak of the rising and the setting of the sun and the moon, but they are very careful to point out the exact minute, when these *unphilosophical absurdities* take place.

Senator. I did not intend to insist on this objection. I have another, of a character more serious. Would not such a suspension of the rotary motion of the earth have introduced confusion, derangement, and ruin into the entire solar system ?

Minister. Your question is this : When the master workman has completed every wheel, spring, lever, and minuter part of the perfect watch or clock, and put the machine together, and set it in motion, can he now stop the minute hand and the hour hand, for one half day, or one whole day, without introducing confusion and ruin into the entire structure ? Joshua "spake to the Lord in that day," and the miracle was performed by that hand which built the stupendous frame of nature. Surely the divine Architect can control the work of his hands as easily as an earthly mechanic.

Senator. Yet the narrative has something about it that strikes my mind as strange and incredible.

Minister. That is owing to our limited and imperfect knowledge in the present life. In the early history of what has been called the *far west,* there was a steamboat built, by the order of the government, for the purpose of exploring the Missouri River. The figure-head of that boat was fashioned like the head of an enormous serpent. It projected some distance in front of the boat, and then the body of the serpent seemed to wind down under the boat till it was lost from view in the water. The head and body of this serpent were painted with bright colors, — red, green, yellow, — in long streaks, so as to give it a very frightful appearance. The machinery was so constructed, that when the fires were kindled up and the vessel was in motion, the steam, smoke, and sparks were thrown out at the mouth of this serpent. In this style it moved up the Missouri River — a monstrous serpent, carrying the great boat on its back, breathing out steam, smoke, and fire in its progress. Indians, of the various tribes along the river, would come to the top of the bluffs that overlook the stream. They would gaze a moment or two in terror at the moving monster, then wheel and yell, and run for their lives.

Now, how perfectly mysterious, to one of these untutored Indians, was the fact, that a skilful engineer, by simply turning a screw, can stop the action of that mighty machinery that throws the boat with such speed against the current of the rapid river, and by giving that screw a turn the other way, can put it all in motion again.

The present life is but our birthday. We but "know in part," we but "see through a glass darkly." In a future state, no doubt, we shall see clearly how a mighty angel could stop the rotary motion of the earth; or take off the fury of the flame of Nebuchadnezzar's furnace, so that Shadrach, Meshech, and Abednego could walk through the midst of it, without having a hair of their head singed, or the smell of fire upon their raiment; or stop the mouths of the lions, so that Daniel could stay all night unhurt in their den. Indeed, there are beings above and around us now to whom these matters are just as plain as the mode of managing a mighty engine is to a skilful engineer. You remember, doubtless, the beautiful lines of Pope —

"Superior beings, when of late they saw
A mortal man unfold all nature's law,
Admired such wisdom in an earthly shape,
And showed a Newton as we show an ape."

Senator. But my great difficulty is yet untouched. I can't see that it was worthy of the great God to perform such a miracle as this, merely to give one nation the advantage over another in battle. Can it be shown that this miracle, at *that time*, and *in that connection*, was worthy of the great God?

Minister. That is indeed the most important question that has yet been brought up. And I assure you that it admits of a most satisfactory answer.

Senator. I shall be much gratified to hear a conclusive answer.

Minister. I think that three points can be established to your entire satisfaction.

1. That there was *then* a critical juncture in the affairs of men, which rendered it worthy of God to interpose and perform that miracle; that the miracle itself was timely, appropriate, and highly instructive.

2. That traditions have come down among heathen nations which show that such an event certainly took place.

3. That the whole matter is in perfect unison with the elevated and sublime spirit of Bible religion.

Senator. If these points can be established, the objection must certainly vanish. I will hear you patiently.

Minister. It must be borne in mind that idolatry, the worship of false gods, was in that age the besetting sin of the world. Infidelity is a somewhat modern device of Satan. His great engine of destruction, in that age, was idolatry.

Egypt, Nineveh, Babylon, all the wealthy and powerful kingdoms of the earth, had been carried away by this destructive and strong delusion. Idolatry had swallowed up the nations. It was triumphant north, south, east, and west. With the single exception of Israel, no nation had escaped the insnaring power of this master device of the prince of hell. The whole land of Canaan was deluged with this hideous delusion. The objects which they idolized were many, but the most notable were the sun and the moon, which they worshipped under the title of the king and queen of heaven.

A memorable conflict between idolatry and the true religion, dates its commencement from the first mission of Moses to Pharaoh, king of Egypt. Many of the wonders performed in Egypt were designed to show that the idols of the heathen are nothing; and that Jehovah, the God of Israel, is the living and the true God. It is essential that this be borne in mind, in order to a correct understanding of much of the Old Testament. The overthrow of Pharaoh and his mighty Egyptian army at the Red Sea, sent terror and trembling to the heart of the heathen world. They realized that it was a fearful thing to fall into the hands of Israel's God. The impression was so deep that it is found among the Philistines many ages afterward, as appears from 1 Sam. iv. 7, 8: "And the Philistines were afraid, for they said, God is come into the camp. And they said, Woe unto us! for there hath not been such a thing heretofore. Woe unto us! Who shall deliver us out of the hand of these mighty Gods? these are the Gods that smote the Egyptians with all the plagues in the wilderness."

As Israel journeyed from the Red Sea toward Canaan, the news of God's wonders among them ran ahead, and spread among the nations west of Jordan. At length, from their mountain tops and temple towers they began to catch a glimpse of that fiery pillar that glided slowly along in front of the hosts of the Lord. Next the immense moving multitude came in view, and the banner of each of the tribes could be distinctly seen. Presently the stream of Jordan is rolled back by an invisible hand, and banner after banner is seen going down on the eastern side into the channel, and soon banner after banner rises on the western shore. Jericho falls before them. City after city is overcome. Presently Gibeon, one of the royal cities, convinced of the folly of their idol worship, send and make a league with Joshua and with Israel, and acknowledge Jehovah as the only living and true God. "Thy servants are come," said they to Joshua, "because of the name of the Lord thy God; for we have heard the fame of him, and all that he did in Egypt." (Josh. ix. 9.) This was a solemn profession of the true religion. They thus publicly renounced heathenism, and acknowledged Jehovah as the only true God. Now, "Gibeon was a great city, one of the royal cities, and all the men thereof were mighty." This was a tremendous blow to idolatry, and it roused to earnest action the advocates of idol worship in all surrounding kingdoms. "Wherefore Adoni-zedec, king of Jerusalem, sent unto Hoham king of Hebron, and unto Piram king of Jarmuth, and unto Japhia king of Lachish, and unto Debir king of Eglon, saying, Come up unto me, and help me, that we may smite Gibeon; for it hath made peace with Joshua and with the children of Israel. Therefore the five kings of the Amorites, the king of Jerusalem, the king of Hebron, the king of Jarmuth, the king of Lachish, the king of Eglon, gathered themselves together, and went up, they and all their hosts, and encamped before Gibeon, and made war against it. And the men of Gibeon sent unto Joshua to the camp to Gilgal, saying, Slack not thy hand from thy servants: come up to us quickly, and save us, and help us; for all the kings of the Amorites that dwell in the mountains are gathered together against us. So Joshua ascended from Gilgal, he, and all the people of war with him, and all the mighty men of valor." Here is the most notable and eventful struggle on the field of battle which the annals of the world have witnessed between idolatry and the true religion. What were the leading idols to which these deluded Canaanites paid divine honors? They were the sun and moon. To these they offered their profane adorations under the title of the king and queen of heaven. When man is in trouble, he calls upon his God. The fears excited among these idolaters by the wonders done by the God of Israel, of which they had been told, would lead them to call for help now on their supreme deities; that is, on the sun and the moon. Breathing prayers to these, they mustered their armies; and officers and soldiers, as they marched to the dreaded conflict, sent up their earnest petitions for help to the sun and to the moon.

Now, what is that which a routed army, flying from a victorious foe, so much desires? It is *night*, that under its dark covert the fugitive may elude his pursuer. At the sanguinary battle of Waterloo, the Prussian army, commanded by Blucher, was strangely tardy in coming into the action; and when the experienced eye of Wellington beheld the frightful waste produced by the columns of the French army, as, led on by its fiery marshals, they charged in terrible succession on the exhausted troops of England, "If that deadly charge continues ten minutes longer," he exclaimed, "I must order a retreat! O that Blucher or night would come!" Yes, *night*, the darkness of night, is that which a flying army preëminently desires. Behold now the scene on the field of Gibeon: the embattled armies of the confederate kings, with courage inflamed by burning appeals from renowned warriors who lead them on, rush with headlong fury against the hosts of the Lord. Along the extended line, the strife of contending champions is stern and terrible. "We come, sustained by the gods we worship!" cries Adonizedec, at the head of his army. "We meet you," answers Joshua, "in the name of Him who dried up the Red Sea!" "The sun and moon are our helpers and our gods!" shout the heathen multitudes, making a desperate onset. "My help cometh from the Lord, which made heaven and earth!" replies Israel, repelling their legions, as the rock repels a thousand waves. Soon the scales of destiny begin to turn. Victory perches on the standard of Israel. And O, what confusion, terror, rout, and ruin have overtaken that idolatrous multitude! Hark! that loud and lamentable cry! that earnest, imploring prayer that bursts from myriads of agonized bosoms, "Ye sources of light, whom we have worshipped! Sun and moon, to whom we have poured out our offerings! Withdraw your rays! withdraw! withdraw! let thick darkness cover us, that we may hide from the sword of our pursuers!"

Then spoke Joshua to the Lord; and he said, in the sight of all Israel, "Sun, stand thou still upon Gibeon! and thou, moon, in the valley of Ajalon! Throw your light around them! Let there be no darkness nor mantle of night, under which the champions of idolatry may hide themselves! Let the heathen nations know that Israel's God made and manages the sun and moon, and can make the very luminaries they have profanely idolized contribute to their overthrow!" "And the sun stood still, and the moon stayed, until the people had avenged themselves upon their enemies. Is not this written in the book of Jasher? So the sun stood still in the midst of heaven, and hasted not to go down about a whole day. And there was no day like that, before it or after it, that the Lord hearkened unto the voice of a man; for the Lord fought for Israel."

There are now three particulars, in relation to this miracle, which I wish you carefully to consider.

1. This miracle was worthy of God, and demanded by the circumstances of the occasion. It was peculiarly appropriate, timely, and instructive. The darkness and delusion that have come over the human soul constitute one of the most mournful results of man's rebellion. God has employed a "long cloud of witnesses" to testify divine truth to men. Patriarchs, prophets, apos-

tles, many of the brightest luminaries that have appeared in the intellectual firmament, have been thus employed for ages. When the Son of God came to earth, the first office in which he engaged was that of a teacher of righteousness. Long did he labor, that man might be delivered from spiritual darkness, and led to a knowledge of the truth concerning God. Now, I ask, was it worthy of Jehovah to employ such intellects as Enoch, and Moses, and Isaiah, that men might be delivered from fatal error, and brought to know the truth? Was it worthy of God to send his only Son to earth, to preach at the sea-side, in the synagogue, and on the mountain, that blinded, erring man might come to the knowledge of the truth? And was it unworthy of God to use any portion of that unconscious matter which his own hand had created, for the same great purpose? Was it unworthy of God to make use of the flood, the fire, the earth, the sun, the moon, to sweep from the soul of man a most fatal delusion, and fasten there a conviction of that great truth which lies at the very foundation of all true religion? The more correctly we understand the actual characteristics of that idolatry which had bewitched and bewildered the nations of Canaan, the more clearly we shall see that in this "notable miracle" the God of Israel appears divinely wise, divinely good, and divinely glorious.

2. Traditions have come down among the heathen nations, that can be accounted for only by admitting the reality of this recorded miracle. Authentic history among the Gentiles fails, by some thousand years, to reach back to the time of Joshua. Yet notable events, which were observed before the days of Hesiod and of

Homer, have been handed down from age to age by tradition. Often, indeed, there is a great deal of fabulous drapery thrown around such events. But when you strip off the covering in which poets and sages have dressed it, the substance of the historical fact is there. Now, among their many traditions is found the following: Apollo being the god of the sun, it was his business to drive the chariot of the sun round the world every day, in order to give light to the inhabitants. The thing was done with great exactness and propriety while Apollo attended to it in person. But Apollo at length became the father of a headstrong, adventurous boy, whose name was Phaëton. A playmate of Phaëton's insulted him, by alleging that his mother had deceived him as to his parentage, and that Apollo would not own him as his son. Phaëton, full of anger and vexation, hurried to the palace of Apollo, and demanded, "Do you, Apollo, acknowledge me as your son?"

"I do," answered Apollo.

"What proof will you give that you own me?" asked Phaëton.

"I will give you any proof you may desire."

"Swear to that by an inviolable oath," said Phaëton.

Apollo accordingly took the inviolable oath.

"Now, Phaëton, what do you ask?" said Apollo.

"I ask," said Phaëton, "the privilege of driving the chariot of the sun round the world for one day."

"Alas! Phaëton," said Apollo, "you know not what you ask. It requires all my strength and skill to manage the fiery horses. It is utterly beyond your strength."

But Phaëton was inflexible, and the oath of Apollo inviolable. So Phaëton is the driver for one day. Ovid says that Phaëton succeeded tolerably well in driving up the ascent of the morning, till the sun reached his noonday station. But when it became necessary to commence the descent by which the sun might go down, the horses became restive, unmanageable, and all Phaëton's efforts were wholly unavailing. The sun strangely remained in the heavens, and refused to go down; and the heathen poet, after enumerating many disasters that ensued, uses almost the very language of the book of Joshua, that "there was no day like that day."

Now, strip off the drapery which the poet's imagination has thrown around this matter, and come to the facts of the case. What ever put it into the head of a heathen sage to get up a story like this? Evidently the fact, that there was one extraordinary day in which the sun strangely refused to go down, as on other days. And heathen sages, attempting to account for the singular phenomenon according to their philosophy and their mythology, very naturally came to the conclusion, that the right driver was not engaged on that day, and that the reins, and the management of the chariot of the sun, had been intrusted to inexperienced and incompetent hands. This heathen tradition is a marked and strong confirmation of the miracle, as recorded in the book of Joshua. Had no such interruption of the sun's course ever taken place, we should never have heard this tradition.

3. This command of Joshua is in perfect unison with the elevated and sublime spirit of Bible religion. "Hallowed be thy name!" is the first petition in our Lord's prayer. The most important end that any created object can answer, is to honor and glorify God.

The song of the church in heaven is, "Thou art worthy, O Lord, to receive glory, and honor, and power; for thou hast created all things, and for thy pleasure they are and were created." The song of the church on earth is, "Praise ye the Lord. Praise ye the Lord from the heavens; praise him in the heights. Praise ye him, all his angels; praise ye him, all his hosts. Praise ye him, sun and moon; praise him, all ye stars of light. Let them praise the name of the Lord; for he commanded, and they were created." Of this religion the soul of Joshua was full to overflowing. He had beheld the wonders of God in Egypt; he had witnessed that great transaction at the Red Sea. The river of Egypt had honored God, and blushed itself to blood when smitten by his rod. The Red Sea had honored God when it made a way for his people. The clouds of heaven had honored God when they sent down the manna. Mount Sinai had honored God with her smoke and her flame when the Lord descended upon it in fire. The earth had honored God when she opened her mouth at his command, and swallowed up Korah, Dathan, and Abiram. Jordan had honored God when it rolled back its tide, and stood in a heap at the approach of the ark of his covenant. Joshua had seen all this, and rejoiced that unconscious Nature honored her God. And now, when the heathen army approached, bearing on their banners profane devices of the sun and moon which they have idolized, the soul of Joshua was roused, and he calls again upon unconscious nature to honor the great God. We are reminded of the language of Christ, when the Pharisees called on him to rebuke the disciples who were speaking his praise. "He answered and said unto them, I tell you that, if these should hold their peace, the stones would immediately cry out." The same spirit was in the prophet when he said, "The stone shall cry out of the wall, and the beam from the timber shall answer it."

The appeal of Joshua may be paraphrased thus: "O Sun! O Moon! Can you bear to have your Maker dishonored and blasphemed? Can you bear to look on and see stupid, rebellious man change the glory of the incorruptible God into a lie, and worship and serve the creature more than the Creator? Remonstrate! remonstrate against such awful profanation! Stand still, in the midst of heaven! Shine to your Maker's praise! Witness to all these deluded nations, that you are upheld and controlled by a hand that is divine." The sublime religion which animated the heart of Joshua taught him that the glory of God is the highest good of the universe, and that the best use that can be made of earth or ocean, sun or moon, is to have them proclaim the wisdom, the power, the grandeur, the supremacy of the great, eternal God. And hence, when Joshua gave this notable command, he was acting in perfect harmony with this elevated and divine religion. I close with two remarks.

1. We are not surprised that "Israel served the Lord *all the days* of Joshua, and all the days of the elders that overlived Joshua." The very companions of such a man would shed a wholesome influence around them as long as they lived.

2. Joshua witnessed more of God's wonderful works than any mere man who ever lived. He saw most, or all, of the miracles performed by Moses. He beheld the works of Israel's God in Egypt, at the Red Sea,

at Mount Sinai, and throughout the wilderness. And then, when Moses was dead, he led the tribes into Canaan, and saw God's wonders there. He nobly sustained his part in life, through a long series of years, and well deserves an honorable rank among "the great men of the Bible."

At this point the stage passengers separated, as earthly travellers must. What effect was produced on the mind of the senator, the writer has not had opportunity to learn. The substance of the conversation is inserted here, with the hope that it may aid others to understand this notable passage in the Bible.

THE SKELETON PREACHER, AND THE CONGREGATION OF DRY BONES.

EXTRACT FROM AN ANCIENT JEWISH RECORD.

The valley was wide, long, and very capacious, but the reign of desolation was there. The green grass had spread no carpet over the ground; neither plant nor flowering shrub was to be seen; nor did the tall forest tree, lifting up its majestic form toward heaven, there wave its beautiful branches in the breeze, or cast its refreshing shade around. The naked earth had long been baked and scorched by the rays of a torrid sun. No living form was seen in that deserted and desolate field. Every beast of the forest kept aloof. Nor was it approached by one of "the cattle upon a thousand hills." Even the birds of the air shunned it, as they are said to have shunned the lake of Sodom, and the very winds of heaven appeared paralyzed and powerless when they came to the confines of this kingdom of the dead.

The valley was "full of bones; and behold, there were very many in the open valley; and lo, they were very dry." (Ez. xxxvii. 1, 2.) While I gazed on the sad scene before me, my ear was caught by a strange, unearthly voice. "I am the pastor of this congregation," said the voice; "this day is the seventieth anniversary of the commencement of my ministry among you, and now I am about to preach again."

I turned to see the speaker, and behold there stood up in the midst of the valley a ghastly skeleton of dry bones. Its naked, fleshless condition gave it the appearance of unusual tallness, and the long bones on which it stood, and of which it was composed, appeared extremely dry. The ribs had a bleached and wasted aspect, from long exposure in the open plain. The skull was bare and weather-beaten, and the empty sockets, where eyes should have been, had a frightful, ghastly look; the teeth were all exposed, and extremely white. Sometimes he stretched out his long, fleshless arm and hand, and then every bone was distinctly seen. Sometimes he brought his hand to his side, and then his dry fingers would rattle on his naked ribs; and then, again, he would clasp his hands, while the bones would clatter and clank one against another. How he could speak without the use of lungs, or lips, or tongue, I could not tell; but there was a strange, sepulchral hollowness in his voice, and his articulation had a supernatural and horrible distinctness.

As he turned his head to address the different parts of his congregation, the naked skull harshly grated and creaked on the dry neck bones; yet there was an air of gloomy satisfaction in the manner of this *skeleton preacher*, while he surveyed the multitude before him, as if their situation delighted him much. A haggard expression of approval looked out through the hollow sockets of his eyes, and there appeared on his naked cheek-bone the dim counterfeit of a ghastly smile.

"O ye dry bones," he exclaimed; "this is the anniversary of my profitable and acceptable ministry among you. It is therefore highly proper that we should mutually rejoice together; yea, that we should mutually rejoice in each other; for few preachers have had such a congregation, and few congregations have had such a preacher.

"O ye dry bones, on this joyful occasion you must allow me to speak freely. I must go into particulars, and rehearse the many things in your present prosperous and promising condition, that afford me rapturous delight.

"First, then, O ye dry bones, I am in raptures while I contemplate you, because you are so *steady.* Steadiness and stillness are well known as the attributes of profound attention, and thus you bestow the highest encomium on your esteemed and beloved pastor; for what congregation have been so long composed and orderly, under stated and regular ministrations, as you have been under mine? For the term of seventy years, you have been entirely steady, and still, no one of you has moved the breadth of a hair. It is true, O ye dry bones, that a superficial observer might ascribe your stillness to a want of life. Indeed, when I have been boasting of my charge, and telling abroad how calm and composed my congregation continue, notwithstanding the surrounding agitations of a troubled and tumultuous world, it has been broadly hinted to me that my church is dead, utterly dead, and that the stillness there is the stillness of death. But, O ye dry bones, none of these things move me. I scorn calumny and misrepresentation. I maintain that we are conservative; not dead, but highly conservative. A mere itinerant preacher, or transient visitor, cannot judge of your state as your judicious and experienced pastor can; and he puts a very different construction on the collected calmness and regular habits that have characterized you through a long series of years; yea, the stability and composure that reign among you are the joy of his heart, and the theme of his daily exultation. But I must proceed to the

"Second characteristic. O ye dry bones, I am exceedingly gratified with the *uniformity* that has long prevailed among you. Who has not heard that consistency is a jewel? Now, O ye dry bones, you are consistent; you are uniform in your habits; *I always know where to find you.* An uncertain church I cannot bear. But here you are just in the same spot where you were seventy years ago, and just as dry. O, what a privilege to be the pastor of such a church! and what a privilege for a church to have such a preacher! The 'fits and starts,' that have agitated many other churches — the 'spasmodic awakenings,' that have disturbed them — have never affected you in the least, since the happy day of my installation as your pastor. You have slept on, O ye dry bones, and taken your rest, from month to month, and from year to year. Indeed, such has been your admirable uniformity, that if I were called on to say which year of my popular ministry among you has been most notable for sound sleeping, and motionless, stagnant inactivity, it would be hard to make the selection.

"In this respect, O ye dry bones, you have been a constant source of comfort and consolation to me. It must be confessed, that our lot has fallen to us in the midst of a restless and agitated world. The kingdom of nature, I am sorry to say, is sadly out of joint. I have no doubt that it is in consequence of the fall; but I find that the wheels of nature and the wheels of time have a mighty propensity to be in motion. Indeed, I am continually disturbed by departures from that standard of excellence, which we have long since set up in our '*model congregation.*' The changes of morning and evening, noon and night, are to me exceedingly annoying. How much more desirable would it be to have *uniformity!* And as light is fleeting and transient in its very nature, I should give my voice for the establishment of the kingdom of perpetual, unmitigated night. I long for uniformity. The clouds of heaven, also, appear restless, and fond of flitting about: one day they are driving over the face of the sky, and another day wholly out of sight. We have fair weather and foul, clear days and cloudy, wet days and dry days. I am perplexed with mutability in the kingdom of nature. I have heard of a happy period, in days of old, when there was no rain for three years and six months. What delightful uniformity the seasons must have had at that time! How happy the lot of those who lived in that day! But now the earth is distracted with successive changes. The streams are, at one time, so low as to show the pebbles at the bottom; and then they will rise, and overflow all their banks. The restless ocean is ebbing and flowing every day, and the earth itself is constantly varying. Scarcely has winter subdued the vegetable kingdom, and established its reign, when spring bursts forth, and sends out its buds, and wakes its flowers, and throws its green robes over 'hill, and dale, and mountain-peak.' And then summer comes, with its harvests, and autumn, with its fruits. Alas for the mutability that prevails in the world! Were it not, O ye dry bones, that you have been in no condition to travel, I should long since have proposed that I and my church would emigrate to the north — to the region of perpetual ice and snow. I learn that there is delightful uniformity in that country. No bud, or leaf, or blossom vegetates there, from age to age. Happy they who dwell in that sweet clime. Ah, the sweetest, beyond all doubt, on which the sun is permitted to shine! But we have not been in a condition to emigrate; and therefore, O ye dry bones, allow me to say, as your honored and much-esteemed pastor, that when I have been vexed and tortured with the changes and revolutions in the natural world, I have found comfort and consolation when I have turned to you. Ah, such delightful uniformity! Here you are, perfectly motionless and cold and dry; yes, as dry as you were seventy years ago. Admirable congregation! Surely your pastor may exclaim, 'To me the inheritance has fallen in marvellously pleasant places.'

"Thirdly. O ye dry bones, another feature in your condition I regard as peculiarly favorable: that is, you are so entirely free from *animal excitement.* Long experience and extensive observation have convinced me that the living principle, the moving principle, is the dangerous principle; and I have found the perfection of prudence among dry bones. Never have I known a dry bone take a hasty step, make a rash, indiscreet movement, or put forth precipitate and inconsiderate action. Ah, there is safety about dry bones! And O that the world were warned of the danger of rash, hasty action, produced by animal excitement!"

Here I discovered, for the first time, a number of

shadowy forms flitting and bestirring themselves around the skeleton preacher. On closer observation, I found that they were skeletons, also, but so perfectly fleshless and bare, and the bones had such a slim, attenuated appearance, that they might have been mistaken for shadows. These, I learned, were volunteer helpers of the pastor — skeletons who spent their time in eulogizing and puffing him to the members of his congregation. They echoed his sentiments, and sung his praises. "Animal excitement!" they exclaimed all at once, as soon as the expression fell from the skeleton preacher — "animal excitement!" Then each deputy or subaltern skeleton took off in his own direction among the dry bones, repeating, "Animal excitement! What a marvellous skeleton our pastor is! how profound! how talented! how judicious! Animal excitement! O ye dry bones, beware of animal excitement!" Over the entire valley of dry bones could be heard the harsh, husky voice of the deputy skeletons — "Beware of animal excitement! beware of animal excitement!" It seemed a strange and needless exhortation, for the bones were very dry. There was not a particle of flesh on them. There was not a fragment of sinew, nerve, or tendon. There was not a drop of blood, or a throbbing pulse, in all their thousands. One would have thought that a more appropriate exhortation would have been this: "Beware of mildew and total decay! beware of being further bleached by the sleet, and snow, and hail-storms, to which you are exposed! beware of being further parched and dried by the torrid rays, which pour down upon you in this naked valley!" The skeleton pastor turned the hollow sockets in his dry skull, as if looking after his deputy skeletons, who were so busy among the dry bones; a glare of hideous satisfaction seemed to issue from those dark caverns, as he surveyed his helpers, and the ghastly smile on his naked cheek-bone assumed unwonted distinctness. After a moment, he resumed his discourse.

"Talk as you will," he exclaimed, "the pastor who encourages the *breath of life* among his people will have trouble. No congregation is so manageable, so perfectly under the control of its pastor, as a congregation of dry bones. Show me a church whose members have flesh on their bones, blood in their veins, and a heart in their body, — a church whose members have eyes and ears, brains in their skull, a tongue in their head, and breath in their bosom, — and I will show you a church subject to *excitements*, and variations, and ups and downs. Yes, such a church will have day and night, summer and winter, cold and heat, seed-time and harvest; in short, there will be no end to their fluctuations. O ye dry bones, I must exult in your stability, your uniformity, your perfect exemption from 'animal excitement,' through all the years of my ministry among you. Some pastors can only commend a part of their flock; but I can commend you all. Though you are very many, yet you are very dry. You have all 'held your own,' and kept free from 'animal excitement.' Yes, I can witness in your behalf, that in all my seventy years' ministry among you, never have I been annoyed with breathing lungs, a beating heart, or a throbbing pulse; no glow of heat, above that possessed by the granite rock, has passed over you; never has there been a drop of blood in your veins, or a particle of flesh or muscle, sinew or nerve, upon you. O ye dry bones, you have chosen, with commendable unanimity, your beloved pastor as your pattern and your model; and each bone of you is naked, and cold, and dry as his own; and each skull of you as perfectly exempt from brains as the great example (modesty will scarcely suffer me to be thus particular) which you have chosen to copy.

"Fourthly. Once more, O ye dry bones, permit me to say, that I admire your *durability*. Here you are, much the same as you were seventy years ago. Flesh will fall off, blood will run out, vital warmth will cool, and life itself will expire; but 'dry bones' hold their own admirably. Indeed, the only remains we have of the early ages are in the form of bones — some of them of most gigantic size. Had the antediluvian churches, like mine, been composed of 'dry bones,' only, they might have remained to this day. I should like to know how those troublesome preachers, who insist on having flesh on the bones, and blood in the veins, breath in the lungs, and life in the heart, would meet this argument. Ah, their churches cannot stand the test of time! The heart may sicken, and the life that is therein may die, the breath may depart, the flesh perish, and the blood, also; but the bones! Ah, there is durability, especially when kept 'very dry'! It is susceptible of demonstration, that the drier they are kept, the more durable they are. He that wishes his church to last, let him keep his bones 'very dry.'

"It is certainly commendable in every preacher, O ye dry bones, to know himself. Indeed, ancient philosophers declare, that the maxim 'Know thyself' has been handed down from Jupiter. In this respect, O ye dry bones, I have the satisfaction to inform you, that your own illustrious preacher has succeeded to admiration. He has mastered the mystery that so long puzzled the contemporaries of Samson; that is, he has found out 'wherein his great strength lieth.' He has ascertained, with the clearness of demonstration, that his enormous talent consists not so much in ability to do any good himself, as to find fault with what others do. By careful experiments, I have discovered that fault-finding is a business that can be set up on very small capital. There is little demand for intellect, learning, or piety, in order to set up the establishment of a fault-finder. Having made this valuable discovery, O ye dry bones, I at once invested all my available means in this business. I find that the delightful work grows upon my hands. It is peculiarly adapted to my genius. O, there is sublimity in fault-finding! Indeed, it is a vocation itself. It demands *all* the energies of the mind. And hence it is not marvellous that those who excel in that business can do nothing else. No man, for example, can expatiate on the evils of revivals like the man under whose preaching revivals never take place. No man can dilate on the danger of spurious conversions like the man under whose ministry there are no conversions of any kind. Ah, give me a fabric of 'dry bones' to creak, and clank, and cry out against 'protracted meetings, inquiry meetings, hasty conversions,' and all such things. Immortal honor to the memory of St. Jeroboam! (1 Kings xii. 26—29.)

"You must be aware, O ye dry bones, that this is a very delicate subject. Indeed, your worthy pastor has had to endure some very broad hints in the course of his labors. Some of these, in fact, have amounted to a perfect insinuation. When I have been declaiming against the indiscretions of others, impertinent persons have presumed to ask, what good I myself had done? what kind of conversions had taken place under my preaching? To such rude and unseasonable inquiries I have given but this one reply, 'Ah, my friend, the less we say on that subject, the better.'

"It will be acceptable to you, O ye dry bones, to hear, on this joyful anniversary, something of your esteemed pastor's experience and personal history. The history of your pastor, O ye dry bones, should be a source of comfort and consolation to a church in your advanced and enviable condition. I was once encumbered with flesh on my bones, and blood in my veins. I was once troubled with breath in my nostrils, and vital warmth in my heart. But a period came, when I was vexed by the discovery that the labor of other preachers was very successful. I felt the rising of envy and jealousy. I resolved to oppose revivals, especially such as took place under the ministry of others. In a short time, I had gone much further than I at first intended. I had invested all my stock in this business. I had become a regular *revival-fighter*. All that I could now do in relation to revivals was to find fault, raise objections, and expatiate on their *evils*. From that moment, *my own ministry was smitten with barrenness!* Yes, my own ministry became bleak and desolate as the mountains of Gilboa, on which 'there is no rain, neither any dew'! From that moment, my flesh withered away, my blood dried up, my vitality departed, my skin cracked and fell off, my bones became bare and 'very dry;' and I have since walked among the churches a naked skeleton, my bones 'very dry.' Yet think not, O ye dry bones, that I complain. I am much pleased with my present meagre and fleshless condition. It is a condition of great *power;* and who does not love power? Did not the seven 'lean kine,' in Pharaoh's dream, eat up the seven that were fat-fleshed and well-favored? These lean cattle, meagre, famished, very ill-favored — 'Such,' said Pharaoh, 'as I never saw in all the land of Egypt for badness;' that eat up all that were better than themselves — were certainly very promising specimens. They were verging toward the condition of 'dry bones,' which I regard as absolute consummation. Ah, if you wish every thing that is well-favored, and lovely, and of good report, utterly eaten up, just set a skeleton of 'dry bones' at the work, and it will soon be done!"

Here the hideous monster paused in his discourse; and in a paroxysm of greediness that was frightful, he snapped repeatedly around to the right and left with his dry, naked teeth, till the valley rang again. Presently he resumed his discourse.

"Another peculiarity, O ye dry bones, in the history of your esteemed pastor, is this: he has been absolutely stationary. For seventy years he has kept his place. Dry bones are admirable in this respect. There is no moving about in them. Many pernicious examples have been set in former days. There was one Abraham, that went out from his country, his kindred, and his father's house, in order to lead a religious life. What fanaticism! Just as if there was any propriety in 'going into all the world,' in order to promote religion. The fact is, that same Abraham seems to have been a very restless man. He went from Mesopotamia to Haran, thence to the land of Canaan, then down into Egypt, then back to Canaan, and then into the country of the Philistines. It is reported, that he and his family 'confessed that they were strangers and pilgrims in the earth.' Some have maintained, that at these various points Abraham was laboring as a missionary, or as an evangelist. But one thing is certain: that is, he departed essentially from that model of perfection which is found in 'dry bones.' After Abraham, arose one Moses, a very unsettled man. Now he was in Egypt, now in Midian, and now in the wilderness. And even when in the wilderness, he repeatedly changed his place — a most injurious example. After Moses, arose one Samuel, who positively 'went in a circuit, from year to year, to Bethel and Gilgal, to Mizpah and Ramah,' performing in those places the duties of a public minister of religion. Nor was the example of Elijah one whit better. In him we find the adage verified, that the ruling passion is strong near the close of life; for, just before his translation, he took Elisha with him, and went on religious errands from Gilgal to Bethel, from Bethel to Jericho, and from Jericho to Jordan. Such are some of the untoward examples, O ye dry bones, which your *model preacher* has had to counteract; and although they have been not a little troublesome, yet he has been able to remain stationary, and keep his bones 'very dry.' I have been grievously annoyed, of late, by the prophecy of Daniel. He has been predicting, that in the latter day 'many shall run to and fro, and knowledge shall be increased.' This Daniel must be an exceedingly indiscreet man, or he would not utter such predictions. They are calculated to disturb dry bones, in my condition. I am resolved to commence the business of prophesying, too. I am driven to it in self-defence.

My prediction is this: 'In the latter day, many shall imitate the sublime example set by the clucking hen!' I have a right to use her as an illustration. Noah had his dove, Elijah had his ravens, and why should not the skeleton preacher be allowed his favorite bird? That bird is the clucking hen. Ah, when I see her settle down on her own nest, and push every egg under her own wings, and then raise the feathers on the back of her head and neck, and peck at every one that comes near her, I am ready to exclaim, 'There is true sublimity! there is an example worthy of all imitation!'

"Again, O ye dry bones, your judicious pastor has rattled every dry bone in his skeleton frame, to keep down special effort in the church, revivals of religion, protracted meetings, and all such things. That blundering man Moses, before mentioned, instituted a number of such meetings, which were attended with many and sore 'evils.' At the feast of the Passover, at the feast of Pentecost, and at the feast of Tabernacles, the people, in great numbers, came up to Jerusalem to worship, and continued their religious exercises for seven or eight days in succession. In the time of Hezekiah king of Judah, 'a very great congregation assembled at Jerusalem, and kept the feast of the Passover seven days.' And then 'the whole assembly took counsel to keep other seven days; and they kept other seven days with gladness.' (2 Chron. xxx. 23.) What extravagance was this! If such measures are suffered to pass without rebuke, who can tell where the mischief will end?

"St. Jeroboam, the son of Nebat — immortal honor to his memory! — yes, St. Jeroboam, the son of Nebat, is the first man recorded in history who took a decided stand against protracted meetings, as ordained by Moses. 'And Jeroboam said in his heart, Now shall the kingdom return to the house of David. If this people go up to do sacrifice in the house of the Lord at Jerusalem, then shall the heart of this people turn again unto their Lord, even unto Rehoboam king of Judah, and they shall kill me, and go again to Rehoboam king of Judah. Whereupon the king took counsel, and made two calves of gold, and said unto them, It is too much for you to go up to Jerusalem: behold thy gods, O Israel, which brought thee up out of the land of Egypt. And he set the one in Bethel, and the other put he in Dan.' (1 Kings xii. 26—29.) The objection of St. Jeroboam to protracted meetings, was not that they would injure the great body of the people, but he feared that they might diminish the importance of a certain worshipful individual, whose aggrandizement he had very much at heart; and rather than hazard any thing in that quarter, he 'took counsel,' and employed his utmost ingenuity to induce them to forsake the altar of God, and worship a calf. And I have known other instances, O ye dry bones, in which such meetings have been violently opposed, when the secret spring of action was anxiety to maintain among the people the worship of some object very little better than Jeroboam's calf.

"Your judicious and venerable pastor, O ye dry bones, has opposed, both by precept and example, 'sudden conversions,' 'hasty admissions,' and every thing in that line. There has not been one conversion under my preaching, during the last seventy years. In all that time, there has not been a foot or a finger moved in any religious duty. Ah, it is delightful to observe how long and how carefully duties are considered, before there is any movement toward obedience among 'dry bones.' I have had immense success in holding back my congregation from precipitate action. St. Pharaoh — honor to his memory — was fully aware of the 'evils' of rapid accessions to the visible church. He commanded the old women in Israel, saying, 'When a son is born in Israel, then ye shall kill him.' Israel was then the visible church; and finding that this edict did not destroy them fast enough, he charged all his people, saying, 'Every son that is born ye shall cast into the river.' (Ex. i. 16, 22.) Thoughtful, judicious, amiable St. Pharaoh! He knew that the beginnings of life in an infant are extremely tender and delicate. He knew — sound and discreet man — that a withered old granny had strength enough to choke a young baby to death. Or, if that failed, he knew that the monsters of the river of Egypt could crush them between their hideous jaws. Even now, my mind delights to contemplate him in the noble stand that he took against the too rapid increase of the visible church. I behold him standing on the banks of the Nile, his venerable form drawn up to its full height, while he pours forth this sublime soliloquy: 'Ha! talk of Abraham's seed becoming countless as the stars of heaven! talk of Israel being 'fruitful, and multiplying exceedingly'! Behold the fate of their children! yes, the children of the church, over whose birth there was such exultation. See the quivering limbs of that one in the midst of the river, in the mouth of that voracious crocodile! Why, the jaws of the huge monster and the waters all around are stained and gory with its blood. And I have the best authority for saying, that on land many infants who were born are dead. The life that was in them was so feeble, that a few minutes' choking, by a withered old granny, could stop their breath forever. The back of my hand to such boasted births in Israel as these!' Such was the soliloquy of St. Pharaoh, while he well knew that the destruction of the lives of these young Israelites was his studied and favorite aim. And sweet experience has taught me, O ye dry bones, that the most effective way to dishonor and disgrace a revival in the church is to choke the young converts to death, while the early dawn of spiritual life in them is yet tender and delicate. A naked skeleton preacher, who judiciously employs his 'dry bones,' can do much of this; and then he can point to the destruction which he himself has made, and triumphantly exclaim, 'There is your revival! there is the end of your converts!' Let the memory of St. Pharaoh be affectionately embalmed in the hearts of all revival-fighting ministers.

"I must further observe, O ye dry bones, that I am delighted with your *deliberation.* You avoid agitating scenes and agitating subjects. You are deliberate. There is no sudden or rash movement with you. I understand that Ezekiel has been preaching about churches 'waking up,' 'prodigals returning,' 'spiritual resurrections,' and things in that line. But, O ye dry bones, such things are agitating in their very nature. You have guarded against them. Ezekiel has been preaching that the angels in heaven rejoice when the wicked turn from their wickedness; that the morning stars sing together when the dead awake to life. But, O ye dry bones, you have stood aloof from Ezekiel and all his enthusiasm; you have let the angels and the morning stars alone. No doubt they are doing very well, up where they properly belong. It would be very 'indiscreet' to drag their attention down to earth, and tamper with their sensibilities. You have allowed the angels to sing their own songs without interruption, while you have remained admirably cold, and dead, and dry. And your beloved pastor has fully sympathized with you in all things. He has been cold among the cold, dead among the dead, and dry among the dry.

"And beyond all this, O ye dry bones, it should be mentioned to your praise, that you have been delightfully exempt from 'backslidings,' 'declensions,' and 'falling away.' You know, O ye dry bones, how many churches, after seasons of revival, have been dishonored by 'backsliding' among their members, 'declensions,' &c. From these 'evils of revivals' you have been marvellously free. The church which takes *no forward step* is proof against *backsliding.* Who ever saw blighted blossoms on trees that were dead and dry? I challenge investigation. What living church, for the last seventy years, has been so entirely free from cases of backsliding as my *model church* of 'dry bones'?

"In the last place, O ye dry bones, another score on which you are entitled to commendation is this: you have been satisfied with my preaching, and have never gone to hear any one else. Some, it is true, have called me a dead preacher; but I have not been too dead for you. You have been satisfied with my sermons. They have been uniform. None of them have made any impression on the audience: therefore they have had the charm and the graces of uniformity.

It is *wearing* on a minister to feel his subject, or to *care* about the salvation of his hearers. I say it is *wearing*. I have been most delightfully exempt from 'excitement' on such subjects. I have kept perfectly cool, and have kept my bones 'very dry.' And beyond all this, let me declare, O ye dry bones, that the admirable condition in which you now are, is the result of my own ministry exclusively. *I have called in no foreign aid.* Your skeleton preacher abhors that practice. *I have allowed of no extra means.* I have jogged on just in my own way. Can ye believe it, posterity! By the dint of my own marvellous genius, I have kept my bones, and the bones of all my church, 'very dry.' O ye dry bones, you have kept around your own minister, and you have refused to run after transient men, itinerant preachers, missionaries, or evangelists. They talk about the duty of 'going into all the world;' but they have no business here. This is no part of the world. This is 'the valley of dry bones.' But ha! what form is that approaching my congregation?" Here the skeleton preacher raised his hollow eye-sockets, as if looking intently, and then exclaimed, "The prophet Ezekiel! that fatal disturber of dead churches; and he is coming here, as sure as my bones are dry!" Here the skeleton preacher made a sign with his long, bony fingers, to the deputy skeletons already mentioned; for I learned that there was a certain kind of work that he wished to have done in his congregation, and he would set these subalterns at it, though he was rather afraid to risk his reputation by engaging in it himself. The deputies, having received the signal, darted speedily among the congregation of dry bones, clattering every where — "The prophet Ezekiel is coming! Don't go to hear him! He is a mere transient preacher — only an evangelist. He has a few subjects on which he can preach tolerably well; but he can't stay long in one place. He don't last like our admirable preacher of 'dry bones'!" In this style these deputy skeletons were tattling and gabbling in all directions, when the whole valley was waked and electrified by the clear, strong, trumpet-like voice of Ezekiel — "O ye dry bones, hear the word of the Lord!" And immediately there was a noise; and behold there was a shaking, and the bones came together, bone to his bone. The skeleton preacher beheld these movements with the utmost alarm and perturbation. He stamped on the naked earth with his skeleton foot, until the dry bones clanked again. "Order!" he exclaimed; "I call to order! This is my congregation. I will sanction no such measures as these. Order! order! I call to order!" But the shaking went on, and the bones came together, bone to his bone; and the prophet Ezekiel continued his address — "O ye dry bones, hear the word of the Lord. Thus saith the Lord God unto these dry bones, 'Behold, I will cause breath to enter into you, and ye shall live; and I will lay sinews upon you, and will bring up flesh upon you, and cover you with skin, and put breath into you, and ye shall live; and ye shall know that I am the Lord.'" And while the prophet Ezekiel spoke thus, lo! the sinews and the flesh came up upon them, and the skin covered them above; but there was no breath in them. "Ha!" exclaimed the skeleton preacher, "they are not alive, after all — a mere 'spasmodic movement' — nothing but 'animal excitement.' I thought it would amount to this. Here's all our ancient order of things broken up, confusion and novelties introduced, and nothing gained at last — a mere 'spasmodic awakening' — nothing but 'animal excitement.'" And here he gave the sign to his deputy skeletons — "Discredit it, discredit it, all you can." Away went the deputy skeletons through the crowd, tattling, "No revival! no revival! only spasmodic awakening! nothing but animal excitement!" But just now they were startled and stunned by the powerful voice of Ezekiel, with which the whole valley rang again — "Thus saith the Lord God, Come from the four winds, O breath, and breathe upon these slain, that they may live;" and lo! the breath came into them, and they lived, and stood upon their feet — an exceeding great army. And there was glory to God in the highest. And there was the joy of life from the dead. The brother greeted the brother redeemed from the grave. The father hailed, blessed, and embraced the son. Glad angels spread their rainbow wings over the enrapturing scene, and sung, "The dead is alive, and the lost is found."

As for the skeleton preacher, he escaped from the living multitude; then turned, and gazed over the scene with more than fiendish indignation. He gnashed and ground his naked teeth, struck his bony hand on the dry ribs of his breast, then turned, and set his face for the Valley of the Son of Hinnom, elsewhere called Tophet, muttering, as he went along, "Yes, this is the result of the revival. I am *unsettled.* The relationship between me and this church is dissolved. Perdition on such revivals! This is the result of allowing such evangelists as Ezekiel to roam over the country, preaching. Perdition on such revivals! Yes, I'm *unsettled;* and now I must look out for another location." As the skeleton preacher went muttering along toward the Valley of Tophet, he was met by one of the sons of the prophets, who perfectly understood the whole case. He was a plain, straightforward, out-spoken man, ardently devoted to the cause of God and the salvation of men. He heard the murmurings of the skeleton for a few moments, and his anger was kindled, and he thus addressed him: "Meagre, miserable skeleton! are you raving and wrathful because your great congregation has awaked to life, and your control over them is at an end? Do you think that the great Majesty of heaven planned the scheme of redemption in eternity, and established his beloved church on earth, for no higher object than that such a wretched rackheap of dry bones as you should be bolstered up in some comfortable location? Do you think that all the wheels of creation, providence, and redemption should be stopped, for fear that such a foul, frightful scarecrow as you should be driven from its roost! Wretched skeleton! What madness has possessed thee! What worse than demon has entered into thee! Yes, you're unsettled, and *deservedly* so. You attempted to hurl back the Spirit of the Almighty. You lifted up your dry bones to resist the growing conquests of the glorious Immanuel. You're unsettled; yes, because you hated light, and hated life. You continued dead, and your bones very dry; and you wished to keep all as dead and dry as yourself. Why did not you hear the word of God? Why did not you awake to life? Why did not you have flesh and sinews, and skin cover your dry bones? Why did not you receive the breath of heaven, and live? You might then have remained in the congregation of the living. You are cast out, because there is no breath in you. Your bones are fleshless, frightful, and very dry. Avaunt, wretched skeleton!" The chop-fallen skeleton preacher made no reply, but went on his way toward the Valley of Tophet. The entrance of the valley was dark and dismal. Heavy clouds hung over it, and shut out the light of heaven. The exhalations of the valley arose like columns of ascending smoke, and from the depths within sounds issued like weeping, and wailing, and gnashing of teeth. The skeleton approached. His "ruling passion was strong" up to the very moment when he entered the gloomy vale. "This," he exclaimed, "verifies the doctrine I have maintained for years. The conversion of souls costs too much, and the resurrection of the dead costs too much. *Here I'm unsettled.* I must look out for a new location; and there is little likelihood that I shall better my condition. Perdition on revivals! Tell me not that God is honored, the Redeemer glorified, sinners saved, the dead alive, the lost found, the angels rejoicing. What are all these things to *me?* Here is an *evil* that outweighs them all — *I'm unsettled!* Perdition on revivals!" Muttering and blaspheming thus, while he gnashed his naked teeth, the skeleton plunged into the horrible valley, and I saw him no more.

THE LITTLE AUGER AND KING SOLOMON.

AN EXTRACT FROM THE "BOOK OF THE ACTS OF SOLOMON," MENTIONED 1 KINGS XI. 41.

Now it came to pass, while King Solomon was building the house of the Lord at Jerusalem, that very many tools and instruments were employed by the king in this great work. "And King Solomon raised a levy out of all Israel; and the levy was thirty thousand men. And he sent them to Lebanon, ten thousand a month by courses; a month they were in Lebanon, and two months at home. And Adoniram was over the levy. And Solomon had threescore and ten thousand that bare burdens, and fourscore thousand hewers in the mountains; beside the chief of Solomon's officers which were over the work, three thousand and three hundred, which ruled over the people that wrought in the work. And the king commanded, and they brought great stones, costly stones, and hewed stones, to lay the foundation of the house. And Solomon's builders and Hiram's builders did hew them, and the stone-squarers: so they prepared timber and stones to build the house." "And this is the reason of the levy which King Solomon raised; for to build the house of the Lord, and his own house, and Millo, and the wall of Jerusalem, and Hazor, and Megiddo, and Gezer. For Pharaoh king of Egypt had gone up, and taken Gezer, and burnt it with fire, and slain the Canaanites that dwelt in the city, and given it for a present unto his daughter, Solomon's wife. And Solomon built Gezer." "And he built Tadmor in the wilderness, and all the store-cities, which he built in Hamath. Also he built Beth-horon the upper, and Beth-horon the nether, fenced cities, with walls, gates, and bars; and Baalath, and all the store-cities that Solomon had, and all the chariot-cities, and the cities of the horsemen, and all that Solomon desired to build in Jerusalem, and in Lebanon, and throughout all the land of his dominion." (1 Kings v. 13; ix. 15—17.)

And it came to pass, that among the great variety of instruments employed in building the house of the Lord, there was a little auger, that had a spirit of high ambition. It is not more strange that a little auger should have a spirit of high ambition, than that the trees, in Jotham's time, should go forth to anoint a king over them, and that the olive, the fig-tree, the vine, and the bramble, should converse together on the subject. (Judges ix. 8—15.) So this little auger was greatly troubled with an ambitious spirit — the same spirit that has often proved a source of anguish and trouble among the children of men.

Now, it came to pass, that on a certain day King Solomon came up to look upon the workmen, and to see the progress of the work. And behold, as the king was passing near the little auger, it opened its mouth and hailed him, saying, "Hear! hear! that I may speak to thee, great king of Jerusalem."

King Solomon stopped, and looked upon it. "Ha!"

said the king; "what have we got here? A little auger, straightening itself up for a speech! But it is not more strange," continued he, reconciling himself to the singular phenomenon — "it is not more strange than that old Pharaoh's bad corn should eat up all his good corn." (Gen. xli. 7.) Then addressing the little auger, which was still standing erect upon a work-bench, drawn up to its utmost height — "What have you to say to the king?"

"Is not this house," said the little auger, "which you are building to the name of the God of Israel, designed to be very great?"

"Yes," said Solomon; "to quote the language of my venerable father, David, 'The house that is to be builded for the Lord must be exceeding magnifical, of fame and of glory throughout all countries.'" (1 Chron. xxii. 5.)

"Great king," continued the little auger, "I beseech you to make me the *only instrument* that shall be employed in building this famous temple. I should love to have *all the honor*. I am grieved deeply with the present state of things. I see the workmen every day handling immense crowbars, great axes, long steel saws, hammers, chisels, wedges, planes, and an almost countless variety of implements, whose shape and fashion differ widely from my own. Now, great king, I have studied the subject thoroughly; and I have felt deeply; and I must say, that these instruments are all wrong. They are useless, and worse than useless. Great king, look at me!" — here the little auger assumed the tallest attitude, and appeared to entertain marvellous conceptions of its own consequence, as though it were prodigious — "great king, look at me! Am not I a *model instrument?* Am not I the *only* instrument that ought to be honored with bearing a part in the erection of this famous temple? Now, therefore, O king, hear my request, and grant my petition. Establish thou a royal statute, and make a firm decree, that every crowbar, poleaxe, steel saw, broadaxe, hammer, chisel, plane, wedge, and each and all other instruments whatever, shall be heated, hammered, and twisted, until they are brought into exact conformity with that *model of perfection,* the little auger; and further, let the royal decree go forth from the king's palace, sealed with the king's ring, that should any tool or implement, great or small, attempt to stand on its reserved rights, or should it shrink from the process of assimilation, or on any account fail to have itself transformed into the likeness of the *model* instrument — a little auger — each and every such refractory, obstinate, and contumacious instrument shall, without favor or affection, be banished from the dominions of King Solomon forever, and suffered to have no share in building the temple to the honor of the great name of the God of Israel."

"Little auger," said the king, "I have heard your speech with mingled emotions of astonishment and pity. It is true, that you have an important part to act in the building of this illustrious temple; otherwise you would never have been forged and fashioned out of the crude ore from which you were taken. Yes, the part that you are called to sustain in the erection of this house is not only important, but, I may say, it is commendable, honorable; but what ever put the idle conceit into your little head, that you are the *only* instrument needed in the putting up of this mighty structure, or that you are the *model instrument?* There is much, very much, to be done in forwarding this building, for which you, little auger, have no capacity whatever — work that is essential to the great enterprise, and that is wholly beyond your tiny powers. Behold that immense wedge of iron, and that great battering-engine, by which it is driven into the mountain quarry, to move the huge masses of stone from their ancient bed. Could you act the part of that strong battering-engine, or that great wedge of iron? See that heavy sledge, which can break the rock in pieces; that great iron lever, that can lift a weight that is beyond the strength of threescore men. Look upon that keen-edged axe, that can hew down the tall cedar of Lebanon; and that bright saw of steel, that can split the block of marble that is seven cubits thick and forty cubits long. Would you have all these, and many other necessary and valuable instruments, banished from the temple service forever, merely to gratify the senseless whim and foolish ambition of a little auger? Tell it not in Gath! Publish it not in the streets of Askelon! And now," said the wise king, "allow me, little auger, to show you a more excellent way. Be content to pass for what you *are*, and never take the flattering unction to your soul, that you shall be able to pass for what you *are not*.

"The great Architect of earth and heaven has not made all men alike. There is a vast variety of talents and of gifts among them. Yet he has use for them all. And each man, who is willing to do his duty, and honor his Creator, is important and honorable in his place. So in the building of this great temple. Many and various instruments are needed. No one should aspire to be considered the *only* instrument, or the *model* instrument. Each is important and respectable in its place. Bear this in mind, little auger. Do your duty, and be contented in your station; and fret not your little soul because others can render service of which you are altogether incapable."

THE GREAT MEN OF THE BIBLE.

ABRAHAM.

A VERY strong argument in favor of the true religion might be drawn from the fact, that in no place does the human soul unfold its powers to such perfection as it does in that land where the light of revelation shines. Dr. Young remarks, concerning heathen Greece and Rome, that "half our learning is their epitaph." The fame of notable men who have risen in the heathen world has been blazed abroad in Christian countries; and very often it would appear, that even the children of the church are not aware that, in all the attributes of *true greatness*, no men, who have ever lived amidst the darkness of idolatry, will compare with the men who have worshipped the God of the Bible. "What manner of men were they whom ye slew at Tabor?" said the victorious Gideon to Zebah and Zalmunna, the two kings of Midian. And they answered, "As thou art, so were they; each one resembled the children of a king." And he said, "They were my brethren." (Judges viii. 18, 19.) Of Jehoshaphat, the king of Judah, it is recorded, that "his heart was lifted up in the ways of the Lord." Indeed, it is the uniform doctrine of the Bible, that true religion exalts the soul of man. I might go into specifications; true religion exalts,

1. The thoughts of man, from low and grovelling objects, to God, and heaven, and eternity.

2. True religion exalts the affections of man.

3. It exalts the hopes of man.

4. It exalts the aims of man.

5. It exalts the destiny of man.

Should we wonder, then, that, under the light and influences of this religion, men have arisen whose greatness the church may contemplate with admiration and with joy? Take Abraham, for example.

How great was his faith in God! Idolatry, in the age in which he lived, was rampant throughout all surrounding lands. Fashion, wealth, power, respectability, public sentiment, were all arrayed against the cause of truth and righteousness; yet in such circumstances Abraham would believe and obey God. He would face a frowning world. He would stand as a rock amidst the billows of the rolling ocean.

Abraham was a man of great *decision* of character. When the Lord said, "Get thee out from thy country, and from thy kindred, and from thy father's house, unto a land that I will show thee," he immediately obeyed the heavenly call, and "went out, not knowing whither he went," but feeling only that God was his leader and his guide. There was no parley; no hesitation with him; no "conferring with flesh and blood." An objector would have said, "Cannot I serve God here as well as in another place? My country is dear to me. I love my native land. I delight in these green hills, these fruitful vales, and these limpid streams, where first I became conscious of existence. The graves of my ancestors are here. My country is dear to me, my kindred dearer, my father's house dearest of all. Why should I go to another land, in order to serve God?" Not so reasoned Abraham. His decision was immediate and final — "I will obey the divine command, and commit consequences to God."

In like manner he acted when called to offer up his only son Isaac on the altar. A wavering mind would have said, "There must be some strange mistake in this command. Offer up Isaac on the altar! Why, it is inconsistent with God's promise, that Isaac shall be the head of a great nation. It is inconsistent with the hope of the saints, that the Messiah shall arise from among the descendants of Isaac. It is at variance with that paternal affection which God hath implanted in every father's heart. It will bring a reproach on the true religion; for the heathen around will confound the act with the sacrifices offered to Moloch," &c., &c. Such would have been the cavillings of unbelief. But to Abraham's mind one point was divinely clear, to wit: It is the command of God. "Yes, the command of God, who sees the consistency of his own ways, though they be too wonderful for me. It is the command of God, who gave me Isaac and all the blessings which I have enjoyed. It is the command of God, who redeemed my soul, and on whom all my hopes depend for time and for eternity. It is the command of God, and I hasten to obey." And Abraham rose up early in the morning, and took two of his young men with him, and Isaac his son, and clave the wood for the burnt-offering, and rose up, and went unto the place of which God had told him. How prompt and wonderful was his *decision* in obedience to the command of God!

How great was his *benevolence!* He stood before

the Lord, and interceded for guilty Sodom with an earnestness and an importunity that could take no denial. Abraham knew that he and his house were in no danger. The plague would not be suffered to come nigh them. Yet he cared for the souls that were in Sodom, on the very verge of destruction. And such was his benevolence, that he wrestled in prayer for them, while they neglected to pray for themselves.

Abraham was a man of great *humility.* "Behold, now, I have taken upon me to speak unto the Lord, who am but *dust and ashes.*" There is nothing here like the boasting Pharisee — "God, I thank thee that I am not as other men. I have stood firm in thy service, while others turned away after idols. I left my native country at thy command. I have believed thy word, and hoped against hope. I have not staggered at thy promise, but have been strong in faith, giving glory to God." Nothing of all this. Though he had set his face steadfastly in the way of God's commandments, and though his feet had moved swiftly in the paths of holy obedience, yet now, like the seraphim, he would veil his face, and even his feet, before the high and holy One. He would speak of himself in the lowliest terms — "I am but dust and ashes."

Great *charity* also appears in the character of Abraham. "Peradventure there be *fifty* righteous within the city." "Peradventure there shall lack *five* of the fifty righteous." "Peradventure there be *forty* found there." Noble, generous-hearted man! *Great* in the exercise of an exalted charity, even in Sodom he hopes to find fifty righteous, or if not quite so many, then forty-five, or, at any rate, forty. What a lovely exhibition of a great and good man! "Charity thinketh no evil." Charity "hopeth all things." How different from that spirit of bitterness which sometimes stalks abroad in the earth! A bitter spirit would have said, "Ha! burn up Sodom and Gomorrah! I'm glad to hear it. It is just what I've been looking for. They richly deserve it. There is not an honest man in all the place, nor a virtuous woman. I'm glad to hear that they are about to get their desert at last." It is no proof that a man is uncommonly good himself, when he shows a severe and censorious spirit, that rejoices to put the worst construction on the condition of others.

Abraham exhibits *greatness* in his holy fortitude. He "stood before the Lord." And while his soul was filled with sacred awe and reverence, he "drew near and said, Wilt thou also destroy the righteous with the wicked? That be far from thee to do after this manner; to slay the righteous with the wicked, that be far from thee: shall not the Judge of all the earth do right?" He came "boldly to a throne of grace."

Abraham was great in *his daily intercourse with his fellow-men*. See the magnanimity of his deportment in relation to Lot, when difficulties had arisen between their herdmen. (Gen. xiii. 5—12.) See his intercourse with the sons of Heth. (Gen. xxiii. 3—20.)

Abraham was great *as a patriot soldier*, who drew the sword in defence of civil and religious liberty. He was a wise and successful leader of patriotic armies. (Gen. xiv. 13—16.) Also observe his noble bearing in reference to the spoil. (Gen. xiv. 22, 23.)

Abraham was great in his relations — "a mighty prince" among men, and a "friend of God."

He was *great* in his destination. The abode of the blessed is called by the Savior "Abraham's bosom."

(Luke xvi. 22.) And the promise to the redeemed is, that "they shall sit down with Abraham, and with Isaac, and with Jacob, in the kingdom of God."

JUDAH.

Recorded facts clearly show that Judah, the fourth son of Jacob, was a very distinguished and powerful man. Jewish tradition, concerning the events which took place in the earlier periods of Hebrew national history, abound with statements of the famous part acted by Judah, and of the preëminence which he maintained among celebrated men in that age of the world. There is also much on this subject found in the Bible history.

We find in the story of Joseph that Judah had great influence with his *brethren*. Led on, it appears, by Simeon, they had conspired to kill Joseph. Reuben had interposed, and prevailed on them to cast Joseph into a pit, where, as they supposed, he would inevitably starve to death. Reuben's design was to deliver Joseph from death, and restore him again to his father. Reuben had withdrawn, it seems, for the purpose of concerting measures for the escape of Joseph, when a company of Ishmaelites passed by. "And Judah said unto his brethren, What profit is it if we slay our brother, and conceal his blood? Come, and let us sell him to the Ishmaelites, and let not our hand be upon him; for he is our brother and our flesh; and his brethren were content." It is likely that Judah was unacquainted with Reuben's aim, and thought this the best method to prevent the death of Joseph in the pit. But should it even appear that he was moved by some motive less praiseworthy, the passage proves that he had great weight in swaying the counsels of his brethren.

Judah had also great influence with his *father*. When the sons of Jacob returned from their first visit to Egypt, they told their father, " The man who is lord of the land spake roughly to us, and took us for spies; and we said unto him, We are true men; we are no spies. And the lord of the country said unto us, Hereby shall I know that ye are true men: leave one of your brethren here with me, and take food for the famine of your houses, and be gone. And bring your youngest brother unto me. Then shall I know that ye are no spies, but that ye are true men. And their father said, Me have ye bereaved of my children; Joseph is not, and Simeon is not; and ye will take Benjamin away: all these things are against me. And Reuben spake unto his father, saying, Slay my two sons, if I bring him not to thee;" just as if the death of two grandsons could console Jacob for the loss of his beloved Benjamin! "And he said, My son shall not go down with you." But when the corn brought up from Egypt was all consumed, and "the famine was sore," their father said unto them, " Go again, and buy us a little food." And Judah spake unto him — " The man did solemnly protest unto us, saying, Ye shall not see my face, except your brother be with you. If thou wilt send our brother with us, we will go down and buy thee food; but if thou wilt not send our brother, we will not go down." And Judah said unto his father, " Send the lad with me, and we will arise and go; that we may live, and not die, both we, and thou, and also our little ones. I will be surety for him; of my hand shalt thou require him: if I bring him not unto thee, and set him before thee, then let me bear the blame forever."

And their father Israel said, "Take your brother, and arise and go; and God Almighty give you mercy before the man." (Gen. xliii. 1—16.)

The whole narrative shows that Jacob entertained a very high regard for Judah, and placed a very exalted estimate on his force of character and trustworthiness — those very attributes on which he expatiates in his last benediction: "Judah, thou art he whom thy brethren shall praise; thy hand shall be in the neck of thine enemies; thy father's children shall bow down before thee. Judah is a lion's whelp; from the prey, my son, thou art gone up; he stooped down, he couched as a lion, and an old lion; who shall rouse him up?" (Gen. xlix. 8, 9.) But it is when he comes to stand before the injured and frowning governor of Egypt, and pleads for the convicted and sentenced Benjamin, that the grandeur of Judah's character is seen. Great exigencies call forth great men. And here was an eventful crisis, in which the greatest earthly interests seemed trembling on the brink of destruction.

The sons of Jacob had gone down to Egypt the second time with troubled apprehensions, such as beset the pathway of the guilty. But on their arrival, they were agreeably disappointed. They meet with a prompt and welcome reception at the governor's house. Simeon is released from prison, and joined to their company; the governor himself comes home at noon, and greets them pleasantly, inquires of the welfare of their father, looks with interest and kindness on Benjamin, and then gathers them all around his well-furnished board, and refreshes them with a plentiful feast. Indeed, it seemed as if, in the profusion of his hospitality, he was anxious to efface every remaining impression of that rough speech and harsh treatment which he gave them when they first came down. They were delighted. They passed the afternoon and night joyfully in the house of the governor; and "as soon as the morning was light," they were sent away, — Simeon, Benjamin, and all, — their sacks filled with corn, as much as they could carry, to supply their families with bread. What glad hearts were there! How joyful were their anticipations! "Soon the high hills of Canaan will rise to view! Soon our homes will be in sight, and the loved form of our venerable father, eagerly fixing his dim eye on the approaching caravan; and how great will be his joy when he finds that his sons have all returned in safety! But hark! What cry is that of one in pursuit? It is the governor's steward." He hurries to overtake them, proclaiming, "The silver cup in which my lord drinketh is stolen. Ye have done evil in so doing."

And they said unto him, "Wherefore saith my lord these words? God forbid that thy servants should do this thing. With whomsoever of thy servants it shall be found, let him die, and we also will be my lord's bondmen. Then they speedily took down every man his sack, and he searched, and began at the eldest and left off at the youngest, and the cup was found in Benjamin's sack. Then they rent their clothes, and returned to the city." The language of the sacred historian is here very instructive. "Then Judah and his brethren came to Joseph's house." Judah alone of the eleven is named. All eyes were now turned to him; and the looks and the lips of all confess that in this awful extremity their only hope is in the wisdom, the eloquence, and the extraordinary resources of Judah.

Indeed, the attempt of Judah, at this dreadful juncture, just as the cup has been found in Benjamin's sack, to head the returning column of his mortified and despairing brethren, and lead them back to the house of the outraged and indignant governor, is itself a proof of astonishing stamina and greatness of soul.

What a moving scene have we here! Pause for a moment, and fix your eye upon it. That accusing steward seizes the cup, and holds it up reproachingly before them all, as incontestable proof of vile ingratitude and enormous guilt. Hear his exclamations — "O, what baseness! What detestable falsehood! What abominable thievishness!" Reuben wrings his hands, crying out bitterly, "Undone! undone!" Simeon, Issachar, Asher, Naphtali, cover their abashed faces, and stepping backward, fall to the earth. Ten of Jacob's sons are utterly unmanned and overwhelmed in the depth of their disgrace. Not so Judah. His powerful spirit rises with the importance of the occasion. Disasters which prostrate others only rouse the slumbering energies of his mind. The more dire the extremity, it is to him but the louder call to prompt, effective action. "Up, my brothers, up! All danger is not death; all darkness is not destruction; rise up, and come with me. We will go back to the governor's house, and try what can yet be done." Rare, exalted, wonderful man! At the distance of thirty-five hundred years, we yet gaze with astonishment and admiration upon thy marvellous fortitude and firmness of soul. Yes, after this long lapse of ages, we yet continue to feel that our nature is honored and ennobled by thy manly and dignified bearing when those thick clouds of blackness were clustering and condensing around thee.

The reception of the sons of Jacob at the governor's house was altogether rough and repulsive. "What is this that ye have done? Wot ye not that such a man as I can certainly divine? Did ye think to practise thievery about my house, and escape detection?" We must bear in mind, that Judah regarded Joseph as a great Egyptian prince, who wielded the power of Pharaoh. "What shall we say unto my lord? what shall we speak? or how shall we clear ourselves? God hath found out the iniquity of thy servants: behold, we are my lord's servants, both we, and he also with whom the cup is found." There is great ingenuity and power in this opening of his plea. He dilutes or neutralizes the guilt of the act of stealing the cup, by diffusing it among all the eleven brethren, and representing their present distress as a righteous judgment from God, for all the sins of their past lives. And then he declares their readiness to submit to a heavier doom than Joseph's sense of justice would allow him to inflict. "God forbid," said the governor, "that I should do so; but the man in whose hand the cup is found, he shall be my servant; as for you, get you up in peace to your father."

Here, now, is the climax of their troubles. They could have consented, if it must be so, all to perish together; but the thought of some returning home with tidings that will break their father's heart, is unsupportable. The reader, who carefully examines Judah's argument, will subscribe to the following sentiment of a celebrated English divine: "Without exception, this may be considered as the most affecting speech that was ever uttered by mere man."

"Then Judah came near unto him, and said, O my

lord, let thy servant, I pray thee, speak a word in my lord's ears, and let not thine anger burn against thy servant; for thou art even as Pharaoh. My lord asked his servants, saying, Have ye a father, or a brother? And we said unto my lord, We have a father, an old man, and a child of his old age, a little one; and his brother is dead, and he alone is left of his mother, and his father loveth him. And thou saidst unto thy servants, Bring him down unto me, that I may set mine eyes upon him. And we said unto my lord, The lad cannot leave his father; for if he should leave his father, his father would die. And thou saidst unto thy servants, Except your youngest brother come down with you, ye shall see my face no more. And it came to pass, when we came up unto thy servant my father, we told him the words of my lord. And our father said, Go again, and buy us a little food. And we said, We cannot go down. If our youngest brother be with us, then will we go down; for we may not see the man's face, except our youngest brother be with us. And thy servant my father said unto us, Ye know that my wife bare me two sons: and the one went out from me, and I said, Surely he is torn in pieces; and I saw him not since; and if ye take this also from me, and mischief befall him, ye shall bring down my gray hairs with sorrow to the grave. Now, therefore, when I come to thy servant my father, and the lad be not with us, seeing that his life is bound up in the lad's life, it shall come to pass, when he seeth that the lad is not with us, that he will die; and thy servants shall bring down the gray hairs of thy servant our father with sorrow to the grave. For thy servant became surety for the lad unto my father, saying, If I bring him not unto thee, then I shall bear the blame to my father forever. Now, therefore, I pray thee, let thy servant abide instead of the lad a bondman to my lord; and let the lad go up with his brethren. For how shall I go up to my father, and the lad be not with me? lest peradventure I see the evil that shall come on my father."

1. What tender affection for his aged father breathed through the whole speech! "Honor thy father and mother, which is the first commandment with promise."

2. With what soundness of judgment does he avoid any particular reference to the crime charged on his younger brother. To have admitted it, would have been to censure Benjamin. To have denied it, would have reflected on the justice of Joseph. He presses only the great argument, that the life of his aged father is bound up in the life of the lad; and if Benjamin goes not back with his brothers, his father will die.

3. How delicately he refers to Joseph's supposed loss! quoting his father's words, "Ye know that my wife bare me two sons; and the one went out from me, and I said, Surely he is torn in pieces, and I saw him not since." How the heart of Joseph must have vibrated at this part of the argument!

4. He offers himself as a substitute for Benjamin. Jewish tradition says he was by far the most able bodied of the two. Joseph would thus be gainer by the exchange. His father could better bear the loss of him, than of the only remaining son of his beloved Rachel. So far is he from being envious at his father's superior fondness for Benjamin, that he is willing to become a bondman himself, in order that it may be gratified. Generous, worthy, wonderful man!

5. The power of his eloquence rose beyond all that

Joseph had anticipated, though he had doubtless been accustomed to hear the most powerful pleaders of Egypt. Joseph had been making experiments with his brethren, testing and trying their temper toward Benjamin; and evidently he intended to carry his experiments further. For he had men present in the house who he did not intend should witness the scene, when he should make himself known to his brethren. According to his plan, the *time* for that disclosure had not yet come; but the tide of Judah's eloquence came upon him like the waters in Ezekiel's vision — now flowing to the ankles, now to the knees, now to the waist, and now a mighty river, whose resistless flood swept all before it. Joseph himself was carried away by the overspreading deluge, and "could not refrain himself before all them that stood by him. And he cried, Cause every man to go out from me; and he wept aloud; and the Egyptians and the house of Pharaoh heard." Who can read this affecting history without coming fully to the conclusion, that Judah deserves a prominent place among "the great men of the Bible"?

6. What an impression this generous proposal of Judah must have made on the heart of Benjamin! It appears that neither he nor his children could ever forget their obligation for this magnanimous devotion. Long afterwards, when ten tribes went off under Jeroboam, Benjamin adhered with unwavering faithfulness to Judah. The ten tribes were carried away captive, and lost; but Benjamin is still found with Judah. In the first age of the Christian church, the children of Benjamin were with Judah. Paul was "of the tribe of Benjamin, a Hebrew of the Hebrews." And till

this day, in their dispersion throughout the whole world, Benjamin is found standing by the side of Judah.

7. Was Judah a type of Christ, when he became *surety* for a younger brother, and made *intercession* for the *transgressor?* Troubles, the most gloomy and appalling, were clustering and thickening around Benjamin. The cup was found in his sack. He alone is singled out, by the frowning governor, as the guilty one. He alone is condemned to a perpetual doom. Yet all this cannot turn away the tender affection of Judah, nor check his burning zeal. I "became surety for the lad unto my father, saying, If I bring him not unto thee, then I shall bear the blame to my father forever." Great *Surety* of our souls, this reminds us of thee! "For I am persuaded, that neither death, nor life, nor angels, nor principalities, nor powers, nor things present, nor things to come, nor height, nor depth, nor any other creature, shall be able to separate us from the love of God, which is in Christ Jesus our Lord."

THE PUBLIC REBUKE.

ANECDOTE OF JUDGE WHITE.

THE late lamented Judge Hugh L. White, of Tennessee, became conspicuous, at a very early period of life, as a jurist and a statesman. He fixed his permanent home near Knoxville, amidst the scenes of his youthful sports, and the companions of his boyish days. Rarely has a young man, continuing in his own country and among his own kindred, so soon attained such literary and political preëminence. From his youth, the judge was characterized by profound reverence for the ordinances of the gospel. He was a regular attendant at the house of worship. And while he was a Presbyterian, that being the church of his fathers, and the church of his choice, he was benevolent and generous towards other branches of the great Christian family. He gave to the Methodist church at Knoxville the ground on which their house of worship was built; and occasionally he would appear in the congregation, and join with them in their worship.

Now, in those days, there was a notable presiding elder in that region, called Father Axley, a pious, laborious, uncompromising preacher of the gospel, who considered it his duty to rebuke Sin wherever it should presume to lift up its deformed head within the limits of his district. And while Father Axley was a man of respectable talents, undoubted piety, and great ministerial fidelity, he had, moreover, a spice of humor, oddity, and drollery about him, that rarely failed to impart a characteristic tinge to his performances. The consequence was, that amusing anecdotes of the sayings and doings of Father Axley abounded throughout the country.

On a certain day, a number of lawyers and literary men were together in the town of Knoxville, and the conversation turned on the subject of preaching and preachers. One and another had expressed his opinion of the performances of this and that pulpit orator. At length, Judge White spoke up — "Well, gentlemen, on this subject each man is, of course, entitled to his own opinion; but I must confess, that Father Axley brought me to a sense of my evil deeds — at least a portion of them — more effectually than any preacher I have ever heard." At this, every eye and ear was turned; for Judge White was known never to speak lightly on religious subjects, and, moreover, he was habitually cautious and respectful in his remarks concerning religious men. The company now expressed the most urgent desire that the judge would give the particulars, and expectation stood on tiptoe.

"I went up," said the judge, "one evening, to the Methodist church. A sermon was preached by a clergyman with whom I was not acquainted; but Father Axley was in the pulpit. At the close of the sermon, he arose, and said to the congregation, 'I am not going to detain you by delivering an exhortation. I have risen simply to administer a rebuke for improper conduct, which I have observed here to-night.' This, of course, waked up the entire assembly; and the stillness was most profound, while Axley stood and looked, for two or three seconds, over the congregation. Then, stretching out his large, long arm, and pointing with his finger steadily in one direction, 'Now,' said he, 'I calculate that those two young men, who were talking and laughing in that corner of the house, while the brother was preaching, think that I'm going to talk about them. Well, it is true that it looks very bad, when well-dressed young men, who you would suppose, from their appearance, belonged to some genteel, respectable family, come to the house of God, and, instead of reverencing the majesty of Him that dwelleth therein, or attending to the message of his everlasting love, get together in one corner of the house,' (his finger all this time pointing straight and steady as the aim of a rifleman,) 'and there, through the whole solemn service, keep talking, tittering, laughing, giggling — thus annoying the minister, disturbing the congregation, and sinning against God. I'm sorry for the young men. I'm sorry for their parents. I'm sorry they have done so to-night. I hope they'll never do so again. But, however, that's not the thing that I was going to talk about. It is another matter, and so important, that I thought it would be wrong to suffer the congregation to depart without administering a suitable rebuke. Now,' said he, stretching his huge arm, and pointing in another direction, 'perhaps that man, who was asleep on the bench out there, while the brother was preaching, thinks that I am going to talk about him. Well, I must confess, it looks very bad for a man to come into a worshipping assembly, and, instead of taking his seat like others, and listening to the blessed gospel, carelessly stretch himself out on a bench, and go to sleep! It is not only a proof of great insensibility with regard to the obligations which we owe to our Creator and Redeemer, but it shows a want of genteel breeding. It shows that the poor man has been so unfortunate in his bringing up, as not to have been taught good manners. He doesn't know what is polite and respectful in a worshipping assembly, among whom he comes to mingle. I'm sorry for the poor man. I'm sorry for the family to which he belongs. I'm sorry he did not know better. I hope he will never do so again. But, however, that is not what I was going to talk about.' Thus Father Axley went on, for some time, 'boxing the compass,' and hitting a number of persons and things that he was 'not going to talk about,' and hitting them *hard,* till the attention and curiosity of the audience were raised to the highest pitch, when, finally, he remarked, 'The thing of which I was going to talk, is *chewing tobacco.* Now, I do hope, when any gentleman comes here to church, who can't keep from chewing tobacco during the hours of public worship, that he will just take his hat, and put it before him, and spit in his hat. You know we are Methodists. You all know that our custom is to kneel when we pray. Now, any gentleman may see, in a moment, how exceedingly inconvenient it must be for a well-dressed Methodist lady to be compelled to kneel down in a great puddle of tobacco-spit!'

"Now," said Judge White, "at this very time, I had in my mouth an uncommonly large quid of tobacco. Axley's singular manner and train of remark had strongly arrested my attention. While he was striking to the right and left, hitting those 'things' that he was not going to talk about, my curiosity was roused, and conjecture was busy to find out what he could be aiming at. I was chewing my huge quid with uncommon rapidity, and spitting, and looking up at the preacher, to catch every word and every gesture; and when, at last, he pounced on the 'tobacco,' behold, there I had a *great puddle* of tobacco-spit! I quietly slipped the quid out of my mouth, and dashed it as far as I could under the seats, resolving never again to be found chewing tobacco in a Methodist church.

THE LIVING AND THE DEAD PROPHETS.

SCENE I. *A half-built Tomb in Judea, in the time of the public ministrations of Jesus Christ. Around the tomb,* ANNAS, *and* CAIAPHAS, *and* JOHN, *and* ALEXANDER, *and others of the kindred of the high priest, with Stone-masons and Attendants.* (Acts iv. 6.)

Annas. This is truly a pious business! Yes, this is what I call religion. We are all here, with one heart, to build the sepulchre of the prophet Elisha. Ah, he was a treasure to Israel in his day! What miracles he performed on Naaman the Syrian, and others! What a life of exemplary piety he led! And after he was dead, there was virtue in his bones. Yes, the sacred record declares, that, while certain men were burying the body of a man who had died, they spied a company of hostile Moabites, who had invaded the land; and they "cast the man into the sepulchre of Elisha. And when the man was let down, and touched the bones of Elisha, he revived, and stood on his feet." (2 Kings xiii. 21.) Ah, he was a prophet, whose like we shall not see again! But there is piety in building his sepulchre. Let us put our own hands to this admirable religious enterprise. Caiaphas, take hold! John, Alexander, — all of you who are of the kindred of the high priest, — take hold! Help me to set this great block of marble in the right position for hewing.

I delight in such work as this. I absolutely believe that I could hew this marble almost as well as a professed mason. (*He takes a stone-hammer, and begins to hew.*) Ah, this is what I call religion!

Caiaphas. How much it is to be regretted that we have no such prophets as Elisha in the church at this day! *Mortar!* bring *mortar!* (*Aloud.*) Have it well tempered and prepared. My heart experiences *the excitement* of the noble enterprise. Ah, there is sublimity in the thought of building the sepulchre of a dead prophet! — especially one who has been so long dead. Yes, I feel the inspiration of the occasion. I am quickened, yea, revived, yea, ennobled, by the animating character of this exalted undertaking. None of that odious modern fanaticism can mingle in such an elevated and dignified design as this. Honor to the memory of the prophet Elisha!

Annas. I hear that there are some very disorderly proceedings over in Galilee.

Caiaphas. Ah! say you so? In what respect?

Annas. One Jesus, a professed prophet, has arisen, and is making quite a number of disciples.

Caiaphas. Disciples! How absurd for such a mere pretender to call men to be his disciples! We are Moses' disciples. We know that God spake unto Moses; but, as for this fellow, we know not from whence he is. That is a most beautiful block of white marble. How it will garnish the sepulchre of the dead prophet! The truth is, no embellishment or decoration should be spared in a pious purpose like this. Drive on the work, masons! Prepare the stone for the good prophet's tomb as fast as you can! *Mortar!* Attendants, keep these masons well supplied with mortar! A pious work, truly! I should take pride in carrying the hod myself, in order to forward such an important religious enterprise.

First Mason. I have heard that the prophet in Galilee does many wonderful works; that the common people hear him gladly; and that many have believed in him, as the promised Messiah.

Caiaphas. Peace, man! hold your peace! Have any of the rulers or Pharisees believed on him?

Second Mason. I saw some officers, that the chief priests had sent to take him. They said that they had listened to one of his sermons, and that they were constrained to declare, "Never man spake like this man."

Caiaphas. I command you, laymen, to hold your peace! Beware how you interfere with the rights of those who have the oversight of the people! If you must speak of the transactions over in Galilee, speak of the disorders, the extravagances, &c.

Annas. I learn that there are great excesses and irregularities among the followers of this "prophet of Nazareth of Galilee." Some four or five thousand men, besides women and children, it is said, continued with him "three days, when they had nothing to eat." This was shocking extravagance. It was a great shame to expose those little children to such suffering.

First Mason. I was told that the prophet fed those four or five thousand men, and all the women and children, with a few loaves and fishes; and that they did all eat, and were filled; and that twelve baskets-full of fragments, or broken meat, were taken up after they had all eaten.

Caiaphas. *Mortar!* Bring on a good supply of

mortar, for the tomb of the prophet! Roll up those large blocks of marble, that the workmen may hew and prepare them! Here, fellow! (*To the mason, in a lower tone.*) If you speak in commendation of that prophet of Galilee, you shall be dismissed from our employment, and put out of the synagogue. Ah, those poor women and children! From my inmost heart, I pity them. Three days, and nothing to eat! There were no such disorderly doings in the days of the good old prophet Elisha.

Annas. I was credibly informed that the roof of a poor man's house was very much injured, but a short time since. They had brought one sick of the palsy; and an immense rabble being collected about the door, they who had charge of the sick man could not enter that way. Being very reckless persons, and having little regard to the rights of others, they ascended to the roof of the house, and broke it up, and let down the sick of the palsy through the great opening which they had made in the roof. I saw a very respectable man, who was at the house on the afternoon of the same day; and he reports that the injury done to the roof was very great. The owner of the house is a poor man, who can ill afford to meet the expense of repairing — particularly at this time, when lumber and shingles are uncommonly high. So, now, the family are there, all exposed to the first squall of bad weather that may chance to blow up.

Second Mason. I understand, however, that the sick of the palsy was perfectly healed; that he took up his bed, and walked through the astonished multitude, calling on all to witness what great things the Lord had done for him; and that all the people glorified God, and declared that a great prophet was risen in Israel.

Caiaphas. Fellow! fellow! no more of that! (*In a subdued tone.*) Take warning from the words I spake to your neighbor there, a moment ago. I tell you that you tamper with a lion, if you disobey the high priest. Most sincerely do I sympathize with that poor, unoffending man, whose roof was so greatly damaged. These are new measures! new measures! Nothing of the kind was sanctioned by Elisha, in his day. He was no house-breaker, or roof-destroyer. I glory in the privilege of building his sepulchre. Confusion to all modern innovations!

Annas. Innovations? The half has not been told you.

Caiaphas. Well, this sepulchre takes my eye. It will be a most beautiful structure, when completed. None will dare to call in question our religion, after this, we have been so forward in this great and good work. What a pity that we cannot have such prophets as Elisha in our day! Admirable man! he has been gone from the earth now more than eight hundred years. But it is to us a source of high satisfaction, that we can build his sepulchre. Ah, a work like this proves the depth of a man's religion! I say again, Confusion to all modern innovations! I cannot keep from thinking of that poor man's damaged roof, and those hungry women and children.

First Mason. (*Aside.*) But it seems that the miracle of the loaves and fishes, and the sick man who was perfectly healed, must not be mentioned.

Annas. As to irregularities, and "mischievous disorders," I repeat, that the half has not yet been told.

I was informed, the other day, that certain unoffending persons have sustained a great loss by the lawless proceedings now prevalent in that region. The persons of whom I speak had invested the principal part of their substance in a large herd of swine. The swine were in fine condition, just ready for the market. The number of the swine was about two thousand, and they were worth more than twenty thousand shekels of silver. By some disorderly proceeding, which I do not understand, — for that professed prophet is said to be in league with Beelzebub, the prince of devils, — the whole herd took fright, and ran down a steep place into the sea, and perished in the waters — a great loss to the owners! certainly, a great loss. I am grieved to hear of such proceedings. But we are Moses' disciples, and we build the sepulchre of Elisha. That is the right kind of religion, beyond a doubt. Away with modern fanaticism and extravagance!

Second Mason. (*Aside.*) But there is not a word about the man that had been possessed by the legion. The devils were cast out; and the wretched man was healed, and restored to his friends, clothed, and in his right mind; and "the people were all amazed, and glorified God." Not a word of all that!

Caiaphas. Sad times! Sad times indeed! Two thousand hogs utterly lost; a valuable roof broken up, and well nigh destroyed; and a large number of women and children almost starved to death! Venerable prophet Elisha! Our only remaining comfort is in building thy tomb. O, had we lived *eight hundred years ago,* we might have found good enterprises in the church, in which we could have coöperated. The revivals, at that day, were of the right stamp; but, now, all that we can do is to find fault, raise objections, build the sepulchres of prophets who are dead, and scowl at those who are living.

SCENE II. *A Church in Scotland in the days of John Knox. Enter three venerable Churchmen.*

First Churchman. I am greatly grieved with the manner in which the reformation is conducted. John Knox seems to be cheek by jowl with the Earl of Murray, and with Morton also, and other ambitious nobles. They evidently are anxious to pull down the old establishment, in order to enrich themselves, and their friends and favorites, with the spoils. The Earl of Morton and the Earl of Murray have had a fierce quarrel about the disposal of the lands and property of the last abbey which they have broken up. And John Knox has such men in the church, and he permits them to be his counsellors! Ah, "birds of a feather" — the old proverb, how true! The fact is, the conduct of John Knox is highly exceptionable. The exigencies of the times demand a better man at the head of the reformation in Scotland.

Second Churchman. I don't believe that John Calvin, at Geneva, is one whit better. True, he has managed to get great influence in that city; but there are many hard things said against him. Alas for the cause of religion, when prominent ministers are obnoxious to so many objections! Indeed, the whole reformation abounds in blemishes and defects.

Third Churchman. And there is Martin Luther, in Germany. The fact is, they are all "tarred with the same stick." Luther is one of those headlong, self-willed, obstinate men, on whom good counsel is absolutely wasted. Ah, I often think of the preachers in the primitive church! Could we only have such ministers now, we should know how to value them. There was Stephen — strange that the men of that age should stone such a man to death!

First Churchman. Yes; and there was Peter — what a treasure to the church! and Paul — wonderful that the men of that day should cast such excellent ministers into prison, and subject them to cruel stripes.

Second Churchman. And there was the amiable apostle John. How wicked it was to banish him to the Isle of Patmos! O that we had such ministers in our day! Let us build their sepulchres, otherwise we may be misunderstood. While we oppose John Knox, and Luther, and Calvin, people may conclude that we are opposed to revivals of religion; but if we build the sepulchres of those primitive ministers, then we can cry out against those of our own day, without forfeiting our religious characters. What say you? Shall we build the sepulchres of the primitive ministers, and thus show that, beyond a doubt, we are religious men, and friends of revivals — that is, revivals of the right stamp?

First Churchman. I will subscribe liberally. Ah, that is a pious work, in which my heart would rejoice!

Third Churchman. And I, too, will gladly coöperate to build the sepulchres of the early ministers, who are long since dead. That is a religious enterprise, that commends itself to my judgment and my heart; but, as for these modern men, — Knox, Luther, and Calvin, — I wholly disapprove of their measures. John Knox comes down like a thunder-storm. I wish for a revival that has not got so much of *man* in it. I wish the Lord to do his own work.

SCENE III. *An American Church in 1742. Enter three venerable Ministers.*

First Minister. What can this Freewill Edwards be aiming at? His mode of writing and preaching is certainly endangering the doctrines of the reformation. Ah, venerable John Calvin! Unparalleled champion of the doctrines of grace! What wouldst thou have thought of such an ally as this Jonathan Edwards? The fact is, the entire man is a curiosity, and all his writings are of an abstruse, metaphysical character. The church knows not what to make of him, or them; but fears of the worst are extensively entertained. O for the plain, unequivocal, and downright manners of the great reformers! John Calvin, John Knox, and the men of *that day*, were an invaluable treasure to the church.

Second Minister. This George Whitefield is not one jot better than Edwards. He professes to believe the doctrines of the reformation; but he is turning the world upside down. It is, moreover, reported that Bellamy, at Bethlehem, sympathizes entirely with Edwards and Whitefield, and the same thing is said of Gilbert and William Tennant, of New Jersey. I am a friend of revivals; but not such revivals as these, that take place under the preaching of Edwards, and Whitefield, and the Tennants. No, no. I wish to see such revivals as blessed the church in Geneva, under the preaching of John Calvin; and such revivals as blessed the church in Scotland, when John Knox proclaimed the gospel. Those revivals were worthy of the name. Ah, they were rich and lasting blessings to the church! But these mere ephemeral, modern excitements awake my indignation. The fact is, Edwards preaches sermons that are perfectly frightful. He seems to wish to take the conversion of sinners into his own hands; and Whitefield and Bellamy do the same thing. Now, I like a revival that has not got so much of *man* in it. I like a revival that gives all the glory to God.

Third Minister. And such were the revivals under the great reformers, John Calvin, John Knox, and their fellow-laborers. Those eminent men should not be forgotten. Would it not be a pious work to build their sepulchres? I would gladly join with you in such an important religious enterprise.

First Minister. I will coöperate with all my heart.

Second Minister. And I, also, for two reasons: First, by building their sepulchres, we shall give honor to men who deserve to be held in everlasting remembrance; and, second, we shall throw around ourselves the influence of the great names of these reformers; and thus we shall be strengthened in our opposition to Edwards, Whitefield, Bellamy, and all such modern fanatics.

First and Third Minister. Amen and amen!

SCENE IV. *Place, not legible. Time,* 184–, *(last figure indistinct.)*
Enter an Aged Man and a brisk, self-important Youth.

Youth. What astonishing men labored in these American churches, before the colonies were separated from Great Britain! Edwards, and his fellows of that day, were noble examples for the faithful, discreet, and judicious minister of the present age to copy; and the revivals, which blessed the church under their labors, are models which we would do well to imitate. There have been many very objectionable things mingled with the revivals in the church of late years. Indeed, I have little sympathy with modern revivals. I absolutely believe that they have done more harm than good. But I am free to express my warmest admiration of such revivals as attended the preaching of Edwards and others, one hundred years ago; and, as for Edwards himself, he was, in his day, "a burning and a shining light." I am decidedly of opinion, that the American church ought to erect a monument to his memory. Yes, a richly-ornamented sepulchre should grace the sacred spot where his ashes repose.

Aged Man. And what do you think of George Whitefield?

Youth. O, I venerate the name of George Whitefield! I understand that a costly tomb has already been erected over or near his remains; otherwise I should have proposed to have his memorial placed beside that of Edwards. And, moreover, I believe that a faithful history of the distinguishing features of the revivals of their day ought to be compiled, as a guide and a model for ministers of this age. It might preserve them from many lamentable indiscretions and extravagances.

Aged Man. My son, listen to the voice of experience. You have fallen into the common error of mankind, who eulogize and build the sepulchre of the prophet that is *dead*, while they stigmatize and reject the prophet that is *living*. With this device Satan has deceived the nations for ages. The dead prophet rebukes no one. Neither the sinner, nor the cold, worldly professor, is interrupted by him. They can, therefore, build his sepulchre, while they continue to live in sin. Thus the tempter deludes multitudes with a persuasion that their spiritual condition is good, because they can eulogize the dead prophet; but let the living prophet appear, teaching and exemplifying the same doctrine which his predecessor once taught, and he is intolerable. The cry is raised, "Away with him from the earth; for it is not fit that he should live." How were the old prophets treated by those among whom they lived? "They had trial of cruel mockings and scourgings, yea, moreover, of bonds and imprisonments. They were stoned, they were sawn asunder, were tempted, were slain with the sword. They wandered about in sheep-skins and goat-skins, being destitute, afflicted, tormented. They wandered in deserts, and in mountains, and in dens and caves of the earth." (Heb. xi. 36—38.) But after they had been dead for ages, then many were eager to sing their praises and build their sepulchres. But when Christ appeared, teaching the same doctrines with the old prophets, "they said, He hath a devil, and is mad: why hear ye him? Crucify him! Crucify him!" And thus Satan manages, from age to age. At the reformation, there were many who would eulogize Christ and his apostles, who were exceedingly bitter against such *living* prophets as John Calvin and John Knox; but when Calvin and Knox were dead, and Whitefield and Edwards were the living prophets, then the same scenes were acted over. Half the pulpits in the country were shut against Whitefield, while he was alive; and Jonathan Edwards was driven from his church, at the age of forty-seven, and took refuge among the Indians. But, now that Edwards and Whitefield have been dead near one hundred years, the devil and revival-fighting men would gladly turn over their great names into the ranks of the enemy, and borrow influence from the reputation of Edwards and Whitefield, to make war against the work of the Spirit of God in this age. It is just as absurd as the conduct of the Jews, when they quoted Elijah and Isaiah, to keep them in countenance while they were denouncing Christ and his apostles. My son, allow me to speak plainly. You have fallen into a great error; nay, you are taken captive in a dreadful snare of the devil, and your danger is imminent. God is the same, from age to age. God's word is the same. "The grass withereth, the flower fadeth; but the word of our God shall stand forever." God's Spirit is the same now as in the days of the apostles and prophets. The sinner that is converted now, is converted by the same Spirit, and the same truth, that turned souls to God on the day of Pentecost. Before Christ ascended up on high, he gave this promise to the church: "Lo, I am with you always, even to the end of the world." That promise he has never violated, nor is it necessary to go back a hundred years, to find tokens and proofs of his presence with the church. There is as much guilt brought upon the soul by blaspheming the Holy Ghost now, as there was on the day of Pentecost. Blasphemy is evil speaking. Beware how you speak against the Holy Ghost, sent down from heaven!

Youth. But — but understand me. I only spoke against spurious revivals.

Aged Man. Yes, and the Jews only spoke against

spurious works of Christ; but, according to them, his works were all spurious. "He cast out devils by Beelzebub;" and in his public preaching they alleged, "He hath a devil, and is mad." So with you — all modern revivals are spurious; and, to find any that you can approve, you must go back a hundred years, among people and preachers who are all dead, and gone to eternity, and who, while they were living, "were men of like passions with ourselves," and were "every where spoken against." You profess to be a preacher of the gospel. Look at your own ministry. Does God bless it? Does God convert sinners by your preaching? or is your ministry bleak and barren as the mountains of Gilboa? Who authorized you to be a barren fig-tree in the vineyard of God? Who authorized you to be an unprofitable servant? "Cast the beam out of thine own eye, and then shalt thou see clearly to cast the mote out of thy brother's eye." But beware of evil speaking. That sin, which shuts the gate of heaven against the soul forever, is a sin of the tongue. All evil speaking does not rise to the aggravation of the unpardonable sin; but very clearly the doctrine is taught, that evil speaking tends to grieve away the Holy Spirit; and this is found in the experience of ministers of the gospel. Mark that man who speaks bitterly, or even lightly, of the revivals which God grants to the church in *this day.* Does God ever own his ministry again, after he has lifted his tongue against revivals? Does God make him an honored instrument in converting sinners? No. God smites his ministry with barrenness, for the sin of his tongue; and he walks, a naked skeleton, among the churches, till the day of his death. There is a peculiar dreadfulness in the rebuke with which God visits that minister who lifts his tongue against the work of the Holy Spirit. See that tall tree, along whose trunk has flashed the lightning of angry heaven! Does it ever bud or bloom again? No. There it stands, desolate, dreary, dead. The spring returns, with its warm gales, its genial showers, and its quickening sunbeams. Other plants feel the reviving influence. Nature all around awakes and rejoices. Gushing streams of life are pushing forth buds, blossoms, leaves, and young formations of fruit, on every hand. But O, that dead tree! No bud, no leaf, no blossom, or young formation of fruit, is there. The quickening power of spring, the warm and strong energies of summer, affect it not. It stands dreary, desolate, dead. Yes, it stands leafless, limbless, barkless — scattering on all around its mouldering and unsavory dust. Sad emblem of the decayed and dead ministry of that deluded man who has lifted a profane tongue against the visitations of the Spirit of God, which accompany the gospel in the present day!

Youth. I must remind you that I am altogether in favor of such revivals as were granted in the days of Edwards and the reformers. It was only of these *modern* revivals that I said they do more harm than good. I spoke lightly of these only.

Aged Man. Yes, so I understand you. And the Scribes and Pharisees were altogether in favor of the revivals under Samuel and Elijah, eight hundred or a thousand years before they were born. It was only of the then modern reformations, under the ministry of Christ and his apostles, that they wished to speak lightly or reproachfully. Let me warn you again, that you have taken a most perilous stand. Know you not that the Father of Lights is the same from age to age, "without variableness, or shadow of turning"? Know you not that Jesus Christ is "the same yesterday, to-day, and forever"? Know you not that the Holy Spirit is unchangeably the same? Know you not that heaven and earth shall pass away, but one jot or one tittle of Christ's gospel shall not pass away? The same divine Redeemer, the same word of truth, the same Holy Spirit, that were with the church, and in the church, on the day of Pentecost, are with the church, and in the church, at this day, and will be, to the end of the world. The guilt, therefore, of blaspheming the Holy Ghost now, is the same as when Christ was on earth, or when the cloven tongues sat upon the apostles. I mentioned that *all* evil speaking against the Holy Ghost may not rise to the aggravation of the unpardonable sin. It is very clear that a Christian minister may be deluded by the devil to so speak against the work of the Holy Spirit, that, while the sin may not actually kill both his soul and body in hell, yet it may *cripple his ministry for life.* He may be saved at last, "yet so as by fire." That is, his soul may be saved, while his works are burned up in the flames of the great day. In conclusion, let me admonish you to read the comments of God's providence on the lessons taught in his word. It is of these lessons that the inspired psalmist says, "Whoso is wise, and will observe these things, even they shall understand." (Ps. cvii. 43.) Now, observe the comments of Providence. Did the men who resisted the work under Edwards and Whitefield ever prosper afterwards, as preachers of the gospel? Was not the rebuke of

God on them till the day of their death ? Look at the comments of Providence, at a later day. Where are the men who made themselves conspicuous in our country, but a few years ago, in opposition to revivals ? Has God blessed their ministry since ? Are they not *crippled for life ?* Has not their ministry, ever since, been like the seven ears of corn, in Pharaoh's second vision, " withered and thin, and blasted with the east wind " ? Ah, my young friend, I have seen enough in the volume of God's word, and, during some years past, in the volume of his providence, to make me tremble for the man who employs his tongue and his breath in stigmatizing, or even mocking, and making light of the manifestations of God's Spirit, at this day, in connection with the truths of his glorious gospel ! Pitiable and forlorn is his condition who is driven to the wretched expedient of building the sepulchre of some dead prophet, in order to quiet a conscience that is troubled in view of his having scoffed at the divine mercy that accompanies the ministry of the prophet that is living.

THE DIVINITY STUDENT.

WHEN the red man, retreating before the face of his white brother, forsook those romantic and beautiful regions that are watered by the Holstein and the Tennessee, divine Providence planted a people there remarkable for their attachment to the Bible. Bible history, Bible doctrines, and Bible religion were "the joy of their heart, and the boast of their tongue." Divine *truth*, revealed in the word of God, was their "meat and their drink." It was their daily study. It was their literature. It was the theme of their social intercourse. It was the source of their consolations on earth, and the foundation of their hopes for immortality. The learned theologian, who chanced to pass that way, was delighted and surprised to find, in a new and comparatively rough country, among a plain, unostentatious people, views of divine truth clearer than the crystal streams that flowed among their towering hills, and sweeter than the salubrious breezes that fanned their mountain country. The following anecdote will show with what accuracy and discrimination the great doctrines of the gospel were studied in the west, at that early day: —

Dr. Anderson, now of the theological seminary at Maryville, had undertaken the supervision of an academy in Knox county, Tennessee, as early as the year 1807. Among his students was Abel Pearson, a youth who had embraced religion, and who, while pursuing his literary studies, exhibited great appetite and capacity for investigating the sublime philosophy of the plan of salvation. This greatly delighted his instructor, who, though then quite a young minister, had already begun to display those gigantic powers, as an expounder of Bible truth, which have since been so astonishingly unfolded to the edification and joy of the church. Learned critics, in comparing the Iliad of Homer with the Odyssey, have alleged that the latter poem, having more narrative and less fire than the former, bears the marks of old age. An elegant writer observes, that if the Odyssey has the marks of old age, it is the old age of *Homer*. In like manner, I observe, that if the academical instructor above mentioned was then but a youth, it was the youth of Isaac Anderson. And of the student I may say, that he was a student worthy of his instructor.

This young man, before completing his studies, was providentially called into a neighboring county, where strong prejudices were entertained against the Presbyterian church, their doctrines were denounced as horrible, and even their ministers were assailed as learned Pharisees, who preached merely from their learning, without any heart-religion, &c., &c., while their assailants claimed a species of inspiration, and professed to preach from the immediate teachings of the Spirit.

Our student, after a long day's ride, stopped for the night at a house where one of these semi-inspired preachers had an appointment to deliver a sermon at candle light. The congregation assembled, the minister came, and our young man took his place in the audience unobserved. The preacher proved to be a red-hot

Arminian, who boasted that his back had never been rubbed against the walls of a college, and whose zeal for the propagation of his peculiarities was sufficiently ardent, though his knowledge of polemic theology was somewhat scant. Endowed, however, with lungs of great power, he commenced and "reported progress," dealing, as he moved along, many a merciless blow at John Calvin, John Knox, John Wetherspoon, and others, all and singular, who have maintained the doctrines of the Presbyterian church, warning his audience, in the mean time, to use his own expression, against "the great, high-learned men," who were preaching in some of the neighboring counties. While in the full tide of his boisterous declamation, it appeared, doubtless, to his own mind, quite problematical whether Calvinism would be able to survive the terrors of that dreadful night; but as all preceding storms had been succeeded by a calm, so it turned out in this case. The sermon closed. The audience dispersed. The preacher, who remained with the family for the night, found himself in company with our student.

Preacher. Do you live in this neighborhood, young man?

Student. No, sir.

Preacher. Where is your home?

Student. In Knox county.

Preacher. Are you a member of the church?

Student. Yes, sir.

Preacher. To what church do you belong?

Student. I am a Presbyterian.

Preacher. What! a Presbyterian?

Student. Yes, sir.

Preacher. Why, do you believe the confession of faith?

Student. Certainly I do, or I should not be a Presbyterian.

Preacher. Why, sir, the confession of faith says, "God has, for his own glory, foreordained whatsoever comes to pass."

Student. It does.

Preacher. And do you believe that?

Student. Certainly I do. Do not you believe the Bible?

Preacher. Yes; but that language is not in the Bible.

Student. The Bible tells you that God "worketh all things after the counsel of his own will," which is precisely the same doctrine.

Preacher. But the doctrine of predestination is unreasonable. My reason revolts, whenever it is presented.

Student. I will examine that point with you, if you will answer each question I ask you, and then stick to the answer you have given.

Preacher. I can easily do that; but you could not make me acknowledge that doctrine in a lifetime.

Student. I should not want a lifetime, unless it were a very short one. Remember, now, this is our agreement: you are to answer each question I ask, and then stick to the answer you have given.

Preacher. Yes, that is the agreement. Now, come on with your questions.

Student. You acknowledge that God foreknows all things from eternity?

Preacher. O, yes; but then foreknowledge is a very different thing from predestination.

Student. Well, we will not dispute about that

now. You admit that God foreknew all events from eternity?

Preacher. Yes, certainly. I am not going to deny God's foreknowledge.

Student. Well, stick to that.

Preacher. I maintain the doctrine of God's foreknowledge as firmly as you.

Student. If God from eternity foreknew all future events, it must have been in one of these three ways: First, he saw that future events would spring into existence by chance, without any cause; or, second, he depended on some other being to bring them about; or, third, he had determined to bring them about himself. Can you think of any other method? or was it not in one of these three ways?

Preacher. I suppose it was in one of these methods. I can think of no other.

Student. Well, was it the first? Did God from all eternity behold all future events springing into existence by mere chance, without any cause?

Preacher. No, I think not.

Student. To maintain that, would be atheism.

Preacher. Yes, to say that God from eternity saw that all future events would spring into existence without any cause, merely by accident, would be atheism.

Student. Well, there was a period when no being existed but God, — I mean the period before he had created either man or angels. Could he then have depended on any other being to bring into existence the future events which he foresaw, when there was no other being in existence?

Preacher. Certainly not. But what next?

Student. What do you say? But one other method

remains: that is, he himself had determined to bring them to pass.

Preacher. Stop! I was too fast. I should not have admitted your statement. There was another method, in which God foresaw the future existence of some things.

Student. This is violating your agreement; for you were to stick to the answer you had given. But let us hear what you were going to say.

Preacher. I say God knew, from "the reason and nature of things," how some events would come to pass.

Student. Pray, sir, what sort of a reason and nature had things, before God created all things, and gave them a reason and a nature? Thus you see your whole foundation is swept away; and you can find no resting-place, until you come back to the good old Bible doctrine, that "all things are of God."

Preacher. Well, rather than admit that doctrine, I will deny that God foreknows all things. I would rather deny the foreknowledge of God, than admit the doctrine of predestination.

Student. If you deny the foreknowledge of God, you may as well deny his present knowledge; for the Bible teaches the one as plainly as the other; and, indeed, there is scarcely a step from the position you have assumed, to the doctrine of him who "says in his heart, There is no God." Now, sir, you see the wretched result to which you come in this discussion with me; and all this family see it. I am no minister. I am but a youthful member of the Presbyterian church. I have no pretensions to distinction among them; and yet you see how you have come out in this discussion with me. In the course of your sermon to-night, you said many things against those "great, high-learned men," who are preaching in the neighboring counties. You arraigned their motives, and denounced their principles. I must caution you to be more modest and moderate, and not hazard too much in this warfare; for if you have come out thus wretchedly in a little discussion with me — a mere stripling — a mere boy in the Presbyterian church — what on earth do you think would become of you, should you fall into the hands of one of those "great, high-learned men," whom you have been so violently and publicly denouncing.

Here the discussion closed. Whether any permanent and profitable impression was left on the mind of the anti-Calvinistic preacher, is not certainly known. Of the divinity student, however, it should be recorded, that, in due time, he entered the gospel ministry. He became distinguished as an able expounder of the holy oracles. Many, very many, of our Lord's disciples in the west have sat under his ministry with great delight, while he has "fed them with knowledge and understanding." Laboring, like the great apostle of the Gentiles, with his own hands, to supply his temporal wants, he has, without cost to the church, preached salvation to destitute thousands. And the author of the "Western Sketch-Book," with emotions of gratitude to the Giver of all good, would record on this page, that he has had the privilege of profiting much by the clear, sublime, scriptural views of the mighty work of redemption, presented in the familiar conversations, the sermons, and the published writings of Rev. Abel Pearson.

JO; OR, THE VOICE OF CONSCIENCE.

ABOUT the year 1820, I became particularly acquainted with a venerable elder of the Presbyterian church in East Tennessee, whom I will introduce to the reader as Mr. M'Clellan. He was a man in humble circumstances, advanced in life, and possessed of a very fine and highly-cultivated intellect. He belonged to that class of *reading* Christians, who were the glory of the primitive Presbyterian church in the west. The Bible, Henry's "Commentary," Doddridge's "Family Expositor," Boston's "Fourfold State," the "Bible Dictionary" of John Brown of Haddington, Edwards "On the Will," Edwards "On the Affections," Newton's "Letters," Bellamy's "Wisdom of God in the Permission of Sin," &c., &c.: such is a sample of the works studied by the church at that period. Ah, "there were giants in the earth in those days," alongside of whom could some of our modern peacock-tail theologians be placed, they would soon learn to sympathize most fraternally with the spies sent out by Moses, when they said, "We were in our own sight as grasshoppers"! The venerable Elder M'Clellan, mentioned above, was remarkable for the fervor, comprehensiveness, and power of his prayers. Although more than a quarter of a century has rolled into eternity since I last heard his voice, yet the very words employed in some of his earnest and thrilling petitions are fresh in my memory at this moment. The truth is, he had been baptized with the spirit of that great western revival in the year 1800, one of the distinguishing characteristics of which was the liberty, compass, and power of prayer, granted to the subjects of that divine visitation.

Near the close of the year 1838, I visited the state of Mississippi, in order to labor, for a limited period, in connection with Rev. Messrs. Newton, Holley, and other esteemed brethren there. We were engaged, for a number of days, in a very interesting and solemn meeting at Grenada, and among those who came before the session and the church, professing "repentance towards God, and faith towards our Lord Jesus Christ," was a young Mr. M'Clellan; and lo, I was presently informed that he was a son of the worthy East Tennessee elder, with whom the reader is already acquainted! Like a good soldier in the Redeemer's service, having taken his stand in the church, he sees to it that his house is a house of prayer, and that his family is consecrated to God. From this son I learned that his venerable father had long since gone to his rest in heaven.

Our meeting at Grenada closed on Monday evening. On that afternoon, or, perhaps, the next, an elder brother, Col. John M'Clellan, who had been up the country, near Holly Springs, and was now returning to his home, near Carrollton, called to spend a night with his brother in Grenada. Learning that his brother had made a profession of religion; that he had joined himself to the church of God; and finding, when the hour of prayer came, that he prayed in his family, and would do it even in presence of an ungodly brother, who was some twelve or fifteen years older than himself, — the discovery of all this, O, it agitated the great deep of his soul. He remembered his pious father. He remembered his counsel, his example, and his prayers. He remembered the warnings, the impressions, and the vows of years, now forever gone. He thought of the prodigal son, who left his father's house, to chase the pleasures of the world. "Is not my word as a fire? saith the Lord; and like a hammer that breaketh the rock in pieces?" Early the next morning, Col. M'Clellan, silent and solemn, set out for home. The character of his meditations and reflections on the road can be more easily conceived by the reader, than described by me.

On the following Thursday, according to appointment, a sacramental meeting was commenced at Carrollton. To that meeting I went in company with Rev. Mr. Newton and Rev. Mr. Holley. It was early when we reached the meeting-house; but Col. M'Clellan and his entire family were already there, though his residence was six miles distant. He was standing, with a few others, who had come early, near the door of the church. When we had arrived, Mr. Newton introduced me to Col. M. I shook hands with him, saying, "How do you do, Col. M.? I am happy to see you." This last remark was made in reference to the fact, that I had been acquainted with his father, and had also seen him in his younger years. I was now introduced to one and another of the gentlemen who were standing round, and engaged in some transient conversation, when brother Holley came, and asked me to step off a little way from the company. "Why," said he, "Col. M. is very much troubled, because you called him 'Jo.'"

"Because I called him 'Jo'? Why, he is altogether mistaken. I didn't call him 'Jo.'"

"Yes; but he says that when you were introduced to him, you said, 'How do you do, Joseph?' And he says that his name is *John*. Jo was a brother in the family; but the colonel says his name is *John*. Jo was the drinking one."

"Very good. I have no doubt that the colonel's name is *John*. I did not know that there was a Jo in the family, and therefore very certainly did not call him 'Jo.'"

About this juncture, brother Newton, our other preacher, came up, and, addressing me, said, "Col. M. is quite vexed, because you called him 'Jo,' when you were introduced to him."

"But I did not call him 'Jo.' I did not say 'Jo,' nor think 'Jo.' The fact is, I did not know that there was a Jo in the family."

"But he is very positive that you did; and he says that his name is *John*. Jo was a brother. Jo was the drinking one."

"Why, this is a very strange affair. What on earth can have put it into the colonel's head, that I called him 'Jo,' when I didn't know that there was a Jo in the family? I am entirely satisfied that his name should be *John*." Such was my reply to brother Newton; but I must here tell the reader what, at that time, I myself did not know — that is, it was the colonel's conscience that had said "Jo," and pronounced it so distinctly, that he thought the name was uttered by me; and he was so affected by it, that he hurried round among his acquaintances, telling them that I had called him "Jo," and resolutely maintaining that his name was *John*.

The people of the congregation were yet in the act of assembling, and, as it was a full half hour until preaching-time, I concluded to step into a house, that was near by, and sit down for a few minutes. As soon as I had entered, Mrs. More, the lady of the house, introduced me to a very respectable-looking, well-dressed Mississippi lady — " This is Mrs. Col. M." I spoke to her, and then took a seat. She immediately turned her fine, broad eye and full countenance upon me, and, with much earnestness, said, " This is not 'Jo.' My husband's name is *John.* Jo was a brother of my husband; but it was *John* that was introduced to you."

" So I learn, madam — so I learn," said I, surprised that the colonel should have found opportunity to communicate to so many persons the unlucky misnomer, though imaginary, which had so greatly disturbed him. Scarcely, however, had the good lady and I come to a satisfactory understanding that her husband's name was *John*, and that Jo was quite another person, when the colonel himself approached. His step, his countenance, his whole attitude and bearing, showed that something of immense weight was pressing on his mind. Wholly ignorant of the number of persons who had already attempted to enlighten me on the subject, he planted his tall, fine figure directly in front of my chair, and, with great gravity, thus began: —

"My name is *John.* Jo was a brother of mine; but my name is *John.*"

" Yes, yes, colonel. So I understand — so I understand."

Now, here was a mighty ado to get the fact established, that the colonel's name was not Jo, when no one had said he was Jo, or thought he was Jo. The exact explanation of this matter I never fully learned. Whether, the colonel being an elder brother in the family, conscience now reproached him that he had not, after his father was taken away, set such an example to his younger brothers as was his duty, and the name of Jo came up in this connection, or whether, as "Jo was the drinking one," and conscience was now arraying before the colonel's agitated mind the long catalogue of his own misdeeds, he felt that these were as heavy as he could bear, and therefore resolved to stand manfully on the defensive, and repel the insinuation that he was Jo, and, consequently, liable to be held responsible for whatever Jo had done amiss. However all this may have been, the hour of preaching was now at hand, and the company left the house of Mrs. More, and went towards the church. When near the door, the colonel paused suddenly, and asked brothers Newton, Holley, and myself, to step aside with him, that he might speak a moment with us, unheard by others. When together thus, said he, "I wish to say to you, gentlemen, that you must not expect me to take any public step in religion at this meeting." Nobody had said that we expected him to take any public step in religion at that meeting. It reminded me of the schoolboy who denies before he is accused, which is not considered the best sign of innocence. "You must not," said the colonel, repeating the caution — "you must not look for me to take any public step in religion at this meeting. At the same time, I don't want you to think that I am indifferent to Christ. I am *not* indifferent to Christ." His eyes filled with tears. His voice trembled. His utterance faltered. After a momentary pause, by a strong effort, he rallied his conversational powers, and proceeded. "The fact is, gentlemen, I have been here in Mississippi, chasing the world, and neglecting the salvation of my soul. I now see that what I have been after is vanity, folly, emptiness. But, gentlemen, here is the point: I am not *informed* in religion. I tell you I am not informed. And, now, this is my plan: I will supply myself with good books, and take a course of reading, — a thorough course, gentlemen, — and will inform myself, before I take any public step in religion. You understand me, gentlemen. At present, I am not informed, and, therefore, you must not expect me to act." All this was said with much gracefulness and elegance of manner; for the colonel was now a man in the prime of life, of fine personal appearance, easy and captivating address, and possessing quite an unusual flow and command of language. When the colonel had ceased his statement, I looked at him steadily, for a moment or two, but remained silent; for having known much of his father, and of the opportunities of his father's family, I was constrained to withhold my assent, absolutely, from the position, that he was "not informed" as to his duty. Mr. Newton, however, observed, "Well, colonel, I am glad to find that you are thinking seriously on the subject of religion." With that, we all turned to enter the meeting-house.

"One word more," said the colonel. "You will not, while here at Carrollton, be all the time engaged in preaching; and now I wish any leisure moments you may have from public duties, during this meeting, to be employed in giving me the information which I need. Instruction, gentlemen, instruction is what I want."

We now went into the church. There was a large audience, and the season of worship was deeply solemn. We then had an interval of some two hours, until the afternoon sermon. The colonel went to his lodgings, and waited anxiously for some of the ministers to come and "inform" him in relation to his duty. But no one came. He thought it strange that his case was not more fully appreciated. To his own mind, his guilt and danger appeared such, that he thought every minister on the ground should be laboring and praying for his salvation; and yet, had any one come, and attempted to guide or direct him while in this state of mind, he would, doubtless, have held back, and fended off in fine style. Such is the contradiction often found in the awakened sinner. He is unwilling to be let alone, and yet he will refuse the best counsel that can be given him. But now the hour of public worship had come, and the colonel returned to the church.

The afternoon service was impressive, and stillness and deep solemnity characterized the congregation. Again there was a recess of some two or three hours, until the time for the night sermon. "Now," thought the colonel, "my request will be regarded, beyond a doubt. Some of the ministers will presently come to labor with me." And he was prepared to "stand upon his reserved rights." But no one came. The first hour passed away, and the second, and the third; but no one came. He now felt a strong temptation to be offended — to look upon himself as a neglected, injured man; and he returned to the church at night, "heavy and displeased."

This night's meeting rose in interest and solemnity beyond either of the others. Judge Shattuck was called on to offer up the concluding prayer. He was a local Methodist preacher, who lived in the near neighborhood, a man of worth and exemplary piety. His prayer was appropriate and powerful. After the congregation was dismissed, Col. M. tarried a little, to give opportunity to any of the ministers, who were so disposed, to address to him a word of counsel or exhortation; but, strange to tell, they all put off to their several homes, without making the attempt, or even noticing the opportunity. This was wholly out of the question. There is a point beyond which patience itself ceases to be a virtue. So the colonel resolved, that, as the Presbyterians were so inexcusably and shamefully negligent, he would go right down to Judge Shattuck, the Methodist preacher; for surely the man who had just offered up such a prayer would be glad to converse with him about the state of his soul. So off he started, through the darkness, blundering along, and finally reached the house. He knocked at the door. It was opened by Judge Shattuck, who received him pleasantly, and helped him to a chair. The colonel sat down in silence, hoping that the judge would introduce the desired conversation. The judge, however, started off into a lively discussion of the condition of the Brandon Bank; the amount of specie in its vaults, compared with its circulation; and the probabilities of its ever being able to meet its liabilities, &c., &c. The colonel was amazed that a minister of the gospel could expatiate so fluently on such themes, when here a soul is before him in perishing need of religious instruction. "But surely he will be through presently," was his comforting reflection, "and then the other subject will come up." And, sure enough, before long, the judge came to a pause, though it was but a short one, when off he dashed in another direction, discoursing earnestly about the whigs and the democrats; the relative strength of the two great political parties in the state at large; and which was likely to have a controlling influence in the legislature, at its approaching session. "This will never do," thought the colonel; "I must introduce the subject of religion myself. — Judge Shattuck, that was a very solemn meeting to-night." "Yes," said Shattuck, rising to his feet; "when you wish to lie down, there is a bed. Good night." And out he went, shutting the door after him. The colonel was astounded. Presently he heard the voice of singing. The family were at worship in another room, to which he was not invited. "Well, well," thought the colonel, "enough is enough. I see how the matter stands. If I wait for preachers, Presbyterian or Methodist, to pull me out of the horrible pit, I'm gone." So down he went on his knees, right there in the room, and told the Lord that if He would let him begin *now*, just with what "information" he had, he would flee from the wrath to come, and strive to enter in at the strait gate, and call for help from heaven, through the Lord Jesus Christ, as long as life should endure.

I never had an opportunity of conversing with Judge Shattuck on this subject; but there is no doubt that he understood the colonel's case fully, and treated it wisely; for he was a very shrewd and judicious man. Most likely he had often tried before to bring the colonel's mind to the subject of religion, when he had utterly refused to hear, and now thought it best to let him wrestle with his awakened conscience, without the intermeddling of a third party. In the above sample of their conversation, I pretend not to give accurately the very words used by Judge Shattuck. The narrative is strictly accurate in this — that it gives a fair specimen of the dexterous manner in which the judge played off from the main question, which the anxious sinner wished to have taken up, and abruptly left him alone, with his conscience and his God. The next morning, we all met at the church. The house was crowded, and the great Master of assemblies was there. In a little time, an opportunity was given to those who were resolved to forsake the ways of sin and follow the Savior, to manifest their determination, by coming forward, in the presence of the church, that prayer might be offered up in their behalf, and suitable instructions given. No sooner was the invitation published, than from the far end of the house, over benches, and blocks, and other obstructions, came the colonel, tears streaming over both his cheeks; and down he knelt, among many others. After a solemn pause, he lifted up his voice in prayer; and the depth of his prostration of soul, the reverence expressed for the high and holy One, the wide range of his desires, the propriety, pathos, and power of his prayer, forcibly reminded me of his venerable father, whom I had heard pray so many years ago. The associations were affecting and overwhelming. I bowed my head amongst them there, to weep with those that wept, and rejoice with those that did rejoice.

I will only add, further, that, during this interesting meeting, some twelve or fourteen gentlemen — a part of them were the heads of families; all of them were in the prime of life — commenced praying publicly in the prayer meetings of the church.

As for the colonel, my esteem for him grew with my acquaintance; and when I returned to Missouri, I wrote him a fraternal letter, as a memorial of friendship. And when I had told him how the Lord had graciously preserved my family during my absence, and desired him to remember me to the many dear friends I had left in Mississippi, and signed my name to the letter, I wrote on the left-hand side of the page, opposite my name, "Col. *John* M'Clellan," making a heavy score under *John.* I then folded the letter, and directed it thus: "Col. *John* M'Clellan, Carrollton, Mississippi," again emphasizing the *John* with a heavy score. I knew that when the colonel received it, he would understand it all, and be satisfied that in my letter, at least, I had not called him "Jo."

RED RIVER.

In the month of January, 1845, I made my first visit to the people on Red River. Some of my acquaintances had emigrated to that region, and had written to me, stating that a number of members and friends of the Presbyterian church were already in that country; and that if some of our ministers could go and labor for a time among them, their hearts would be strengthened and encouraged, infant churches might be organized, and a foundation laid for extensive permanent good.

On landing at Shreveport, about seven hundred miles above New Orleans, I was astonished to learn that the American settlements on Red River were already so extensive. While I was there, a steamboat, loaded with cotton, came down from a point some four hundred miles higher up on the river; and the oldest merchants in Shreveport — that is, those who had been there seven or eight years — were expressing their amazement at the rapidity with which the American settlements were extending west.

I was led to the reflection, that we should look with much indulgence on the mistakes of English travellers, and travellers from the eastern sections of our own country, concerning the condition of the west, when we find that its growth and advancement outstrip the conceptions of those who have been born, and have spent all their days, in its bosom.

Much of the population in this part of the country was from the extreme south — Georgia, Alabama, and South Carolina. Many of them were religious people, of highly cultivated minds, and ardent piety. Not a few of them were the acquaintances and personal friends of John C. Calhoun. Their admiration and esteem for the great statesman were wonderful — not as a politician merely, but as an eminently good man. Repeatedly was I assured by them, that we, who know the honorable senator only as a political man, know but little of his sterling worth, compared with those who have had access to his society, as a citizen at home, a neighbor, and a member of the church of Christ.

While laboring at Shreveport, I was called on by a Baptist preacher, who told me that he lived in Texas, and that he would be pleased to travel with me, if I would consent to spend some time in that republic; and as he was well acquainted with the country, and the roads were few and obscure, he could be serviceable to me as a guide. I accepted his kind offer, and set him a time when I would meet him at Greenwood, within four miles of the Texas frontier. At this period, Texas was no part of the American Union. When the appointed time had come, my Baptist preacher met me at Greenwood; and we started for his home, which was at the distance of eighteen miles. We passed the broad lane, cut through the tall timber, which showed the boundary line between the United States and the young republic; and after swimming some streams, and traversing divers canebrakes, we reached the house of my friend in safety. Many of the neighbors were assembled, according to an appointment previously made; and on that night I had the privilege, for the first time in my life, of preaching the gospel beyond the limits of the United States.

Early the next morning, my friend and I set out for Marshall, the county seat of Harrison county, Texas. It was eighteen miles; yet he uttered no word of reluctance about going so far; and the country was so new and *pathless*, that I should scarcely have found the way without a guide. When we had gained an eminence that overlooked the town, the Baptist preacher reined up his horse, and took a survey of the prospect before us. It was not very promising. The buildings were mostly small log houses, covered with clapboards; and the bushes were growing all over the public square, and along the streets. "Stop," said he; "there is not an ear of corn in this place." I did not, at first, comprehend his meaning, and asked what it was that he had remarked. "There is not one ear of corn in this place. We cannot find accommodation even for our horses. Come, let us go back. I have an appointment for the Sabbath in my neighborhood. Our people will be glad to hear you preach. Come, let us go back."

"I think I am too old a soldier to adopt that course," was my reply. "I have been on many a hard campaign; and I think I must go down into the town, and see who live here, before I can consent to leave the neighborhood."

"Very well," said he; "if that is your determination, I will go with you." So on we rode into the public square of the town of Marshall.

After reconnoitring for a little time, we entered a

lawyer's office, that bordered on the public square. He was from the state of Georgia. His name was William Pinkney Hill. I told him that I was a Presbyterian minister; and that I had come to visit them, and would be pleased to have the opportunity of preaching to the people of Marshall and the vicinity. He received me in a manner the most gentlemanly and cordial, expressed a high degree of satisfaction that I had come on such an errand, and said he would forthwith take measures for having a congregation assembled on the next day. Moreover, he kindly invited me to make his house my home while I should remain in the country, which invitation I very gladly accepted; and, truly, I found it a most delightful home. Yes, the recollection of the interesting and worthy family into which I was thus introduced, has often, in succeeding years, awaked in my soul the most lively and pleasing emotions.

In this neighborhood, at that time, resided also Mr. Van Zandt, the former minister from Texas to the United States. From him, and from his family, I received many kind attentions. Other names, and other families, occur to my mind, that might, with much propriety, be mentioned here, were it not for swelling the record beyond the intended bounds. I must not, however, omit the mention of a young lawyer, whose state of mind interested me greatly. He was possessed of a fine intellect, good habits, and a warm heart. He was a native of New Hampshire, and, after completing his education, had gone to Texas, hoping to earn a livelihood by the practice of the law. He had been successful. His worldly prospects were now very flattering; and, like "the younger son, in a far country," he began to call to mind the privileges of his father's house. He attended our meetings, and appeared to take a lively interest in the preaching of the gospel. I first noticed the expression of deep and strong emotion in his countenance when the following appeal was made, near the close of a sermon: "It is true, friends, that your country is yet new. As the night draws on, you still hear the howl of the hungry wolf, and that howl is answered by the shrill scream of the fierce panther; and brief is the space since your hills and valleys echoed the wild yell and the ominous warwhoop of the savage and hostile Indian. Yes, your country is yet new. Its inhabitants are thinly scattered here and there, mostly strangers to each other; and the church of the blessed Savior has scarcely begun to put on a visible form among you. But this land is Immanuel's land. It has been given to Christ in the covenant of redemption, and it will yet be filled with his glory. The beautiful house of God will rise in your village, and its tall spire will point to that heaven that is above. The Sabbath bell will swing its loud summons over these plains, and glad multitudes will assemble and worship God. Here the long table will be spread, in commemoration of the Savior's dying love; and thousands will join their voices, and send up hallelujahs to the Lamb that was slain." While these and similar thoughts were expressed, the countenance of the young lawyer evinced strong feeling, and his eyes were dimmed with tears. Not long afterwards, I was walking slowly in a small path near the outskirts of the little town, when I saw the young lawyer approaching. It was evident that he wished to speak with me. I at once afforded him the opportunity.

19

"When I was in New Hampshire," said he, "I thought there was no particular urgency why I should attend to the subject of religion. My parents were both living. They were examples of piety. I had also around me many other Christian friends, who were ever ready to impart to me good counsel, and to remember me in their prayers. I persuaded myself, therefore, that there was no special call for me, individually, to be much concerned on the subject. But it is far otherwise now. I see the broad road is open wide before me. My parents and pious friends are distant three thousand miles. There is no one here to watch, to counsel, or to rebuke me, in case I should go astray. I feel that there is a solemn responsibility resting on myself. I must think, I must watch, and I must care for myself, or ruin is before me." The statement of this interesting young man affected me much at the time; and it never recurs to my mind without awaking the liveliest emotion. What a precious treasure is granted to that youth who has been blessed with pious parental training!

In this country I spent more than three months, preaching sometimes in the towns, and sometimes from house to house. I organized a church of twenty members in Shreveport, and another, of fourteen members, in Marshall, Texas, and formed, moreover, many delightful friendships among the citizens. No person, unacquainted with the character of the population in the new settlements of the west, would imagine the amount of educated mind which I found in the Red River country. I became acquainted with quite a number of men, comparatively young, whose talents and acquirements would have entitled them to a high station in society in any part of the United States. The hospitality for which new countries are proverbial was here in its full perfection. The stranger was welcome at every house, and welcome to stay as long as suited his convenience; and, more than all this, there was a strong desire for the gospel, that stood out as a marked peculiarity of this population.

A physician and his lady, who had been members of the Presbyterian church in Virginia, rode with me twelve miles on the morning of the day on which I preached my last sermon at Greenwood. As we drew near the house of worship, the lady expressed her gladness and her gratitude that she could hear the gospel preached so near to her home, by a minister of her own church. And the physician, her husband, told me that he had been united with the church in Virginia — indeed, had been a ruling elder — but that he had sustained great spiritual loss by emigrating to this destitute region. After the sermon at Greenwood, a lady came to me, and said, "I have a certificate from a church in New York. If a Presbyterian church can be formed in this neighborhood, I wish you to take my name, as one that desires to unite in its formation." Five gentlemen then came to me, and said, "We do not consider ourselves worthy to be church members; but we wish to give you our names, as those who desire to be enrolled as members of a Presbyterian congregation, and who are willing to combine, for the purpose of sustaining divine worship in this community."

These facts are recorded as samples of the state of the public mind in the Red River country, on the subject of religion, in the year 1845. I remember conversing with but one person who professed to entertain any doubts of the divine authenticity of the Bible; and he was not a scoffer, but professed to be in search of more light on the subject. I preached at this man's house, and was treated by him with much attention and kindness. Indeed, the entire Red River country, on both the Louisiana and Texas side of the line, seemed a field "white to the gospel harvest." In this interesting and promising field, I met with the Right Reverend Bishop Polk, of the Episcopal church. He was laboring, with truly apostolic zeal, for the advancement of the Christian body of which he is a member. I was greatly gratified to meet the good bishop in such circumstances; and the interview made an impression on my mind too deep to be passed over in silence, in this sketch of my excursion through the Red River region. I understood that a bountiful Providence had bestowed on the bishop the good things of this world in great abundance; that his home abounded in all that can render home desirable; yet, instead of nursing himself up in the lap of luxury, he was here in the open field, fulfilling the duties of a hardy soldier. He seemed to shrink from no personal exposure; was willing, if necessary, to subsist on the coarsest fare; and would lodge in the flat-boat at the river-side, in the half-faced camp, or in the rudest log cabin, if, by any means, he might find the lost sheep that was wandering and bewildered amidst these extensive wilds, exposed to ravenous beasts, and ready to perish, and might have an agency in leading the wanderer back to the fold of the great Shepherd. I looked on this self-denying bishop of the Episcopal church with much regard and veneration. I could not but "esteem him very highly in love for his works' sake." It was, indeed, a beautiful example of ministerial consecration, and the constraining power of the love of Christ. And when I saw this zealous Episcopalian traversing the rough face of the wide and pathless wilderness, in order, like his divine Master, "to seek and to save that which was lost," I felt rebuked for my own church — yes, my own beloved Presbyterian church. In that "long cloud" of emigrant population, that now stretches from the great lakes of the north to the Gulf of Mexico, and, like the pillar in front of Israel, gradually moves westward, the Presbyterian church has many valuable families, and very many valuable members; but who of our prominent ministers have been willing to devote even a small portion of their ministerial life to the feeding of these hungry sheep? Methodist bishops and Episcopal bishops can see the importance of an early occupancy of this immense field; and they are found "lengthening the cords and strengthening the stakes" of their Zion through all the extent of this mighty territory. Many thousands of our people are dispersed abroad over this land. But, I ask again, what prominent Presbyterian ministers have been willing to spend even three months in twenty years, laboring to plant branches of the blessed vine in this promising soil?

In the summer of 1843, a venerable elder of our church at Richmond, Ray county, Missouri, gave me the following statement. I record it here because it is worthy of being made known to all our ministers. The excellent elder has now departed from the church below; but his words will long remain imprinted on my memory.

"A large number of the early settlers in the upper counties on the Missouri were either members of the Presbyterian church, or persons who had a decided preference for that branch of the great Christian family. Indeed, this preference — or I should rather call it *attachment* — was so strong, that, for a number of years, they could not brook the thought of identifying themselves with any other Christian denomination. Our hope was, that some of our experienced and able ministers would visit our people, preach to them, encourage them, organize churches where members in sufficient numbers could be found, and cause our population to feel that they were noticed; that the body of the church cared for them; and that there was something for them in prospect. Young men, just from the college or the theological seminary, however important and useful in their place, were not exactly what we wanted here. We wanted men of some age and experience, who would know how to collect and combine the material already on the ground, and lay the foundations for coming ages. This is, in substance, what we desired. We looked, we waited — yes, *we waited long;* but our ministers did not come. Those of other denominations came, — the Methodists, the Campbellites, or Reformers, the Baptists, also, — and began to occupy important locations; but the Presbyterians — such men as we needed — were looked for, and waited for, in vain. That part of the population," continued the old man, with a flush of strong emotion in his visage, and his eyes suffused with tears, — "that part of the population who loved our church, persevered in waiting. For twelve or fifteen years, there was scarcely the shadow of wavering in their ranks; and, had there been any cheering prospect ahead, they would willingly have waited longer. But there was none. The men that we needed and desired did not come. Finally, the children in our families began to approach maturity. They had known but little of our church, and, of course, had but little of that strong attachment of which I have spoken. A young daughter, approaching womanhood, would be impressed at a Campbellite meeting, and join that body. A sister would follow her example. Then, perhaps, a brother. At length, the mother would conclude that she had better follow her children; and, last of all, the father would be overcome, and go with his entire household into another communion. Such is, substantially, the history of a vast number of valuable families that have gone from our beloved church, to return no more. Ah, had the Presbyterian church, for the last twenty-five or thirty years, kept a proper number of her experienced and effective men employed among the destitute in the new settlements, those who pray for her prosperity might now have contemplated the results with glad and grateful hearts. The neglect of some such efficient system for the benefit of her scattered population has occasioned an immense loss to the Presbyterian church — yes, a loss that cannot be retrieved in many generations."

Such was the substance of the worthy elder's statement, in the year 1843, concerning the upper counties on the north side of the Missouri River. I saw its correctness; I felt its force; and deeply did I sympathize with him in his regrets. Now, in 1845, I found in the Red River country the same state of society, in all essential particulars, which had existed at an early day in Northern Missouri. I saw that there was a rich harvest there, of very great extent, which might be gathered, if laborers could be found to enter into that harvest.

I stood on the bank of Red River, by the side of a dear brother, whose "heart trembled for the ark of God." Said he, "We are glad that you have come to preach to us, and that you have staid so long. But now that you must leave us, what can we do? You see the condition of our country. A little labor, seasonably bestowed on this field, would secure great results. What shall we do? Cannot some of the middle-aged ministers, up in your country, be persuaded to make us a visit, and continue with us a few months? There is scarcely a man, of any note, who has been preaching fifteen or twenty years in Missouri, Illinois, Kentucky, Ohio, or the states farther east, but would find, on visiting this country, many of his former hearers and acquaintances. We have been so very destitute, that a little preaching would do us great good. We cannot expect to have ministers permanently settled in each neighborhood, in a country so new as ours. The day, we hope, is coming, when that rich blessing will be enjoyed even here; but the whole country should be explored, as speedily as practicable, by men of experience and judgment, that the religious population already on the ground may be embodied and organized. An organization, even though it be small, will hold together and subsist for years, when the same materials, left in an unorganized state, would be dissipated and scattered to the four winds."

Said I to this friend, "What is the extent of the country, west of Red River, which is already settled?"

"I would say that it is six hundred miles in length, by four hundred in breadth."

"Well, you know that when our divine Savior sent out his disciples to preach, he sent them 'two and two.' The promise to Israel by Moses was, that 'one should chase a thousand, and two should put *ten* thousand to flight;' that is, two of God's Israel, when acting together, can do tenfold more than one would be able to accomplish alone. When Paul and Barnabas, and Paul and Silas, went together, according to Christ's original plan, what mighty results followed that ministry! Now, could the condition of this country, and the importance of the present crisis, be laid before our brethren in the better-supplied portions of our church, peradventure ten or twelve ministers might be found, who would be willing to come and explore this broad land, two and two, travelling together according to the Savior's plan. Could not much be accomplished in one campaign of five or six months, by ten or twelve enterprising and self-denying ministers?"

The countenance of my friend kindled up at the suggestion. His eye sparkled, his features glowed with ardent anticipation, as he exclaimed, "It would be as 'life from the dead,' to the cause of religion throughout all this region. The fact, that the church *cared* so much for her scattered and destitute children, expressed in that unequivocal and affectionate form, would be of great importance and value. The labors of such self-denying ambassadors of Christ would doubtless be accompanied with the happiest results. A good impression would thus be made on the whole population, that would be remembered while the present generation remains alive. An impetus would be given to the cause of religion in this land, that might go down to the end of time."

Such was the substance of my last conversation with that pious friend, as we stood together on the bank of Red River. I returned to the country up the Mississippi. I brought the subject of this great missionary enterprise before many of our ministers and people. They saw at once its importance, and its feasibility. But such an undertaking requires time; and before the suitable men could be found, and the necessary arrangements completed, we were startled by the thunders of the Mexican war. The smoke arose, and darkened all the land, and multitudes of armed men were called to muster on the very field of our contemplated mission. Without interfering at all with the political question concerning the war, it was evident that the opportunity of doing a great work was, for the time, cut off. But though at that time we were constrained to a temporary abandonment of this important enterprise, I hope our church will yet resume it under happier auspices. Yes, I hope that our church will wake up to that great enterprise — an early occupancy of the frontier settlements by missionaries of talent and experience. Much, very much, has been lost irrecoverably by the neglect of this momentous work during the last thirty years. "O that my head were waters, and mine eyes a fountain of tears, that I might weep day and night for the slain of the daughter of my people!"

Those, only, who have traversed the mighty west in its length and in its breadth, can properly appreciate the importance of its moral culture to the church, to our country, and to the world. I stood on the bank of the Mississippi, opposite the mouth of the Missouri River, where, after its long career from the Rocky Mountains, the wild and turbid Missouri unites with the clear and tranquil wave of the "father of waters." I was meditating on the connection of this great country with the kingdom of Christ. I looked south, and thought of the twelve hundred miles from the point where I then stood to the Gulf of Mexico. I looked north, and thought of the sixteen hundred miles to the head of the Mississippi. I looked east, and thought of the thirteen hundred miles to the head of the Ohio valley. I looked west, and thought of the three thousand miles to the head of the Missouri. I thought of the immense capacity of this land to sustain human life. I thought of the teeming millions who will presently be here. I seemed almost to hear the tread of coming generations; and I lifted my hand to heaven, and said, "Lord Jesus, this land shall be thine! We will preach and pray. We will hold up the banner of thy dying love, and call for help from on high, till waves of redeeming mercy shall roll over these wide plains, and along the shores of these mighty rivers. And among the multitudes of people that shall dwell here, every knee shall bow, and every tongue confess, to the Lamb that was slain."

AN INDIAN TRADITION.

That part of Louisiana which borders on Texas, in the region where I labored, is called Caddo Parish. The name is taken from a tribe of Indians that once occupied this country. The remains of their villages are yet to be seen in several neighborhoods. This ancient tribe of Indians, when first visited by the Americans, had among them a tradition of the flood altogether remarkable, and as worthy of being preserved as any of the traditions on that subject, that have been found amongst the East Indian Brahmins, or the inhabitants of Peru, in the southern part of our own continent.

Thomas Jefferson, while president of the United States, about the year 1805, communicated to congress the following report of certain American officers, who had explored the Red River country : —

" About forty miles above the mouth of Little River, which empties into Red River two hundred and seventy-seven miles above its mouth, there is a large prairie, forty miles long. Near the middle of the prairie there is a lake, of about five miles in circumference. It is of an oval form, and neither tree nor shrub near it; nor is there any stream of water running either into it or out of it. This lake is very deep, and the water so perfectly limpid, that a fish may be seen at the depth of fifteen feet from the surface. By the side of this lake, the Caddo, or Caddoque, tribe of Indians have lived from time immemorial. About one mile from the lake is a hill, on which, they say, the Great Spirit placed one Caddo family, who were saved when, by a general deluge, all the world were drowned; and from that one family, they declare, all the Indians have originated. To this little natural eminence, all the Indian tribes, for a great distance, as well as the Caddoques, pay a devout and sacred homage."

The report of this exploring party further goes on to say, that " the whole number of what they call warriors of the ancient Caddo nation, is now (that is, in 1805) reduced to one hundred, who are looked upon somewhat like the knights of Malta, or some distinguished military order. They are brave, despise danger and death, and boast that they have never shed white man's blood."

THE RED RIVER BUZZARD.

When the time drew nigh that I had set for leaving the Red River country, I announced to the people of Shreveport and the neighborhood, that if they would collect their children at the court-house, I would attempt to preach a sermon particularly adapted to them. The people were pleased with the proposition; and on the last day of my stay among them, a beautiful company of children were brought together, and I gave them the best instruction I could for the life that now is, and also for that which is to come. I then bade adieu to many highly-valued friends, and started down the river. Our progress was slow; for the boat was taking in cotton, — forty bales at one plantation, sixty at another, — and thus we were some two or three days moving slowly towards New Orleans. Many of the passengers were from the region where I had been laboring, and with some of them I had formed a pleasant acquaintance. At their request, I had preached a few sermons in the cabin of the steamboat as we journeyed. When we had made considerable progress down the river, a great, brawny, broad-shouldered, six-feet-two or three inches high backwoodsman appeared among the passengers. I was not aware at what point he had come on board. He looked as if he might have been brought up in the neighborhood of ironworks. The lineaments of a strong mind were distinctly marked in his visage, and his whole bearing was that of a shrewd, forward, self-confident man. It is extremely rare, in the western country, that you find a man who designedly treats a minister of the gospel with disrespect. I have travelled long, and travelled far, yet have scarcely failed, in twenty years, when on a journey, to receive courtesy and gentlemanly treatment in every company, and from every individual with whom I had any particular intercourse. But here was a notable exception. The rough, stout man, above mentioned, had found out that I was a minister of the gospel; in fact, I had preached once, perhaps oftener, on the boat after he had come on board. He now concluded he would show his smartness, by holding up to reproach and ridicule religion and religious men. From his manner, I had little doubt that he had often before attempted the same thing, and, perhaps, with a considerable degree of success and imaginary triumph.

He now, with an air of great complacency and self-importance, commenced telling a story of a certain minister of his acquaintance. It was an awful story; and he told it remarkably well. He had, in fact, a quantity of that ready, rough wit, which enabled him to set the laughable points of a ludicrous story in a very clear and strong light. When he was through his statement, the company looked somewhat blank. Most of them felt that there was a high degree of impropriety in his telling such a story before the minister who had preached to them only a few hours before; otherwise they might have been prompted to a hearty laugh. As it was, however, some of them twisted their mouths a little, and all remained silent.

But the fellow who had told the tale was no way abashed at its cold reception. Determined to have some amusement, he turned round to me, and, in a manner most impertinent and haughty, said, "Well, sir, what do you think of that?" I replied with much indifference, "I am a stranger in the country, and not acquainted with the circumstances." I should have taken particular notice of neither him nor his story, had he told it and just let it pass. But the fellow appeared by no means satisfied, and, after a momentary pause, he set in and told, either of the same preacher or some other, a second story, which was rather an improvement on the first. A genuine story it was, and astonishingly well told; for in this department he possessed a talent equalled by few. He now turned to me a second time, and said, "Well, sir, what do you think of that?" Again I replied, "I am a stranger in the country, and not acquainted with the circumstances." By this time, it was perfectly plain to me and to the other passengers, that he was disposed to show his smartness at my expense. So I resolved to "give him rope;" and, perhaps, by the time he had run his full career, he might find that he had "waked up the wrong passenger."

He now told a third story, rising still in interest, like the steps in a flight of stairs. The story was certainly an original one, and the style in which it was told "hard to beat." There was a young Texas officer in the company. He was a native of Kentucky, had been brought up in the neighborhood of Mount Stirling, educated at the military institution at West Point, and had now been a number of years in Texas, during her revolution. This young officer now became quite restless. He afterwards told me that he was so indignant, that he was on the verge of breaking out on the fellow in real Kentucky style, and telling him that he was insolent, ill-mannered, and did not know how to behave himself genteelly in company; though, he said, as the thing turned out, he was very glad that he had restrained his temper, and held his peace.

Our orator now proceeded, and told a fourth story, and then a fifth, which lost nothing in comparison with those which had gone before, and fully sustained his claims as a retailer of calumny, and an "accuser of the brethren." When he had finished his fifth story, I saw, by the appearance of the whole company, that they were fully prepared to see the impertinent fellow severely chastised. I turned to Major Jenkins, a very respectable farmer, who lived near Shreveport, and was well known to many of the company, and, in a tone of voice sufficiently loud to be distinctly heard by all in the cabin, called out, "Major Jenkins!" Every eye was now turned, and every ear was attentive. "You were at Shreveport on the day that I made the address to the congregation of children?"

"I was there," replied the major.

"You remember, then, the account which I gave the children of the patriarch Abraham — how that, when the Lord told Abraham that he was about to destroy Sodom, 'because the cry of Sodom was great, and because their sin was very grievous,' Abraham stood up before the Lord, and interceded for Sodom, and said that he calculated there were 'fifty' good men there; and if there were not altogether fifty, he thought there surely must be 'forty-five,' or, at any rate, 'forty.' I called upon the children to notice particularly what a delightful view is here given of the character of Abraham; what an exalted man he must have been; how noble and elevated in principle; how high-minded and lofty the frame of that spirit by which he was animated. Abraham knew that the great mass of these 'men of Sodom were wicked, and sinners before the Lord exceedingly.' He must have known this; for he lived near them, and must necessarily have had transactions with them, more or less, for a number of years. He could not but have known that the multitude there was very depraved, and far gone in wickedness. But Abraham was one of those men of superior mould, who 'rejoice not in iniquity.' He neither sought nor wished to know all that was improper, and all that was censurable, in the conduct of those around him. He would throw the broad, generous mantle of his charity over the imperfections and faults of others, and hope for the best. He would hope that there was an under-current in society, better than what appeared on the surface; that there were many others, who, as deeply as himself, regretted the degeneracy of the times; and he drew near before the Lord, in behalf of Sodom, and said, 'Peradventure there be fifty righteous found there, within the city, wilt thou not spare all the place for the sake of the fifty righteous that are therein?'

"Venerable patriarch! through the long vista of four thousand years, we love to look back and dwell upon thy character. It is an instructive and beautiful example in the annals of a dark and fallen world; and a benevolent God has spread the record on the pages of his sacred book, and has determined that it shall stand there till the end of time, for the edification, the wonder and the imitation of the sons of men. It reminds us of that sweet paragraph in the history of Israel, where, after toiling over the burning sands, exposed to the hot winds of the desert, and the scorching rays of a torrid sun, parched with thirst, weary and exhausted, they at length came to 'Elim, where there were twelve wells of water, and threescore and ten palm-trees; and they encamped there by the waters.' (Ex. xv. 27.)

"It must be confessed, however, that in our world there are characters widely different from that of Abraham; persons who rejoice in iniquity, 'every imagination of the thoughts of whose heart is only evil continally;' persons whose supreme delight is to rake and root among the sewers and filth of a city like Sodom. Had the doom of this city been announced to one of these, he would have exclaimed eagerly, 'Ha! burn up Sodom with a tempest of fire and brimstone! I'm glad of it. They richly deserve it. That's just what I've been looking for. I've been watching these people of Sodom. I know them well. There isn't an honest man, there isn't a virtuous woman, in all the city. The merchants are all roguish, the mechanics are all cheats, the professional men are all false and abandoned. I'm glad to hear that they are about to get their deserts at last.' Such would have been the sentiments and exclamations of a low, depraved, dirty spirit. Not so Abraham. He was far from pretending that all excellence in the whole country was summed up in his individual person. He would hope that even in Sodom there were fifty righteous; and if not fifty, why, certainly forty-five, or, at any rate, forty.

"I mentioned to the children what an excellent member of the community Abraham must have been

— what a pleasant and valuable neighbor; and told them how I should love to live beside such a man, exchange visits with him, and have his intimacy and his friendship. And I illustrated the whole subject to the children in this way: —

"'You may send a dove over a beautiful landscape, where there are rich waving meadows, and extended fields of ripening grain; lovely flowers unfolding on the margin of the bright, lively stream, that is rippling, bubbling, and murmuring along; flocks and herds feeding, thriving, and growing; lambs frisking, skipping, and playing; and where there are all those things that are charming in a beautiful landscape. Now, the dove, its taste is so refined and delicate, will be delighted with the beauties that are here in these cultivated and fruitful fields. Every thing here is in perfect harmony with its prevailing desires, and its capacities for the highest enjoyment; and the genius of the dove revels and luxuriates amidst the congenial scenes by which it is surrounded. It will cast its eye over the broad meadow, undulating in the breeze, and experience delightful emotions. It will gaze on the rich grain field, and be extremely happy in the prospect of such abundance for the wants of man and beast. It will hover over the newly-opened flower, and admire each lovely tint that is there. It will rejoice with the flocks and herds that are feeding and thriving on the plain, and sympathize with the sportive and joyous lambs that are leaping and gambolling in the gladness of their heart.

"'And when the dove returns to its home, if it could talk and tell of its travels, and of the interesting and memorable things which had fallen under its eye, it would speak of the broad meadows, the bright flowers, the beautiful streams, and the fruitful fields it had found in its delightful excursion. It would describe the frisking lambs, and the fine cattle, that almost equalled the first company that old Pharaoh saw in his dream, coming up from the river of Egypt, denoting the seven years of plenty that should come on all the land. These are the objects that are in perfect unison with the delicate and refined taste of the dove, and these are the favorite themes on which it will delight to expatiate.

"'But now, children, suppose you send a buzzard over that same lovely landscape; none of the things which I have named will interest him in the slightest degree. The buzzard goes to search for carrion. He has no taste for the beauties of nature. Carrion alone suits his appetite; and as soon as he starts, he begins to snuff and scent for tainted air. The beautiful meadows, waving in the breeze, have no charms for him. The rich grain field, where the golden harvest is ripening, he regards not. The fine flowers, bending over the bright, meandering stream, he sees not. The flocks and herds, and playful lambs, rejoicing in their green pastures, give him no delight. But if there be a dead pig, or a dead 'possum, or the putrid carcass of a rat, in all the wide range over which he has passed, the buzzard has found that out. That corresponds with his taste, and the developments of his genius are all in that line. And he will light down where he can find carrion, and spread his wings, and strut and parade round, and rejoice more over the half-rotten carcass of a dead calf, than over ninety and nine living cattle, feeding and thriving in a meadow.'"

At this point, the company in the cabin of the steamboat broke out in unrestrained and boisterous expressions of approbation. They clapped, they stamped, they cheered, and gave the most decided demonstrations of entertainment and delight. The young Texas officer shouted aloud, "It is the best thing I have heard in all my life!" And when through with one volley of clapping and cheering, he and the company would set off again on a fresh score, and seemed wholly unwilling to cease their boisterous expressions of approbation and mirth.

It has often been said, that he who excels at giving a joke, or jest on another, is not apt to excel in bearing one that is pointed against himself. The reason is plain. That very shrewdness, which enables him to say severe and biting things against another, enables him to see the point or edge of any severe remark that is aimed at him. A dull man can bear a jest like a philosopher. He does not see the point of the wit, and, of course, does not feel it. It is whipping a sheep on its wool. But not so with the wit himself. He sees all the point of a severe remark aimed at himself, and feels it, too. This was clearly exemplified in the rough, rude man who had brought on this discussion. Not a man in all the company saw the whole application of the above remarks more clearly than did he himself. He had been altogether engrossed with the story of Abraham, and of the dove. Eyes, ears, and mouth were attentive. He seemed to suspect nothing. He neither saw nor "smelt danger," till the buzzard was on him, flapping its wings about his head and ears. He sprang to his feet, stretched himself, and gaped,—one of the most awkward gapes I have ever seen,—and looked as if he was in an agony of effort to think of something to say, that might relieve him. Gladly would he have kindled up into fierce anger, in self-defence ; but, then, not a word had been said to him. My remarks were all directed to Major Jenkins, and contained merely a rehearsal of what had been addressed to the children at Shreveport. The crest-fallen calumniator walked out from the cabin to the boiler-deck, "heavy and displeased," though totally at loss in what direction, or on whom, to vent his bile. He was followed by a number of young men, still laughing in full volley, and exclaiming, "O that buzzard! O that buzzard!" At the first wood-yard that presented itself, our hero left the company, and went ashore; and if he be capable of profiting by the lessons of that excellent teacher, Experience, he will most likely, hereafter, when he enters the cabin of a steamboat, "count the cost," before he attempts to play off his rude jests on any of the passengers.

SUDDEN CONVERSIONS.

In the autumn of 1840, I concluded to visit the mineral region in Wisconsin. I had understood that a tide of population was pouring into that country; and I resolved to spend a few months in laboring there. Peradventure some Christian might be comforted, whose lot had been cast in a destitute neighborhood; peradventure some sinner might be converted to God, over whom the angels of heaven would rejoice; peradventure some little church might be planted, on which the early and the latter rain might descend, until it would grow, and become strong, and eventually prove a blessing to hundreds — perhaps, even, to thousands — of immortal souls. There is something very delightful, to my mind, in establishing a new church in the heart of a great, rising country. When you plant the acorn in the rich western soil, you cannot tell how deep that plant may strike its roots into the earth. You cannot tell how high its stem will shoot up towards heaven. You cannot tell how wide its branches will spread, how great will be the abundance of its fruit, or how many living creatures, in ages to come, will feed upon its fruit, and find shelter under its shadow. I had no connection with the Home Missionary Society. I went under the authority of that primitive commission, "Go ye into all the world, and preach the gospel to every creature. He that believeth, and is baptized, shall be saved." (Mark xvi. 15, 16.) I had then no expectation of publishing an account of these labors. They were known to God, and to the community where they were bestowed. I desired for them no further notoriety. Nor should even a sketch of them be published now, but that I see, that, by doing so, I can illustrate great principles, and place important truths before the church, and before the world.

I took passage in a steamboat, commanded by Captain Miller, and ascended the Mississippi, to a point some ten or twelve miles above the town of Dubuque, in Iowa. I there went ashore, on the Wisconsin side of the river. There was no village, no farm, no improvement of any kind at the landing. A dim path put off from the river, across the wide Mississippi bottom. I took that path, and followed it through the tall cotton-wood timber, some six or eight miles. There I found a small village, stretched along a narrow ravine, that came down through the bluffs of the highlands. The name of the location was "Snake Hollow;" and the village was called by that name far and near. I learned that a miner, at an early day, while searching for mineral, had dug into a den of rattlesnakes; and that circumstance had given a name to the place, and afterwards to the village. I took up my residence, *pro tempore*, with a Jew, who was there selling goods, a very gentlemanly and hospitable man, who kindly invited me to make his house my home. And I commenced preaching to these people. We were greatly incommoded by the want of a suitable house. The small room in which our meetings were held, would not contain one half the people who were desirous to attend; and, after spending a few days in this place, I went to Plattville, a village about twelve miles distant, where the opportunity of a house for preaching was better. But scarcely had I reached Plattville, when Mr. Gay, a prominent man in the other neighborhood, came after me in behalf of the people of Snake Hollow. "You must return," said he, — "you must return with me. I believe that God has begun a good work among our people." I determined, at once, to go with this man; and soon after we had returned, a Kentuckian, who resided there, came to me, and said, "You need a larger house for your meetings."

"We do, sir, very much," was my reply.

"Well," said he, "I have a house, that was fitted up for some play-actors, that were here not long ago. If you will go with me, and look at it, it shall be at your service, provided you think it suitable."

I went with him, and lo, a room, about forty-two feet in length, by some thirty feet in breadth, well prepared to accommodate an audience! Some part of the fabric erected by the play-actors was still standing; but we soon had that removed, and commenced our meetings; and the Spirit of the Lord was in the midst of us, of a truth. In this place I preached three times a day, for about five weeks. Persons came in from all the country round, and many consecrated themselves to the Lord. A church was organized, and members added to it to the number of forty-four. Soon after our series of efforts commenced, I appointed an inquiry meeting, to be held early in the morning. The first person who appeared at the place for that meeting, was a young merchant. I must sketch a little of his history, because it illustrates the subject of "*sudden conversions.*"

He came into the inquiry room, and told me, very frankly, that he had been living in sin, and that unmerited grace alone had held him up from a deserved hell. Said I, "Are you now willing to turn from sin, and consecrate your heart and life to the service of God? Are you now willing to trust in Christ for pardon and eternal life, and spend your days in keeping his commandments?"

"That is my determination," said he. "Relying on the grace of God for assistance, I wish to confess Christ before the world, and to unite myself with his church, that I may honor and obey him in all his ordinances."

"How long have you resided in Wisconsin?"

"I have been here about eighteen months."

"From what place did you emigrate, when you came here?"

"I had been, for very nearly two years, with the American Fur Company, among the Rocky Mountains."

"And where were you before you joined the American Fur Company?"

"I had spent four years in Texas, during the period of her revolution."

"But where were you brought up?"

"I was brought up at Brownsville, in Pennsylvania, on the National Road."

"Were your parents pious people?"

"O, sir, I had at Brownsville a Christian mother, who taught me the Savior's name when I was very young. She prayed with me, and for me, and taught me to fold my little hands, and say, 'Our Father, who art in heaven!' And as long as I remained with her, she endeavored, by her counsel, her example, and her prayers, to win me over to the service of God. And O, sir," exclaimed this young man, weeping profusely — "O, sir, the prayers, the example, the counsel, the warm solicitude of that pious mother have followed me all the while I was roving through Texas — have followed me all the while I was wandering up and down among the Rocky Mountains — yes, and they have followed me here to Wisconsin. I can resist no longer. I must obey the call of the Holy Spirit, and give my life to God."

This is a sample — *a fair sample* — of what the world, and, alas! a portion of the church, denominate "sudden conversions." A cold-hearted professor, dozing and dreaming over his privileges and his opportunities, sees his neighbor living in sin, but has not got religion enough to speak one warning word to the sinner of his guilt and his danger. And he takes it for granted, the Spirit of God, and the man's conscience, are as silent, concerning the things of eternity, as his own unfaithful tongue; whereas the light of the gospel, the presence of the Holy Spirit, and voice of conscience are causing a mighty struggle in the bosom of that man. This struggle continues for months — perhaps for years. At last, the troubled sinner resolves, "I'll resist no longer. I'll yield to the Spirit of God.

'Here, Lord, I give myself away —
'Tis all that I can do.' "

And the torpid professor near him hears this vow, and starts up, rubbing his eyes, and exclaiming, "How sudden! How very sudden!" when the only sudden thing in the whole affair, is the sudden impression in his own sleepy soul.

I said the case of the young man detailed above is a *fair sample* of what the world calls "sudden conversions." I repeat the assertion, from a deep conviction of its truth, and the importance of having the subject properly understood.

I would here, also, record another instance of "sudden conversion," which took place during the same series of meetings; and I desire to mention it with gratitude and praise to the name of the blessed God. After the Divine Spirit was poured out on the population of this village and the neighborhood, a general reformation in morals was diffused in all directions among the citizens; and, finally, the "sign-board" was taken down from above the door of the last grog-shop in the place.

There lived in that community a man quite advanced in life, who had been intemperate for many years. This man came to hear the preaching of the gospel. He appeared deeply affected with divine truth; and presently he opened his house for the weekly prayer meeting, which was now established. He was soon enabled to trust in Christ for salvation. In a little time, according to the example of the apostolic age, he offered himself to the church; and the evidences of his conversion to God were such, that he was accepted. From time to time, after I left the neighborhood, I had opportunity to learn that the old man was walking worthy of the high and holy gospel vocation, and that his house was still opened for the weekly prayer meeting. About six years afterwards, I was at Edwardsville, in Illinois. I there became acquainted with a respectable lawyer, who, at that time, was a senator in the legislature of that state. "I am happy to meet with you," said he. "I have long wished for an opportunity to make your acquaintance. I wish to express my gratitude for the great benefit which my father received during your ministerial labors at 'Snake Hollow.'" And lo! the senator before me was the son of the old gentleman whose house was opened for the weekly prayer meeting, and of whose conversion the reader is already informed.

Many years ago, there lived at Knoxville, Tennessee, a prominent and amiable man, who was by profession a lawyer. His treatment of religious men was respectful and kind. At the house of worship he was a regular attendant; but he had taken for himself no decided stand in relation to the service of God. His wife, at length, came forward, and united herself to the church. After the solemnities of the sacramental season at which she was received, a brother in the ministry walked home with the family to their house. When they were near the door, the lawyer turned to the minister, and said, "I know that religion is very important. It is every man's duty to serve God. But it is a very solemn matter; and surely we ought not to be hasty."

"How old are you?" asked the minister.

"I am forty-one," was the reply. And the tear started in his eye as he spoke.

"Then you have not been *hasty*. Surely, if you have persisted in sinning against God through forty-one years, you have not been hasty in renouncing your rebellion. If you have jeopardized your soul for forty-one years, you have not been hasty in caring for its welfare. If you have been rushing towards the gate of death for forty-one years, you have not been hasty in flying from the wrath to come."

I now close this article with two remarks: —

1. We are liable to much mistake, when we suppose that the subject of religion is new to those to whom *we* have said but little. God has many methods for diffusing abroad the knowledge of his will, independent of our agency. The voice of his word, the voice of his Spirit, and the voice of conscience have been heard far and wide. "I say, Have they not heard? Yes, verily, their sound went into all the earth, and their words to the end of the world." (Rom. x. 18.) I have rarely, in a ministry of thirty-four years, attempted to talk with an inquirer, but I found that the Spirit of God, and a faithful conscience, had been speaking to that soul long before it was addressed by me. God is doing a great and solemn work, while he is leading immortal souls to eternity. And O, how small a portion of his ways do we comprehend! Let us, therefore, put a restraint upon our tongues, when tempted to speak lightly of "sudden conversions."

2. Most, if not all, of the conversions recorded in the Bible are of the description which the world would now pronounce "sudden." See the case of Abraham. "Now, the Lord had said unto Abram, Get thee out of thy country, and from thy kindred, and from thy father's house, unto a land that I will show thee: and I will make of thee a great nation, and I will bless thee, and make thy name great; and thou shalt be a blessing: and I will bless them that bless thee, and curse him that curseth thee: and in thee shall all families of the earth be blessed. So Abram departed, as the Lord had spoken unto him." See the conversion of Naaman the Syrian. (2 Kings v. 15—19.) See the conversion of the men of Nineveh, under the

preaching of Jonah. And yet Christ declares that their religion will stand the scrutiny of the judgment day. See the conversion of James and John, Simon and Andrew. "And Jesus, walking by the sea of Galilee, saw two brethren, Simon called Peter, and Andrew his brother, casting a net into the sea; for they were fishers. And he saith unto them, Follow me, and I will make you fishers of men. And they straightway left their nets, and followed him. And going on from thence, he saw other two brethren, James the son of Zebedee, and John his brother, in a ship with Zebedee their father, mending their nets: and he called them. And they immediately left the ship and their father, and followed him." (Matt. iv. 18—22.) See also the thousands on the day of Pentecost.

When I think of the rich and varied opportunities which God has granted to the present generation, I must believe that there are many important and permanent religious impressions among that part of the community who have as yet given no public manifestation. How many Bibles have been thrown before the eye of the educated and intelligent neglecter of the great salvation! How many religious tracts! How much wholesome religious instruction has been imparted in Sabbath schools! In these respects, the last twenty years have surpassed all the years that have ever gone before them. And, moreover, how great has been the amount of sound, instructive, and powerful preaching, which God has granted to the souls of men within the same period! I speak not now of any one section of our country, exclusively. I speak of the whole, — east, west, north, and south. With how much enlightened, discriminating, and scriptural preaching has the present generation been blessed! I fully believe that, in this respect, few among the ages that are passed have been raised so high in point of privileges. We may fairly infer, therefore, that much thoughtfulness and valuable impression have been produced, that have not yet appeared on the surface of society; and that when, "after so long a time," men come to the determination, that they must and will confess Christ in the church, we greatly err, if we suppose that religion is a new theme of thought to them, or that, in their pious resolves, there is any thing "sudden," in such a sense as implies a want of serious consideration, or the absence of a thorough acquaintance with the solemnity and sacredness of the Christian profession.

Now, at the opening of the year 1850, I cast my eye over our highly-favored land. It is a mighty field, where the fallow ground has been broken up, the clods have been pulverized, and the good seed put in, and covered with earth. Why should we not expect an abundant harvest? God has wonderfully taken hurtful influences out of the way. The thunders of war are hushed. The din of political strife has died away. The ravages of cholera are, at least for a time, arrested. We wait only for the showers of divine grace to make the plants in the garden of God spring up, and produce fruit in rich abundance, beyond all that "kings and prophets" ever saw. No such extensive preparations preceded the revivals under John Knox and his fellow-laborers, when, in a single generation, a nation was born to God. No such extensive preparation preceded the "great awakening" under Edwards and the Tennants. Why, then, should not the church, at this day, "expect great things," and "attempt great things"? Why not hope for the return of sinners to the ark of safety in such multitudes, that the prophet, in vision beholding it at the distance of many centuries, was constrained to exclaim, "Who are these that fly as a cloud, and as doves to their windows?"

GROWTH IN KNOWLEDGE.

The Holy Spirit hath said, "The path of the just is as the shining light, that shineth more and more unto the perfect day." Absolute perfection is not possessed by the newly-converted soul, and hence the command to "grow in grace, and in the knowledge of our Lord Jesus Christ." There is a growth in *knowledge*, as well as in grace, enjoined on the believer. Inattention to this fact has often occasioned erroneous sentiments among pious people. This life is but our birthday. Saints will grow in acquaintance with God and things divine through all eternity. And yet how prone are we, in the very commencement of our religious course, to fancy ourselves fully qualified to pronounce without hesitation on the most high and solemn questions that relate to the things of God! Many a Christian has been kept in darkness for years, by reason of some hasty decision concerning the doctrine of the gospel, rashly made in the very infancy of his Christianity. O that all Christians, and especially the young, would treasure up in their minds that precious counsel of the Holy Spirit, "Trust in the Lord with all thine heart, and lean not to thine own understanding"! God has given us a "sure word of prophecy" for our direction, to which we do well to "take heed, as unto a light that shineth in a dark place." But O, what mournful inroads has error made in the church, when the professed friends of the Redeemer have not followed the light of God's word, but have "leaned to their own understanding"!

In a clear night, when the multitude of stars that are scattered over the heavens, apparently without any regularity or order, are visible to the naked eye, should you tell the man who is utterly unacquainted with the science of astronomy, that these luminous specks are worlds, many of them larger than the globe on which he stands, and that they are all moving with admirable harmony, according to the plan of their Author, he would think your statement altogether incredible; for he sees nothing like order or harmony in all that strikes his eye. In like manner, the man who leans to his own understanding, and is not sufficiently attentive to the voice of God, when he looks around him on the multitude of events which daily occur, and sees in them much that to his eye is confusion and disorder, he feels confident that those who maintain that God is "working all things after the counsel of his own will," are grossly mistaken. He fancies that he sees conclusive proof that Satan and wicked men are driving the world before them, and that the counsel of God does not prevail. Your assertion of the regular movements and harmonious revolutions of the heavenly bodies, is confidently denied by the ignorant man. He tells you it cannot be true; for it contradicts the testimony of his senses. Why does he think so? Because he concludes he has a full view of the whole creation; whereas it is but a small portion that his eye is capable of taking in at once. And the man splits on the same rock, who, because the events which take place around him are different from what he thinks are wisest and best, therefore affirms absolutely that God cannot have appointed them so, and is not "working all things after the counsel of his own will."

> "One part, one little part, we dimly scan,
> Through the dark medium of life's feverish dream,
> Yet dare arraign the whole eternal plan,
> If but that little part incongruous seem."

We have a record of excellent men, in ages long past, who, for a time, were in darkness on this subject. When Joseph was forced away from his aged and affectionate father, and sold in Egypt for a slave, and there for many years confined in a dungeon, how dark, how full of perplexity, was the whole transaction! Indeed, there is no evidence from the history that as yet it had ever entered Joseph's head, that this was God's plan for advancing the glory of his great name, and the interest of his Zion; and that one day he would see the harmony, and beauty, and grandeur of that whole dispensation, now so mysterious and dark. Joseph appears to have looked only at the *agency of man* in the transaction — the agency of his brethren who sold him, the merchants who brought him to Egypt, the Egyptians who imprisoned him. Hear his language to the chief butler: "For I indeed was stolen away out of the land of the Hebrews; and here also have I done nothing that they should put me into this dungeon. Think on me when it shall be well with thee, and show kindness, I pray thee, unto me, and make mention of me unto Pharaoh, and bring me out of this house." (Gen. xl. 14, 15.) But Joseph lived to see the day when the plan of God was ripe for accomplishment. Then his eye discerned a higher hand than that of his brethren, the Ishmaelites, and the Egyptians, in this whole matter. The wonderful ways of God thrilled his soul with admiration. He saw the church preserved, the kingdoms around kept alive, through a long and destructive famine, and the honor of the God of Israel exalted in the view of the nations. Then he saw that the whole transaction was planned and moved forward by the counsel of the Almighty. Hear his language to his brethren: "I am Joseph, your brother, whom ye sold into Egypt. Now, therefore, be not grieved nor angry with yourselves, that ye sold me hither; for God did send me before you to preserve life. God sent me before you, to preserve you a posterity in the earth, and to save your lives by a great deliverance. So, now, it was not you that sent me hither, but God; and he hath made me a father to Pharaoh, and lord of all his house, and a ruler throughout all the land of Egypt. But as for you, ye thought evil against me; but God meant it unto good, to bring to pass, as it is this day, to save much people alive." (Gen. xlv. 4, 5, 7, 8, and l. 20.) Take another instance. When "Jesus began to show unto his disciples how that he must go into Jerusalem, and suffer many things of the elders, and chief priests, and scribes, and be killed," Peter, "leaning to his own understanding," quite confident that such a dreadful event as the killing of the holy, harmless Jesus could form no part of the plan of a wise and holy God, "began to rebuke" his Master for holding and teaching such doctrine — "Be it far from thee, Lord: this shall not be unto thee." Jesus, with unusual severity, reproved him — "Get thee behind me, Satan: thou art an offence unto me; for thou savorest not the things that be of God, but those that be of men," plainly teaching that his "*suffering many things, and being killed*," of which Peter did not approve, was the plan of God. (Matt. xvi. 21—23.) But Peter lived to see the day when light from on high shone on this wonderful transaction. He saw that the death of his Master brought life to the world, and that heaven should be peopled, and the praises of the Lord celebrated through all eternity, by multitudes which no man can number, washed from their sins in that fountain opened on Calvary. And now he glories in "Jesus Christ, and him crucified." Now he sees that what astounded him at first, as altogether incredible, is the plan of that God "who is wonderful in council, and excellent in working." Hear him, on the day of Pentecost, addressing the crucifiers of his Master: "Him, being delivered by the determinate counsel and foreknowledge of God, ye have taken, and with wicked hands have crucified and slain." (Acts ii. 23.) And a few days after, to the same people he says, "And now, brethren, I wot that through ignorance ye did it, as did also your rulers. But those things which God before had showed by the mouth of all his prophets, that Christ should suffer, he hath so fulfilled." (Acts iii. 17, 18.) And, indeed, all the disciples, though at first, perhaps, as reluctant as Peter to believe it, were now so thoroughly imbued with this doctrine, that we find it not only in their sermons, but in their prayers. In Acts iv. 27, 28, we find them uniting, with one heart, in this address to God: "For of a truth against thy holy child Jesus, whom thou hast anointed, both Herod and Pontius Pilate, with the Gentiles and people of Israel, were gathered together, for to do whatsoever thy hand and thy counsel determined before to be done."

Now, it is not strange that, while the church is in a low condition, and the power of Satan is great among the nations, there should be many pious people, who, like Joseph in the dungeon, and like Peter in the infancy of his Christianity, are disposed to deny that many events which they witness belong to the wise and good plan of the great God. But as Joseph and Peter advanced in divine knowledge until they obtained more exalted views of the truth of God, so all true Christians shall grow in the knowledge of God until all their errors shall be cast away. The path of the just, like the shining light, shineth more and more until the perfect day. And thus, when the church attains the full maturity of her glory in the millennial day, all her children shall see eye to eye; and in the heavenly state God shall wipe all tears from the eyes of his people; for he will then show them *that he has done all things well.*

SAINTS TO EXCEL ANGELS IN GLORY.

THE prospects which the gospel presents to Adam's children are wonderful. God has created a great variety of intellectual beings. We read of angels, cherubim, seraphim, principalities, powers, thrones, dominions, &c., &c., all which terms, doubtless, denote other orders of intelligent beings, who have been formed by the hand of the Almighty. But among all creatures in God's wide empire, MAN, alone, finds *his nature united to the Divinity.*

In the person of Jesus Christ, humanity is joined to the uncreated Godhead. The second person of the Holy Trinity put on our nature when he came to earth. In our nature he lived. In our nature he received the stroke of death. In our nature he arose from the grave and ascended to heaven. In our nature he now reigns above. And through the long periods of immortality, he will be clothed in the mantle of humanity. This single fact promises, to the redeemed from among men, an elevation in the kingdom of their Father, to which, while on earth, our boldest conceptions cannot rise.

It is clearly held out in the word of God, that those who are ransomed by the blood of the Lamb will, in the progress of eternal ages, ascend beyond all the angel hosts in holiness, in happiness, and in nearness to the throne of God. The angels are "all ministering spirits sent forth" at his command. They are his *servants.* They were created to serve his church; and, however holy, happy, and glorious, they can approach God in no other character than as servants. But of the redeemed, it is declared, that the Lord of glory "is not ashamed to call them *brethren.*" They have a peculiar relationship to Christ that angels have not. They are *his kindred;* and he is their *elder Brother.* None of all the heavenly family are thus united to the Divine Being except the followers of the Lamb; and this single fact—I repeat it—promises to the saints an exceedingly exalted station among the children of their Father.

The same thing appears from the intercessory prayer of our Lord Jesus Christ, where he speaks of the peculiar and wonderfully intimate connection between him and his children. His prayer is, "that they all may be one, as thou, Father, art in me, and I in thee, that they also may be one in us. And the glory which thou hast given me have I given them; that they may be one, even as we are one; I in them, and thou in me." Wonderful petition! Blessed Savior, how high is the hope which thou hast set before thy people! The apostle James tells us that God designs the saints as a "kind of first-fruits of his creatures." In Rev. ii. 17, God promises to bestow on those who overcome through the blood of the Lamb, a glory beyond the *knowledge* of all created beings save those who receive it. And, in Rev. xiv. 3, we are told that, among the anthems of eternity, the song of Redemption is peculiar and transcendent; and that, among all the bright spirits above, none can learn that song but the thousands who are redeemed from the earth.

This truth is also implied in what we are taught respecting the manner in which the perfections of the invisible God are revealed to his creatures. Christ says, "No man hath seen God at any time; the only-begotten Son, which is in the bosom of the Father, he hath declared him." "No man knoweth the Father but the Son, and he to whom the Son will reveal him." The apostle asserts that God created all things by Jesus Christ, to the intent that "now unto principalities and powers in heavenly places might be made known by the church the manifold wisdom of God." It is through the church, then, that the perfections of God are chiefly revealed to other orders of beings. Accordingly, the redeemed family of Jesus Christ is set forth in Scripture as the admiration of all heaven. In the beautiful language of the poet,—

> "Nearest the throne, and first in song,
> Man shall his hallelujahs raise;
> While wondering angels round him throng,
> And swell the triumph of his praise."

"And one of the elders answered, saying unto me, What are these which are arrayed in white robes? and whence came they? And I said unto him, Sir, thou knowest. And he said to me, These are they which came out of great tribulation, and have washed their robes, and made them white in the blood of the Lamb. Therefore are they before the throne of God, and serve him day and night in his temple; and he that sitteth on the throne shall dwell among them. They shall hunger no more, neither thirst any more; neither shall the sun light on them, nor any heat." (Rev. vii. 13—17.) There is a charming imagery used by the sacred writers to set forth the glory of the various orders of holy beings in the dominions of the great God. They are mentioned as brilliant luminaries, reflecting the light that issues from the uncreated throne. The Lord declares to Job that, when he laid the foundations of the earth, "the morning stars sang together, and all the sons of God shouted for joy." The morning stars were doubtless holy and happy spirits that his hand had formed. Paul says, "There is one glory of the sun, and another glory of the moon, and another glory of the stars; and one star differeth from another in glory." Daniel, in view of the events of the resurrection day, declares, "They that be wise shall shine as the brightness of the firmament, and they that turn many to righteousness, as stars forever and ever." Of the same day the Savior says, "Then shall the righteous shine forth as the sun in the kingdom of their Father."

What a delightful idea does this imagery present to the mind, of the glory of Jehovah's upper kingdom! On the great white throne is seated the everlasting I AM. Before him are the several orders of angelic beings, as stars of various magnitudes in the firmament of heaven, ever growing in capacity, increasing in brilliancy, from glory to glory, and rising to higher and higher stations before the great Eternal. But the Son of God has been sent on an errand of mercy to a revolted world; and behold, in virtue of his mediation, "a great wonder is seen in heaven." On the verge of the celestial horizon new lights are discovered; stars of uncommon brilliancy begin to appear; constellation after constellation rises into view. Who are these? These are the companies of patriarchs, and prophets, and martyrs. These are the redeemed from the earth. They increase more rapidly in brightness and glory. They move in swifter courses up the heavenly firmament. They pass by the shining ranks of angels, cherubim and seraphim, and draw nearer to the divine throne. Hark! what music rolls from the triumphant multitude over all the heavenly plains! "Unto him that loved us, and washed us from our sins in his own blood, be honor and glory forever and ever!" Blessed Jesus! are these the travail of thy soul? O, give us a place among thy saints when thou shalt make up thy jewels!

THE DOCTRINES PREFERRED IN HEAVEN.

"And the seventh angel sounded; and there were great voices in heaven, saying, The kingdoms of this world are become the kingdoms of our Lord and of his Christ; and he shall reign forever and ever. And the four and twenty elders, which sat before God on their seats, fell upon their faces, and worshipped God, saying, We give thee thanks, O Lord God Almighty, which art, and wast, and art to come; *because thou hast taken to thee thy great power, and hast reigned.* (Rev. xi. 15 – 17.)

This life is but the birthday of the children of God. Their attainments, while on earth, in knowledge, in grace, and in every excellency, are small in comparison with what they shall be in that world to which they go. Our Savior, when on earth, said to one of his disciples, "What I do thou knowest not now; but thou shalt know hereafter." Paul observes, "Now, I see through a glass darkly." "We know *in part.*" And he refers to a period "when that which is perfect shall come, and that which is in part shall be done away." The variety of conflicting opinions on divine subjects that now exist among the friends of the Redeemer, are chiefly owing to the small advances they have made in acquaintance with the word and wonderful ways of God. It is delightful to reflect that a day is coming, when all who love the Lord shall "see eye to eye," and "know even as they are known."

When we see different denominations, each containing many zealous and excellent Christians, divided in sentiment, and each earnestly laboring to maintain their peculiar doctrines, the following question frequently presses on the mind: "When these disciples leave this world of darkness, and the light of eternity shines around them, which class will find that they had been mistaken while on earth, and discover that the doctrines they had thought so objectionable are full of perfection, beauty, and glory? With respect to those points on which, while in this world, pious Calvinists and pious Arminians differ so widely, without attempting to say who will be found in the right at last, it may not be improper to inquire which of the systems, on being found the true one, appears best calculated to fill the inhabitants of heaven with triumph and joy. It is plain, from the texts recorded at the head of this article, that when the Almighty has wound up all the affairs of our world, the glorified saints and holy angels, on reviewing all that has taken place under his reign, from the beginning to the end of time, will be exceedingly gratified. "We give thee thanks, O Lord God Almighty, who art, and wast, and art to come, because thou hast taken to thee thy great power, and hast reigned." Now, which of the above-named systems of doctrine, on being found true, appears to furnish the broadest ground for such high transport — such unbounded triumph? And here let it be carefully remarked, that the very same number of souls will then be found in heaven, whether Calvinism or Arminianism proves to be true. There will be no more of the human family in heaven, and no fewer in hell, if the Arminian scheme is then pronounced correct, than there will be if Calvinism should then be declared the true system. Both parties now acknowledge that as to those who have lived and died in ages past, a number have been saved, and a number have been lost. The exact number of both classes is now known to God. Our Arminian brethren will not contend that, if their doctrines are found true, any who have already died impenitent will enter into heaven; and they will admit that, if our doctrines are then found true, all who in past ages have not died impenitent will be crowned with glory. And with respect to those who shall live in ages to come, the omniscient God knows now, with infinite certainty, who will reach heaven, and who will not. So that as to the number of souls who will reach heaven, and the number that will perish, Arminianism, in the judgment of saints and angels, will have no advantage over the doctrines we maintain.

Let us now inquire which of the systems appears calculated to impart the highest ecstasies to the heavenly hosts. Suppose Arminianism should prove to be true. What are the facts that will stand out to the view of saints and angels, when they look back, from the judgment day, over all the events that have taken place in our world, from the creation to the end of time? If Arminianism be true, saints and angels will then see that when the great Creator formed man, he had no desire nor intention that the affairs of our world should take the course they have taken. They will see that it was his desire that the fall of man should not take place, but that Satan prevented that desire from being gratified. They will see that when the Supreme Being found that his first design of having all the human race holy and happy was defeated by Satan, and things had come to pass which he would gladly have avoided, he then, in order to mend matters as much as possible, set on foot the scheme of redemption. They will see that the scheme of redemption was accomplished at immense cost; and although it answered a considerable purpose, yet it did not, by any means, accomplish all that its Author desired. Satan made prodigious headway against it for thousands of years; and although repulsed in many instances, and deprived of a number of his subjects, yet, on the whole, his success was great; and the Almighty would have rejoiced if the gospel could have had much greater success, and Satan had lost many more of his subjects. They will see that the Most High had been baffled and frustrated in many of his benevolent designs, and had desired many things which were never accomplished. If Arminianism be true, these facts must meet the eyes of saints and angels at every period in eternity, when they look back over the history of our world; and it is difficult to conceive that, with these mournful facts continually in view, their rejoicings will be altogether unmingled with regret. Must they not regret that the good designs of their Creator had not been more successful? Must not clouds of sorrow bedim their eyes, when they see that the malignant enemy of their God succeeded in his malicious schemes to so great an extent, and that he was only defeated in some instances? O, how would their hearts leap for joy, could they only find that all the schemes and designs of the old serpent had been effectually frustrated and crushed, and had been so overruled, as to advance the honor and glory of the great God whom he opposed! O, how would the triumphant hallelujah roll from each heavenly tongue, could they only find that the high and holy One had never, in a single instance, been disappointed, and had, from the creation to the judgment day, "worked all things after the counsel of his own will," had caused the "wrath of man" and the wrath of devils to "praise him," and had "restrained the remainder of the wrath," had completely gratified all his benevolent desires, and accomplished "all his pleasure!" But alas! these are raptures which, if the Arminian doctrines be correct, the inhabitants of heaven will never enjoy. According to that plan, it will be true, till the remotest periods in eternity, that the great Jehovah, after all the efforts he has made, has failed to accomplish many of his benevolent desires; and that the inroads of Satan on his kingdom in the world were vastly more extensive and successful than he ever designed.

But should the doctrines for which we contend, after all the high-handed and diversified opposition they have had to encounter in this revolted world, be found true at last, will they furnish any greater reason for the glorified armies above, to celebrate, in anthems of unmingled triumph, the victories of their King? We think that in this respect the difference between the two systems is immense, and that the advantages possessed by our doctrines over those of our Arminian brethren are high as heaven and lasting as eternity. If the Calvinistic doctrines are true, then the following facts will stand as long as immortality endures, conspicuous and bright in the view of saints and angels. They will see that the glorious plan of man's redemption was no afterthought of the great I AM, when he found that his first plan was frustrated by his artful and implacable enemy. They will see "that, from the beginning," it was the determinate purpose of the unchangeable God to manifest, by this great work, his adorable perfections to an admiring universe. They will see that Jesus Christ, the Redeemer of men, who was manifest in these last times, "was verily foreordained before the foundation of the world," (1 Pet. i. 20;) that, in the purpose and plan of God, he was "the Lamb slain from the foundation of the world," (Rev. xiii. 8;) that his saints were "chosen in him before the foundation of the world," (Eph. i. 4;) and that, from that early date, their "names were written in the Lamb's book of life," (Rev. xiii. 8.) They will see that this amazing development of his wonderful perfections in the scheme of man's redemption, is the grand object Jehovah had in view, when he undertook to build the universe. They will see that he "created all things by Jesus Christ; to the intent that now unto principalities and powers, in heavenly places, might be made known, by the church, the manifold wisdom of God, according to the eternal purpose which he purposed in Christ Jesus our Lord." (Eph. iii. 9—11.) They will see that by Jesus Christ, the Redeemer of men, "were all things created that are in heaven, and that are in earth, visible and invisible; whether they be thrones, or dominions, or principalities, or powers; all things were created by him and for him." (Col. i. 16.) He formed the angels in heaven "all ministering spirits, and sent them forth to minister for them who shall be heirs of salvation." (Heb. i. 14.) They will see that all the dark devices and malicious schemes of

Satan have never, for a moment, ruffled the tranquillity, or disconcerted the plan, of the great God. In no instance has he been overmatched — in no design has he been disappointed — in no benevolent effort has he failed. "With omniscient eye he has ever beheld his unshaken counsels, and with almighty hand he has rolled on his undisturbed decrees." They will see that when the raging dragon cast out of his mouth "waters as a flood," to overwhelm the church, He who "dwelleth in the high and holy place" has looked down, with placid serenity, on the foam and dashing of the billows; and, whenever the interest of his Zion required it, he said, "Peace, be still," and "there was a great calm." They will see that he has always had Satan under his control, and that, as in the case of Job, where Satan could not touch his property, nor touch his person, but when God saw it wisest and best to suffer it to be done, so, in every age, he has had his "hook in Satan's nose, and his bridle in his lips," and has restrained and controlled him at pleasure. They will see that the Almighty could have "bound Satan, and cast him into the bottomless pit, and shut him up, and set a seal upon him," as easily before he first came to the garden of Eden, as at the commencement of the latter-day glory. (Rev. xx. 1—3.) But he did not. He saw it wisest and best, on the whole, to suffer the fall of man to take place, having determined, by this means, to make the universe of created beings sensible of the instability and mutable nature of all creatures, and fasten on their minds a deep and everlasting conviction of their absolute dependence on the one immutable God; designing also to send his beloved Son, and in his suffering and death to show forth the immeasurable wisdom and power, truth and justice, love and mercy, of the uncreated One. They will see that, from the first morning of creation, the Lord has sat on his holy throne, and has held, with almighty hand, the reins of universal dominion; has "done according to his pleasure in the armies of heaven," and among the inhabitants of the earth; none have been able to baffle his designs, or defeat his purposes. Those eyes that "neither slumber nor sleep" have constantly been "in every place." The hand of the Lord has been stretched out in all the earth; and, while kingdoms and empires, and all the weighty concerns of the universe, have been upon his hands, he has carefully attended to the minutest matters. He has clothed the lilies, fed the young ravens, hearkened to the cry of the widow and the fatherless, attended to the wants of the little sparrow, and numbered the very hairs of the head of his children. They will see that, from first to last, he has moved every wheel, controlled every event, disposed of every being, and directed every atom, so as to promote, in the highest degree, the glory of his great name, and the joy of his holy kingdom. And although it was Satan's malevolent aim, when he seduced the human family, to rob God of his glory, and fill his kingdom with ruin, yet He who is "wonderful in council, and excellent in working," has so managed all events, that in the end God is more glorified, and his kingdom more exalted, in holiness and happiness, than could have been if angels had never revolted, and man had never fallen! Thus the "head of the old serpent is bruised," his aim totally defeated, his hopes all overthrown. "O the depth of the riches both of the wisdom and knowledge of God!"

All the inhabitants of heaven will gaze, with ineffable delight, on the wonderful counsels and perfect works of God. They see that he has "done all things well;" that such is the infinite perfection of that plan which he formed before the foundation of the world, that if all were now to be done over again, not one jot, not one tittle, could be altered for the better. Their satisfaction is unbounded. They prostrate themselves before his throne. "We give thee thanks, O Lord God Almighty, who art, and wast, and art to come, because thou hast taken to thee thy great power, and hast reigned!"

Millions of ages roll around. The saints and angels, cherubim and seraphim, and all the happy family of the great God, make astonishing advances in holiness, in happiness, and in knowledge. Again they review the history of our world; and still, in all the management of God, from first to last, they behold boundless perfection, beauty, and glory. Still they gaze with increasing rapture on the wonderful work of redemption, transcendently glorious amidst all the works of God — a tall column of light, streaming from the summit of Calvary above creation, and throwing its radiance to the utmost boundaries of Jehovah's dominions. They look down; and still they see the "roaring lion," that so long fought against the cause of God, utterly overthrown, bound in chains, and buried deep among the ruins of his kingdom. They look up; and they behold immortal victory still perching on the standard of Immanuel. Still they behold the banner of the Son of God waving in everlasting triumph over all the empire of the Almighty. Amen! Hallelujah! "And a voice came out of the throne, saying, Praise our God, all ye his servants, and ye that fear him, both small and great; and I heard, as it were, the voice of a great multitude, and as the voice of many waters, and as the voice of mighty thunderings, saying, Alleluia! for the Lord God Omnipotent reigneth." (Rev. xix. 5, 6.)

THE MILLENNIUM.

"They shall not hurt nor destroy in all my holy mountain; for the earth shall be full of the knowledge of the Lord, as the waters cover the sea." (Isaiah xi. 9.)

THE church of God in our world has, for many ages, passed through the deep waters, and through fiery trials. Satan has, for a long season, led the nations at his will. Barefaced impiety has stalked undaunted through the earth, and flung defiance at Heaven. To support and cheer the hearts of his children during this season of spiritual desolation and darkness, God was pleased, at an early day, to pledge his word to the church, that he would grant her a brighter day; that a period should come when Satan should be bound, and the whole earth be filled with the knowledge of the Lord.

This was clearly implied in that notable promise, "The seed of the woman shall bruise the serpent's head." The head is the seat of intelligence, and, as such, the seat of *counsel*. By "bruising the serpent's head," is evidently meant giving an entire defeat to the counsels of the old serpent.

The promise to Abraham more fully announced God's design to make his church triumphant. "In thy seed shall all the families of the earth be blessed." Abraham believed God. Wonderful instance of the power of faith! He stood in the midst of a revolted world. He looked around; he saw the nations, on every hand, casting off the fear of God, and sinking down into idolatry. He looked back on the past history of the world; he saw that in all former ages the impetuous current of depravity had swept the children of men away from God, and from heaven. He saw that the flame of piety, which was kindled, at first, among the children of Seth, had dwindled to a spark — the spark that glimmered in the house of Noah, while the whole earth was covered with darkness. The earth had now been peopled anew, from that one pious family. Abraham had lived till he was a hundred years old among them. The mournful fact was now notorious, that all the terror of God's wrath, displayed in the destruction of the old world, was forgotten. He saw the children of pious Noah, in crowds and nations, turning away from the Creator of the heavens and the earth, and worshipping serpents, and four-footed beasts, and fowls, and fishes. He saw that such was their predilection for idolatry, that they would take their hammer and chisel, and make themselves gods of gold, and silver, and brass, and iron, and then fall down, and worship them. They would take their axe, and their saw, and make gods of logs and stumps, and then prostrate themselves, and pay divine honors. Such were the circumstances, when the Lord comes to Abraham, and tells him, that, aged and childless as he now is, he shall be the father of many nations; and that among his descendants a deliverer shall arise, who shall turn away ungodliness from the earth; and all nations shall forsake their idolatry, and worship the living and true God. Such were the words of the Almighty; and, dark as prospects were, Abraham "staggered not at the promise of God, but was strong in faith."

Is any one ready to say, "The Lord is slack concerning his promise; and the day that Abraham expected will never come"? I reply, the Lord has made good his word, when, to the view of man, it appeared altogether as unlikely as in the present case.

On the last clear day that preceded the deluge, it appeared as unlikely to scoffers of that age, that the huge vessel which Noah had built should float fifteen cubits above the top of the tallest mountains, as it can appear to infidels now, that the knowledge of the Lord shall cover the earth, as the waters cover the sea. Such a thing had never been heard of since the day that God created man upon the earth; and the finger of derision was pointed, and the lip of scorn was curled, while Noah, "warned of God, and moved with fear, prepared an ark, to the saving of himself and house." But on the same day that Noah entered into the ark, the fountains of the great deep were broken up, and the windows of heaven were opened, and the scream of a drowning world was unheeded by an insulted God; and, at this day, the infidel who would deny the Bible is constrained, by the science of geology, to acknowledge that, for some cause, this earth has been overwhelmed with a universal deluge.

That the kingdom of Jesus Christ shall yet triumph in every nation, is not more unlikely now, than the deliverance of Israel from Egypt, and their settlement in Canaan, were on that day when Moses turned aside to gaze on the burning bush. Egypt was at this time, perhaps, the most powerful monarchy on earth. Israel was trodden into the very mire of the streets. So completely dispirited and heart-broken were they, that officers and men of note among them were beaten without resistance, and tamely submitted to the unreasonable demands of Pharaoh's taskmasters. The land of their fathers, the graves of Abraham, Isaac, and Jacob, seem to have been forgotten. How unlikely that such a people would burst the chain that bound them, and march forth in all the majesty of freedom! But granting they were freed from the grasp of Egypt, how shall they obtain possession of Canaan? That land is possessed by seven nations, "greater and mightier" than Israel, (Deut. vii. 1,) — nations that dwelt in cities that were walled, and strongly fortified — nations terrible in battle, and trained in all the arts of war, of which the sojourners in Egypt were utterly ignorant. Could any thing have been proposed, that, in the view of short-sighted man, would have appeared more egregiously fanciful and extravagant, than an attempt by this people to shake off the fetters of this gigantic monarchy, and conquer and take possession of the land of seven warlike and powerful nations? Pharaoh and his courtiers laughed at it, and pronounced the whole scheme a mere whim of idleness and folly. But the hand of God is made bare. Egypt is shaken with judgment after judgment. Pharaoh and his lords rebel and blaspheme. But the hand of God is heavier and heavier upon them. It was midnight. The laborers had sunk in deep repose. But "He that keepeth Israel neither slumbers nor sleeps." At his bidding, the angel of death goes abroad. Every family is visited. The king, and all his servants, spring from their couches in the night. "There is a great cry in Egypt." In every house, the first-born is dead. Moses and Aaron are called. "Rise up; get you forth from among my people." The Egyptians were urgent that they might send them out in haste; for they said, "We be all dead men." Israel is thrust out of Egypt in the night. But how shall they know, amidst the darkness, the way they must go? A sudden gleam of new-created light flashes around them; and, behold! flaming high in mid air, is a pillar of fire, to direct their steps. They gaze on the heavenly signal, and bless the God of their fathers. It begins to move off from Egypt, and takes the direction of the promised land. Judah unfurls his banner, and calls his thousands to follow. The standards of Reuben, and Ephraim, and Dan rise in front of their tribes. The whole assembly is in motion. The sun rose upon the earth, and beheld the march of the ransomed armies of God. On, and still on, they move. The Red Sea rolls its dark waves before them; but Moses stretches forth his rod, and they march through on dry ground. Their provisions are spent; but the heavens supply them with bread. The wilderness is parched and dry; but the smitten rock sends out a stream. Jordan divides at their approach. The walls of Jericho fall. Terror seizes the inhabitants of Canaan. Host after host is routed. The war-horse is cut down. The chariot of iron is broken. The sun pauses in the heavens, and the moon is stayed; but the cause of God goes forward, till all the land promised to Abraham is divided among his children. God had promised it, and God made good his word.

That the whole earth shall be filled with the triumphs of the gospel, is not, in the view of man, more unlikely now, than the victories of the gospel, in the first ages of the Christian church, were, when Jesus hung by nails to the cross on Calvary. What were the circumstances? An obscure personage had arisen in Judea, so plain in appearance that he wore a seamless garment. A few tent-makers and fishermen constitute his train. The wealthy and the powerful of the Jewish nation hold him in unqualified abhorrence. At length he is betrayed by one disciple, denied by another, and forsaken by all. By the most influential men in the country he is accused of high treason before the Roman governor, and pronounced worthy of death. He is led from the hall of judgment to the place of execution, followed by the imprecations of that immense crowd which the passover had brought to Jerusalem. Thus he dies in circumstances of the most aggravated infamy. What rejecter of the gospel, that witnessed this scene, believed that in a few days Jerusalem would be filled with worshippers of Jesus? Who, that disregarded the promise of God, believed that in that age his religion would overrun the Roman empire, and his disciples, then living, would salute the saints in Cæsar's household? What infidel then imagined that in a few ages the emperor of Rome would be baptized, and publicly avow himself a disciple of that Jesus who was crucified without the gates of Jerusalem?

That the church shall enjoy a day of millennial glory, is scarcely more unlikely now, than her present condition was fifty years ago. Many now living remember well the haughty brow and lofty step of infidelity at that time. And many a prediction was then uttered, that in ten years there would not be a Christian in America, nor a Bible acknowledged as the word of God. Had it been alleged at that time, that, in fifty years, thousands of Bible societies should be in vigorous operation, to put the sacred book into the hands of every human being; that the Cherokee Indian, and the Greenlander, and the Chinese, should be reading the word of God in their own language; that the song of salvation should be heard on the mountains of Asia, and on the plains of Africa; that the islands of the sea should be seen stretching forth their hands to God; that thousands of hardy sailors should quit their blasphemy, and revere the God of the ocean and the storm; that millions of children, in Sabbath schools, should begin to lisp hosannas to the Son of David; that millions of tracts, with the news of mercy, should travel abroad through the nations; — had these things been alleged, fifty years ago, by an angel of light, many would have thought them utterly incredible, and the answer would have been that given when plenty was predicted in the gate of Samaria — "If the Lord should make windows in heaven, might such a thing be?" But we have lived to see it. "It is the Lord's doing, and marvellous in our eyes." I have mentioned these instances to show you that if the Lord has said he will fill the earth with his glory, and subdue all nations to the obedience of the gospel, we need not doubt that he will do it, because the event appears to us improbable, and difficult of accomplishment; for we find that in all past ages he has made good his word, and performed all that he had spoken, when prospects, in the view of men, were just as dark, and just as unpromising.

Let us now open the sacred book, and see what Jehovah has said.

"And it shall come to pass in the last days, that the

mountain of the Lord's house shall be established in the top of the mountains, and shall be exalted above the hills; and all nations shall flow unto it. And many people shall go and say, Come ye, and let us go up to the mountain of the Lord, to the house of the God of Jacob, and he will teach us of his ways, and we will walk in his paths; for out of Zion shall go forth the law, and the word of the Lord from Jerusalem. And he shall judge among the nations, and shall rebuke many people; and they shall beat their swords into ploughshares, and their spears into pruning-hooks: nation shall not lift up sword against nation, neither shall they learn war any more." This remarkable passage, written upwards of seven hundred years before Christ appeared in Bethlehem, not only contains an animated description of the latter-day glory, but also distinctly notices the *means* by which it shall be introduced. Zion and Jerusalem denote the church as it has existed and now exists in the world. From Zion and Jerusalem the word of God is to be sent abroad among the nations, and the consequence is their conversion to God — an evident prediction of the present exertions of the church, by her Bible societies, to send the word of God into all the earth. "And many people shall go and say, Come ye, and let us go up to the mountain of the Lord, to the house of the God of Jacob; and he will teach us his ways, and we will walk in his paths; *for out of Zion shall go forth the law, and the word of the Lord from Jerusalem.*" (Isaiah ii. 2—4.)

In Isaiah xi. 6—9, we find this prediction of the church's prosperity: "The wolf also shall dwell with the lamb, and the leopard shall lie down with the kid;

and the calf and the young lion and the fatling together; and a little child shall lead them. And the cow and the bear shall feed; their young ones shall lie down together: and the lion shall eat straw like the ox. And the sucking child shall play on the hole of the asp, and the weaned child shall put his hand on the cockatrice's den; they shall not hurt nor destroy in all my holy mountain: for the earth shall be full of the knowledge of the Lord, as the waters cover the sea."

"Violence shall no more be heard in thy land, wasting nor destruction within thy borders; but thou shalt call thy walls salvation, and thy gates praise. The sun shall be no more thy light by day; neither for brightness shall the moon give light unto thee: but the Lord shall be unto thee an everlasting light, and thy God thy glory. Thy sun shall no more go down; neither shall thy moon withdraw itself: for the Lord shall be thy everlasting light, and the days of thy mourning shall be ended. Thy people also shall be all righteous: they shall inherit the land forever, the branch of my planting, the work of my hand, that I may be glorified. A little one shall become a thousand, and a small one a strong nation: I the Lord will hasten it in his time." (Isaiah lx. 18—22.)

"And it shall come to pass, that from one new moon to another, and from one Sabbath to another, shall all flesh come to worship before me, saith the Lord." (Isaiah lxvi. 23.)

"And they shall teach no more every man his neighbor, and every man his brother, saying, Know ye the Lord: for they shall all know me, from the least of them unto the greatest of them, saith the Lord: for I will forgive their iniquity, and I will remember their sin no more." (Jer. xxxi. 34.)

"And I saw an angel come down from heaven, having the key of the bottomless pit, and a great chain in his hand. And he laid hold on the dragon, that old serpent, which is the devil, and satan, and bound him a thousand years, and cast him into the bottomless pit, and shut him up, and set a seal upon him, that he should deceive the nations no more, till the thousand years should be fulfilled; and after that he must be loosed a little season. And I saw thrones, and they sat upon them, and judgment was given unto them: and I saw the souls of them that were beheaded for the witness of Jesus, and for the word of God, and which had not worshipped the beast, neither his image, neither had received his mark upon their foreheads or in their hands; and they lived and reigned with Christ a thousand years. But the rest of the dead lived not again until the thousand years were finished. This is the first resurrection. Blessed and holy is he that hath part in the first resurrection: on such the second death hath no power; but they shall be priests of God and of Christ, and shall reign with him a thousand years." (Rev. xx. 1—6.)

On these passages, I would remark, first, that they clearly teach, not only that the church shall enjoy a season of unusual prosperity, but that every individual shall be converted to God. For if any, even the smallest number, remained in rebellion, *all* would not know the Lord. There would still be need for one to teach another, and there would be some to *hurt* and destroy in God's holy mountain. It is plain, then, that in the day of millennial glory, there will not be found, in the wide world, a solitary child of Adam but shall love and serve the Lord.

Secondly. This prosperity of the church shall continue a very long season — a thousand years, says the apostle. It is well known that, in prophecy, each day stands for a year. Daniel's seventy weeks are to be thus interpreted. The forty-two months, twelve hundred and sixty days, of Antichrist's reign, are thus understood. And surely the one thousand years of Christ's reign on earth should be interpreted by the same rule — three hundred and sixty thousand years, in which righteousness shall be triumphant, and holiness to the Lord shall cover the earth.

But how shall these things come to pass ? In what way shall the whole earth be converted to God ?

In the first place, it is evident that the reason why the whole earth will then embrace the gospel, is not because unsanctified human nature will gradually grow better, and the tone of depravity abate, until all men will fall in with that gospel which the majority has hitherto rejected. There is no evidence whatever, in Scripture, that as the world grows older, the rancor of man's hostility to God is diminished. The reverse is rather intimated. The Amorites, in the days of Joshua, were more wicked than the Amorites in the days of Abraham. Their " iniquity was full." When Jesus Christ was on the earth, in the cities of Bethsaida, Chorazin, and Capernaum, vice had grown to gigantic stature, such as it had never attained in Tyre or Sidon, Sodom or Gomorrah. The carnal mind is as perfect enmity against God now as it was on the first day after the fall. It is plain, therefore, that the conversion of the world will not take place in consequence of any abatement in the tone of man's natural depravity.

Secondly. We may remark, that the millennium will not take place by reason of the gospel growing better, and holding out stronger inducements for sinners to embrace it. The gospel, in the days of Christ, was the same that it now is. It will continue the same to the end of the world. Like its Author, it is "without variableness or shadow of turning." In all ages, it unfolds the same divine character, offers the same Savior to a lost world, brings to light the same immortality, tells of the same heaven, the same hell, and points to the same judgment bar. And in that day when all flesh shall see the salvation of God, it will be found that they have all closed in with that very gospel which the nations for many ages past have neglected and despised.

Thirdly. The reason why all hearts shall fall in with the gospel in the latter day, is not because the gospel will then be better preached than it had ever been before. There is no doubt but that the heralds of salvation will then possess much higher qualification for their work than they now do. But this is not the chief reason why every heart will then bow to God. There was once a Preacher on earth who far surpassed any who will appear during the millennium. "Never man spake like Jesus Christ." Never man *will* speak like him. Those who sat under his sermons "were *astonished* at his doctrine," and "*wondered* at the gracious words that proceeded out of his mouth." Yet, instead of giving him their hearts, they assailed him with insult and violence; they crowned him with thorns, and stained the summit of Calvary with his blood.

Thus we find that the heart of man has stood out

against the gospel when it was more powerfully preached than it will be during the millennium.

How, then, shall all hearts be subdued? This day will be preceded by tremendous and desolating judgments. Hear the language of Isaiah, ii. 10—21: "Enter into the rock, and hide thee in the dust, for fear of the Lord, and for the glory of his majesty. The lofty looks of man shall be humbled, and the haughtiness of men shall be bowed down, and the Lord alone shall be exalted in that day. For the day of the Lord of hosts shall be upon every one that is proud and lofty, and upon every one that is lifted up; and he shall be brought low; and upon all the cedars of Lebanon, that are high and lifted up, and upon all the oaks of Bashan, and upon all the high mountains, and upon all the hills that are lifted up, and upon every high tower, and upon every fenced wall, and upon all the ships of Tarshish, and upon all pleasant pictures. And the loftiness of man shall be bowed down, and the haughtiness of men shall be made low: and the Lord alone shall be exalted in that day. And the idols he shall utterly abolish. And they shall go into the holes of the rocks, and into the caves of the earth, for fear of the Lord, and for the glory of his majesty, when he ariseth to shake terribly the earth. In that day, a man shall cast his idols of silver, and his idols of gold, which they made each one for himself to worship, to the moles and to the bats; to go into the clefts of the rocks, and into the tops of the ragged rocks, for fear of the Lord, and for the glory of his majesty, when he ariseth to shake terribly the earth." Isa. lxvi. 15, 16: "For behold, the Lord will come with fire, and with his chariots like a whirlwind, to render his anger with fury, and his rebuke with flames of fire. For by fire and by his sword will the Lord plead with all flesh: and the slain of the Lord shall be many." But judgments alone never did, and never will, turn sinners from the error of their ways. Judgments destroy, but are insufficient to convert sinners to God. The "balm of Gilead" alone can heal the diseases of the soul. And all nations will be turned to God, by the omnipotent energies of the Holy Spirit applying to their hearts the truths of the gospel. Without this, all the Bibles, and Sabbaths, and sermons, with which a sinner can be favored, produce no saving effect. The inhabitants of the earth, at the millennium, will be converted just in the same manner as the three thousand were on the day of pentecost — by the powerful operation of the spirit of grace. When the Holy Spirit was poured out, more souls were brought to God, under one sermon of Peter, than had been converted during three and a half years by the preaching of Him who "spake as never man spake;" and doubtless God designed this remarkable fact to teach the world that the most advantageous means, without the *special influences* of the Holy Spirit, would avail nothing.

Sinners, in the latter day, will all be turned to God, just in the same manner that Paul was. His heart was in high rebellion; but the Spirit of God overtook him, the enmity of his proud spirit was broken down, and he cast himself at the feet of that Savior whom before he had blasphemed. When the Savior was on earth, he often said, "Many are called, but few chosen." That is, many hear the general invitation of the gospel, but few, comparatively, have their hearts subdued. It was so in that day. But it will be far otherwise when the "new Jerusalem shall come down from God out of heaven, prepared as a bride adorned for her husband;" for then the converting influences of the Holy Spirit shall come down on every heart. "They shall be all taught of God." "The Lord will make bare his arm in the eyes of all the nations, and all the ends of the earth shall see his salvation." (Isaiah lii. 10.)

There is a notable fact, which the prophets have testified of this day, to which I would now call your attention. All Christians shall then "see eye to eye." They will all understand the Bible alike. There will not then be such a variety of dialects in the "language of Canaan" as there now is; but all the disciples of Jesus will most cordially agree respecting the grand system of doctrines taught in his word. Isaiah says, "The watchmen shall lift up their voice; with the voice together shall they sing; for they shall see eye to eye." Jehovah says, "They shall be my people, and I will be their God; and I will give them one heart, and one way, that they may fear me forever." And not only so, but the truths of the gospel shall then be seen with uncommon clearness. "The light of the moon shall be as the light of the sun, and the light of the sun shall be sevenfold." All the doctrines of the gospel shall then stand out, in bold relief, with amazing brightness, in the view of all nations.

Let us now pause, for a moment, and notice some of the great gospel doctrines which the people in the millennial day, from the very circumstances in which they are placed, must see with peculiar clearness.

1. The doctrine of God's absolute sovereignty: that he gives his favors when and where he pleases; that

none of Adam's race have the least claim to a single crumb of his mercy; and that he has a right to do just what he pleases with his own; and that no man on earth has a right to dispute his awful will, or say unto him, What doest thou? In the present and past dark ages of the church, many have opposed this doctrine, and contended that, if it be true, the conduct of God towards men is partial and unjust, as he does more for some than he does for others; but in the days of the millennium, this doctrine will be clearly seen, and universally acknowledged; for they shall all see eye to eye. They will see that God has done for them what he never did for any other people, since the day he created man upon the earth. He has come down among them with power and great glory, and has turned every heart from sin to holiness, and brought every human being from Satan to God. And while the Bible tells them that God conferred favors on Abraham and his family above the antediluvians, and distinguished Israel above the nations around them, and performed works in Chorazin, Bethsaida, and Capernaum, beyond any thing that was ever known in Sodom and Gomorrah, the people of the millennium will see and feel that God has distinguished them, above all people that ever lived upon the earth. They will admire the sovereign, distinguishing grace of God; and every heart will joyfully adopt the language of the Savior, "Even so, Father; for so it seemed good in thy sight."

2. The doctrine of effectual calling, or that sinners are converted to God by the special influences of the Holy Spirit, will be seen, and universally acknowledged, by the people of the millennium. They will

see how the dispensations of the Holy Spirit in their day differ from what they were during the ministry of Jesus Christ, when "many were called, but few chosen." For now, behold! kings have become nursing-fathers, and queens nursing-mothers, to the church. They will know that the "king's heart is in the hand of the Lord: as the rivers of water, he turneth it whithersoever he pleaseth;" and that "it is the Lord" that hath turned the hearts of kings and queens to righteousness. And when they see piety prevailing among all classes of men, from the least to the greatest, they will not conclude that the glorious change has taken place just because all men, at the same time, happened to take a notion to make a good use of their self-determining power. No; they will ascribe it to God; they will confess it is the "Lord's doing, and marvellous in our eyes;" and they will unite with the holy Psalmist in saying, "Not unto us, O Lord, not unto us, but unto thy name," be all the glory.

3. There is a doctrine plainly taught in the Bible, which, in the past dark ages of the Christian church, and even in the present age, has received much unkind treatment; but in the days of the millennium it will be "established in the top of the mountains, and exalted above the hills; and all nations shall flow unto it." I mean the doctrine of God's determinate counsel — his eternal purposes. Many professors of religion have an idea that there is something very dreadful in the doctrine of God's immutable decrees. They believe in foreknowledge; but speak not of God acting now — "according to the eternal purpose which he purposed in Christ Jesus our Lord;" say not that "his counsel shall stand;" that he "worketh all things after the counsel of his own will."

But when the knowledge of the Lord shall cover the whole earth, this subject will stand in a clearer light. The people of that day will have before their eyes the happy results of God's operations for thousands of years. They will look around them, and see that what he promised many ages before, he has now fulfilled. They will look into the holy book; and they will see that God had not only foretold that there should be a day of millennial glory, but had promised that he himself would bring it about. "I the Lord will hasten it in his time." They will believe in God's foreknowledge; but their belief will go further. They will see that the Lord not only foresaw there would be a millennium, but that from the beginning it had been his determinate purpose to grant his church this blessed day; that, thousands of years ago, he had revealed his design to "build up Zion, and appear in his glory," when "the set time to favor her is come." (Ps. cii. 15.) They will hear a voice proceeding from the holy oracles, "The Lord of hosts hath sworn, saying, Surely as I have thought, so shall it come to pass; and as I have purposed, so shall it stand. This is the purpose that is purposed upon the whole earth; and this is the hand that is stretched out upon all the nations. For the Lord of Hosts hath purposed, and who shall disannul it? And his hand is stretched out, and who shall turn it back? I am God, and there is none else. I am God, and there is none like me; declaring the end from the beginning, and from ancient times the things that are not yet done, saying, My counsel shall stand, and I will do all my pleasure." (Isa. xiv. 24, 26, 27, and Isa. xlvi. 9, 10.) The people of the millennial day will hear this from the sacred book. They will see the glory of the church around them; and with the venerable old apostle they will exclaim, "O the depth of the riches both of the wisdom and knowledge of God!" And earth will roll back the anthem that comes down from heaven, "We give thee thanks, O Lord God Almighty, who art, and wast, and art to come; because thou hast taken to thee thy great power, and hast reigned." (Rev. xi. 17.)

4. The doctrine of the perseverance of the saints in holiness will then be understood and acknowledged by all "nations, and kindreds, and people" under heaven." In the present state of the church, the wheat and the tares grow together. Many assume the badge of Christianity from base motives, mingle a while among the children of God, and then turn back to the world. This has led some well-meaning people to conclude that real saints sometimes fall from grace, and perish. But in the days of the millennium this mistake will be corrected. There will then be no hypocrites in the church. "All shall know the Lord, from the least to the greatest." And there will be no apostasies; for every soul will be the subject of genuine conversion. It is plain that the doctrine of "falling from grace," however numerous its advocates may now be, will be utterly exploded by all nations during the long periods of the millennium; for if any should fall from grace, then *all* would not "know the Lord." There would still be need for "one to teach another," and there would be some to "hurt and destroy in God's holy mountain." These apostates would be very troublesome — the very kind of people to create disturbance. But there shall be none. Perfect peace, and undisturbed tranquillity, shall prevail through all God's holy

mountain. Thus we see that, when Jesus shall come to reign in our world, the doctrine of falling from grace shall "flee away, and no place be found for it."

5. The harmony between the agency of God and the agency of man will be much better understood by the people during the millennium, than it has been in ages past. Many excellent men have been greatly in the dark on this subject. They have supposed that God cannot convert all sinners, without destroying their free agency, and turning them into machines; and this they think is the great reason why God has not converted all sinners long ago. They have also maintained that God cannot keep all saints from falling from grace, without destroying their free agency, and turning them into machines. This is one of the main pillars on which they build their doctrine of falling from grace. But when the "light of the moon shall be as the light of the sun, and the light of the sun shall be sevenfold," all the people of that day will see that, however devout and useful in other respects the advocates of the above opinions may have been, yet on those points they were sadly mistaken. They will see that God has, in fact, come down among them, in the powerful influences of his Spirit, and subdued the heart of every sinner. The loftiness of man is bowed down, and the haughtiness of man is made low, and the Lord alone is exalted. All flesh see his glory, and rejoice in his love; and yet not a man on earth has lost his free agency — not one has been turned into a machine. And as age after age rolls by, they will see that all saints persevere in holiness — none fall from grace — "all are kept by the power of God through faith unto salvation;" yet no

saint is turned into a machine, but all retain their free agency. Thus they will see that their brethren, who, in former ages, contended so stoutly for the foregoing opinions, were altogether mistaken; and that the light which they thought they had on these points was darkness.

Now, it is just as evident that the system of doctrines at which I have glanced is the system that will be received, and rejoiced in, during the millennium, as it is that that glorious day will come. Indeed, the fact itself, that a day is coming when the church shall be blessed with a period of millennial glory, furnishes incontestable proof of the doctrines I have mentioned; for on no other plan can such a day be reasonably expected. Destroy these doctrines, and you destroy the only foundation on which the church can build her hope that Jesus shall yet fill the whole earth with his glory. Deny the doctrine of God's immutable purposes; say that he has no "set time to favor Zion;" say that he as much designed to convert and save all men, in ages that are past, when but few were converted, as he does in any ages that are yet to come, — and how is the whole earth to be converted? Deny the doctrine of effectual calling; say that God has already done all that he can do, consistently with man's free agency, to convert and save all men; and that his Spirit will take no mightier method to subdue the hearts of all sinners hereafter, than he has taken already, — and I ask, how are all hearts to be turned to God? We have seen that the tone of enmity in the carnal heart will not abate. We have seen that the gospel will undergo no change — will hold out no stronger inducements to sinners. We have seen that the gospel will not be preached better in time to come, than it was when multitudes despised it. Where, then, is the hope of the church, that all nations shall learn righteousness, and the saving knowledge of God shall cover the earth ? It is lost. Yes, it is lost ; and it never can be found, till you come back to those grand doctrines of revelation we have mentioned, and acknowledge that the bright period of Zion's triumph is certain ; because God, in his counsels, has determined it. It will come ; because "the Lord will hasten it in his time," "according to the eternal purpose which he purposed in Christ Jesus our Lord."

In like manner, reject the doctrine of the perseverance of the saints ; deny that the great Shepherd of Israel "keeps" every converted soul, "by his power, through faith, unto salvation ;" and where can there be any certainty that, through the long periods of Christ's reign on earth, "there shall be none to hurt or destroy in all his holy mountain" ?

Thus you clearly see that the fact that God will, at his "set time," make his church triumphant in all the earth, furnishes incontestable proof of those precious doctrines which have "been every where spoken against."

REFLECTIONS.

1. This subject shows us that God's ways are higher than our ways, as the heavens are higher than the earth. We would have thought it best that the millennium should have been introduced immediately after the fall of man ; and that the career of human wickedness, and the reign of Satan, should have been as short as possible. God could have bound Satan

then, and cast him into the bottomless pit, and converted the world, as easily as at the day he has appointed; but he did not. He is acting for the universe, and acting for eternity. He is doing that which he sees best on the whole, taking into view the whole extent of his dominions, and the whole duration of his reign. He has seen it best that mankind should be taught by experience what is in their revolted hearts, that they may know how much they are indebted to God for his redeeming mercy. It is a divine maxim, that to whom much is forgiven, the same will love much; but to whom little is forgiven, the same will love little; and just in the same degree that men are acquainted with their depravity, will be their gratitude to God for redemption. Had God led the Israelites directly from Egypt to Canaan, which was but a few days' journey, they would never have known that such wickedness was in their hearts as they acted out when God "proved them, and tried them, forty years in the wilderness." God knew all this before; but he took this course, that they might know it too, and become acquainted with themselves. And had he introduced the millennium immediately after the fall of man, it never would have been known to saints on earth — it never would have been known to glorified spirits in heaven — how deep and how dreadful the depravity into which man has fallen. It would have been known to God and to him only; but from created beings he never would have received all the honor to which he is entitled for man's redemption. He chose a different plan. Soon after the fall, he gave a single intimation that he would be merciful to penitent and returning sinners. But how did men treat it? Did they hail with joy the prospect of reconciliation to God? Did they, with one heart, follow this beam of light, that had come to our dark world, to the mercy seat from which it issued? No. Proud in his rebellion, and pleased with his distance from God, man turned away in scorn from the proffers of pardon. "All flesh corrupted his way." "The wickedness of man was great in the earth," and "every imagination of the thoughts of his heart was only evil continually." Thus matters went on for more than two thousand years.

In the days of Abraham, God gave a further development of his gracious designs. The nations paid no attention to it, but with madness pursued every folly and every abomination. And thus four hundred and thirty years rolled by. Then God came down on Mount Sinai, proclaimed his law, and gave numerous institutions, most significant and impressive, all pointing to the great Messiah as the only hope of a lost world. But it made no impression on the nations. Not one of them forsook idolatry, and turned to God for the hope of redemption. And even Israel, who heard God's thunder, and saw his lightning, at Sinai, were with difficulty restrained from casting away the oracles of God, and plunging into all the abominations of the heathen. Thus matters stood for fifteen hundred years. He then sent his Son into the world. "Surely they will reverence my Son." But they cried, "Away with him from the earth! Crucify him, crucify him!" And now he has caused the light of the gospel to shine upon our world for near two thousand years; and how have mankind acted? How have they chosen the lusts of the flesh, the lusts of the eye, and the pride of life, in preference to communion and fellowship with God, and the joys of his holy kingdom! Thus mankind have been proved and tried in a great variety of circumstances, and have shown their deep-rooted hostility to God, and their determination that he shall not rule over them. An impression is made far and wide through the universe, how deeply they deserve eternal banishment from God, and from glory. It is a history that will never be forgotten while immortality endures. And now, when God's "set time to favor Zion" is come, and he shall cause every heart to bow, and wave the banner of salvation over every tribe, and kingdom, and people on our globe, the pride of man will be stained; heaven and earth will acknowledge that it is the work of the Lord. No flesh shall dare to glory in his presence. But, as it is written, "He that glorieth, let him glory in the Lord."

Blessed Jesus! thou shalt see the travail of thy soul, and shalt be satisfied. But O, what a day of salvation! what a renovated world! — Holiness to the Lord inscribed on every object; all classes of men, from the least to the greatest, clothed with righteousness; fervent piety in every heart; anthems of praise ascending from every habitation. The young man consecrates to God the morning of life; the aged man worships, leaning on the top of his staff; and children stretch their little hands to heaven, and cry, "Hosanna to the Son of David."

2. And now, my Christian friends, what encouragement does this subject impart to you, to be active and energetic in your efforts to advance the cause of your Redeemer! God carries forward his cause in the

world by human instrumentality. Thus he grants to us the high privilege of being "workers together with God," in advancing the interest of his kingdom, and the glory of his great name. And what a privilege is this! Look at the old soldier who fought by the side of Washington, when our country was struggling for liberty; see him now surrounded by his children and his children's children, casting an eye of admiration over this great, this highly-favored nation; and how does his heart swell with rapture inexpressible, when he reflects, "Under the direction of the God of battles, my exertions contributed to procure these blessings; these hands had an agency in raising my country to happiness and glory"!

Now, King Eternal is building up a kingdom, which, in importance, surpasses all earthly kingdoms, as far as eternity surpasses time. And in advancing this great cause, he employs the agency of rulers and subjects, ministers and people, husbands and wives, parents and children. He employs the agency of all who love him. And what a privilege is it to be employed in such a cause! And when the Leader of the armies of Israel has put down all opposition, and filled the whole earth with his glory, what holy rapture will possess the hearts of all who have fought under his banner! And O, how the plains of immortality will resound with Alleluia! Alleluia! when Moses, and Isaiah, and Daniel, and all the old soldiers that fought, and bled, and died in the service of King Immanuel, look down from heaven, and see that the cause of their Master is triumphant, and "the kingdoms of this world have become the kingdoms of our Lord and of his Christ." Christian, do you desire to have a part in the rejoicings of that day? Then consecrate all your powers to the service of Jesus, and he will give you "a crown of life that fadeth not away."

3. When the Redeemer has finished his reign on earth, a scene of the deepest interest will ensue. He will cause the graves to open, and all that sleep in the dust of the earth to come forth; he will separate the righteous from the wicked; he will call the angels of God to draw near; he will summon the inhabitants of every world he has formed to approach and witness his proceedings. All his conduct towards the human family, from the day that Adam was created till the judgment trump was blown, he will cause to pass in review before the assembled universe. The wisdom and holiness, the mercy and truth, the perfection and beauty of all his dealings with the children of men, will stand out in the light of eternity; and from the countless throng of holy beings will burst the acclamation, "Amen! Alleluia!"

Then, before he pronounces on the impenitent the irrevocable sentence, he will cause all the treatment he has received from them to pass in review before the vast assembly — the conduct of those who set at nought and sold him, pierced and nailed him to the tree; the quibbles of infidels who denied his truth, and labored to falsify his word; the "hard speeches" which bold blasphemers had spoken against him; the deep-laid schemes to injure his cause and destroy his kingdom; each guilty soul, on the left hand of the Judge, will see his most secret crimes, and his long-forgotten acts of impiety, rising in dark array before the eyes of the immense assembly. O Daniel! is this the "shame and everlasting contempt" foretold by thee? Lord Jesus, is this the "resurrection of damnation"? Unthinking traveller to eternity, is it in view of this, that Jesus warns you to "prepare to meet your God"? Is it in view of this, that he entreats you to "flee from the wrath to come"? Careless sinner, you came from God, and to God you are going; from his presence there is no escape. "If you ascend into heaven, he is there; if you make your bed in hell, behold, he is there." You are going to meet him; O, how unprepared! Yet meet him you must; the grave cannot hide you; rocks and mountains cannot cover you; death and hell can furnish no hiding-place from God. And yet you may meet him in mercy. O, look to Calvary! Who is that, with the nail-prints in his hands, and the spear-wound in his side? It is Jesus, who died for sinners. Escape for your life to him, in whom alone there is redemption.

Impenitent man, what you do must be done quickly: you stand on critical ground; you live in a most eventful age. Look abroad through the earth, and behold the footsteps of the Almighty. The arm of the Lord is awake. He is sweeping the nations and shaking the earth. Your father never saw a day like this. God's purposes are ripening fast; his church is fast filling up. Soon the door will be shut. God lifts his hand to heaven, and declares he "will make a short work in the earth." The sinner that will not bow he will "kill with death." The soul that will not surrender he will consume with the "breath of his mouth, and the brightness of his coming." Already you have trifled with his mercy long; already the cry of your sins has gone up before God; already the tempest is gathering; the dark cloud is seen, and the distant thunder is heard. But you are not yet lost. There is yet within your view, on the mediatorial throne, "one like unto the Son of man." See, round about his head is the rainbow of mercy, in token that as yet the storm is stayed. Delay not a moment. Fly to Jesus, and your soul shall live.

BEL AND NEBO.

A WESTERN gentleman, of wealth and respectability, said to a clergyman of his acquaintance, "There are portions of the Bible that seem to me to have little or no meaning. Can I believe that such passages are a part of the inspired word of God?"

"Please mention the passages to which you refer," said the clergyman.

"One of them," answered the gentleman, "is found in the commencement of the forty-sixth chapter of Isaiah. It runs thus: 'Bel boweth down, Nebo stoopeth; their idols were upon the beasts, and upon the cattle: your carriages were heavy loaden; they are a burden to the weary beast. They stoop; they bow down together; they could not deliver the burden, but themselves are gone into captivity.' I can see no meaning in this passage."

"Shall I give you a brief exposition, which I think will render the text plain and interesting?"

"I shall be gratified to hear you," added the gentleman.

"Observe, then," said the minister, "that Bel and Nebo were the two principal idols of Babylon. Their kings and heroes often bear names and titles in which there is a reference to these notable idols, as *Bel*shazzar, *Nebu*chadnezzar, *Nebu*zaradan, &c. They had, it is true, other inferior deities, which they worshipped; but Bel and Nebo were the great chiefs among their imaginary gods. The kings of Babylon had been a dreadful scourge to the surrounding nations. They had slaughtered their population; they had plundered their temples and their treasuries, and had carried all the wealth which they could thus collect to Babylon. And the glory of these conquests they ascribed to Bel and Nebo. When they were about engaging in some important military expedition, they invoked the aid and benediction of Bel and Nebo; and when their incursion into a neighboring nation had been successful, they crowded the temples of Bel and Nebo, and offered sacrifices of thanksgiving, and paid to these idols the most costly honors. At length, the king of Babylon invaded Judea. As he made war under the patronage of Bel and Nebo, the conclusion was, that, whenever he conquered, these idols of Babylon had proved too mighty for the god of the conquered people. When Jerusalem fell into the hands of the king of Babylon, these idolaters did not wish to believe the truth. They did not wish to believe that Israel were smitten for their sins against God. They loved darkness. They loved to believe a lie. They exulted in the opportunity of blazing abroad, that now the idols of Babylon had proved too strong for the God of Israel. The city called by his name was destroyed. The beautiful house built for his praise was burned with fire; and his people were carried into captivity. And now they devised honors for their favorite idol beyond all parallel. The king, the princes, and the people, all combine. 'Nebuchadnezzar the king made an image of gold, whose height was threescore cubits, and the breadth thereof six cubits: he set it up in the plain of Dura, in the province of Babylon. Then Nebuchadnezzar the king sent to gather together the princes, the governors, and the captains, the judges, the treasurers, the counsellors, the sheriffs, and all the rulers of the provinces, to come to the dedication of the image which Nebuchadnezzar the king had set up. Then the princes, the governors, and captains, the judges, the treasurers, the counsellors, the sheriffs, and all the rulers of the provinces, were gathered together unto the dedication of the image that Nebuchadezzar the king had set up; and they stood before the image that Nebuchadnezzar had set up. Then a herald cried aloud, To you it is commanded, O people, nations, and languages, that at what time ye hear the sound of the cornet, flute, harp, sackbut, psaltery, dulcimer, and all kinds of music, ye fall down, and worship the golden image that Nebuchadnezzar the king hath set up. And whoso falleth not down, and worshippeth, shall the same hour be cast into the midst of a burning, fiery furnace.' (Daniel iii. 1—6.) Such were the honors publicly given to Bel, after Jerusalem had fallen before the armies of Babylon. And the honors given to Nebo were scarcely inferior. Long ago, these idolaters had heard the fame of the God of Israel — the wonders wrought in Egypt, at the Red Sea, and in the wilderness. They had trembled in dread of the power of Jehovah. But now his worshippers are vanquished, and carried into captivity. His temple is destroyed; and the land called by his name is made a desolation. Their exultation is unbounded; and invention is tortured for methods to give demonstrations of their joy. And now the prophecy of Isaiah comes before them, that Jehovah, the God of Israel, will accomplish the downfall of Babylon. 'Behold, I will stir up the Medes against them, which shall not regard silver; and as for gold, they shall not delight in it.' 'And Babylon, the glory of kingdoms, the beauty of the Chaldees' excellency, shall be as when God overthrew Sodom and Gomorrah. It shall never be inhabited, neither shall it be dwelt in from generation to generation: neither shall the Arabian pitch tent there; neither shall the shepherds make their fold there; but wild beasts of the desert shall lie there; and their houses shall be full of doleful creatures; and owls shall dwell there, and satyrs shall dance there. And the wild beasts of the islands shall cry in their desolate houses, and dragons in their pleasant palaces; and her time is near to come, and her days shall not be prolonged.' (Isaiah xiii. 17, 19—22.) In the forty-fifth chapter, the prophet goes into particulars, and gives specifications concerning the destruction of Babylon.

"1. Cyrus, the Persian, shall command the conquering enemy, (v. 1.)

"2. Cyrus, though a heathen, unacquainted with the true religion, is called to this great work by the God of Israel, (v. 4, 5.)

"3. God will 'open before him the two-leaved gates, and the gates shall not be shut,' (v. 1.)

"4. The 'treasures and hidden riches of Babylon shall be given to him,' (v. 3.)

"5. He shall 'let go the captive Jews.'

"6. 'Not for price nor reward;' that is, he shall not demand a ransom, (v. 13.)

"7. He shall rebuild Jerusalem.

"8. 'And rebuild the temple,' (chap. xliv. 28.)

"But the Babylonian unbeliever demands, 'Where is Bel — where is Nebo — while this destruction is coming on their favorite city? Where are those powerful gods of Babylon, that have dashed the nations in pieces before her conquering armies? Such an overthrow of Babylon is incredible, while she is upheld by Bel and Nebo.' The prophet replies, 'The Medes and Persians will pull down these senseless images, and break them to pieces, and put the metal of which they are composed on mules and pack-horses, and into carriages, and bear it away to Persia.' 'Bel boweth down, Nebo stoopeth; their idols were upon the beasts and upon the cattle: your carriages were heavy loaden; they are a burden to the weary beast. They stoop, they bow down together; they could not deliver the burden, but themselves are gone into captivity.' (Isaiah xlvi. 1, 2.)"

The effect of this exposition on the mind of the gentleman who introduced the discussion I have not the means of knowing. The elucidation of the text is inserted here, with the hope that it may prove acceptable to the readers of the "Western Sketch-Book."

EXPOSITION OF SCRIPTURE.

"And there are also many other things which Jesus did, the which, if they should be written every one, I suppose that even the world itself could not contain the books that should be written." (John xxi. 25.)

The plain Christian reads this assertion of the apostle in much astonishment. No declaration in the New Testament appears to him more mysterious and strange; and, after reviewing it again and again, he finds himself utterly unable to form even a plausible conjecture of what the inspired writer intended. He could not mean to assert that if every one of the things which Jesus did in the presence of his disciples, before his death and after his resurrection, were committed to writing, the number and size of the books would be so great that there would not be in the world itself, or in the whole world, room enough to contain them; and yet this seems to be the direct import of the language employed. After many fruitless efforts to extract the apostle's meaning, he leaves the passage in despair, deeply regretting that, to his mind, "shadows, clouds, and darkness rest upon it."

Elsner, one of the most famous of European critics, explains this text as if the apostle had said, "If all the works that Jesus did were recorded, the unbelieving world would not admit them, so as to be moved by them to faith and obedience." But the sacred writer well knew that unbelievers would scoff and reject what he had written. This, therefore, could not be assigned as a reason for his not writing more.

"God is his own interpreter." Many parts of his holy book, which at first are difficult of comprehension, become perfectly plain when compared with the events of his providence. After the apostles had witnessed the life and death of Jesus Christ, they had a much clearer understanding of the Old Testament predictions concerning him than the prophets had, by whom those predictions were uttered. (1 Pet. i. 10—12.) And many things which Christ did and said were at first unintelligible to the disciples; but after his resurrection, they were clear as the light of heaven. Accordingly, we read, (John xii. 16,) "These things understood not his disciples at the first: but when Jesus was glorified, then remembered they that these things were written of him, and that they had done these things unto him."

In like manner, the Christian who now attentively surveys what the Lord is doing for the advancement of his church, will be enabled to understand declarations contained in his word, which, a few ages back, were shrouded in impenetrable obscurity. The Lamb is opening seal after seal, and as he moves forward, "conquering and to conquer," the light of revealed truth will shine upon our dark world more and more, until the perfect millennial day. The passage under consideration is one of this description; it can be more fully comprehended now than in any former age. But it must be remarked, that the Greek word which in the text is translated *contain*, more properly signifies to *receive;* the best Greek lexicons render it thus, χωρησαι, *recipere,* to receive. "The world itself," or "the whole world, could not *receive* the books that should be written." God designed that the inspired record of the doctrines, and miracles, and death of Jesus Christ should be put into the hands of the whole world, as an infallible rule of faith and practice. He mentioned this, by the mouth of Isaiah, as taking place in order to the conversion of all nations. "Out of Zion shall go forth the law, and the word of the Lord from Jerusalem." His Omnipotent Spirit is now arousing the Christian church to the mighty enterprise ; already the holy book is spreading among the nations with unexampled rapidity; already the benighted tribes of Europe, Africa, Asia, and America, begin to feel its amazing influence ; already, in large and populous districts, every family has been visited and supplied with the sacred oracles. Nor shall the glorious work stop until every kindred and people under heaven read, in their own tongue, wherein they were born, "the wonderful works of God."

But says the apostle, if all the things which Jesus said and did in the presence of his disciples had been written in the inspired book, "I suppose that the whole world could not receive the books that should be written." No. It would have swelled the sacred writings to an extent too great; it would have been impracticable to have put the whole human family in possession of them, and thus fill the earth with the knowledge of the Lord. The spirit of inspiration, therefore, chose only to record so much as is necessary for the salvation of souls. "These are written, that ye might believe that Jesus is the Christ, the Son of God; and that believing, ye might have life through his name." And when the redeemed soul enters eternity, a part of the delightful employment of that heavenly world will be to hear from our blessed Lord himself, and from those who conversed with him while on earth, many other particulars of his life, which will be worthy of everlasting admiration.

A VISION.

I PURSUED my way over a desolate and uninhabited land. The sun, "rejoicing as a strong man to run a race," rushed through a clear sky up to his midday throne, and flooded "hill, and dale, and mountain-peak" with the profusion of his radiance. Silence, profound and wide, reigned over the mighty landscape, save when the doe bleated to her fawn, or the proud eagle, wheeling in airy circles on high, screamed to his distant mate. In every land, Nature has her grandeur, and her loveliness; and yet God has made nothing in vain. The language of inspiration is as applicable to those objects which constitute the furniture of the wilderness, as to those that "garnish the heavens." "For his glory they are and were created." It is only in relation to man that the beautiful sentiment of Mr. Gray is correct —

> "Full many a gem, of purest ray serene,
> The dark, unfathomed caves of ocean bear;
> Full many a flower is born to blush unseen,
> And waste its sweetness on the desert air."

Who can think of the full-blown rose on the lonely hill; the wild apple-tree in the solitary glen, sustaining its pyramid of, flowers, and enriching the air with its perfumes; the unvisited solitude of the mountain cascade, with its ceaseless music, which man sees not, hears not; — who, in short, can think of the wonders of earth, and the wonders of ocean, which, to Adam's children, seem to exist in vain, without being forced to the conclusion, that our world rolls in the view of other intellectual beings than those of the human family?

> "Millions of spiritual creatures walk the earth
> Unseen, both when we wake and when we sleep."

God's work of creation, as well as his work of redemption, contains countless "things which the angels desire to look into."

As the evening approached, I perceived before me a remarkable eminence. Its elevation was great, and the summit was crowned with a lofty grove of majestic cedars. The cedar is much celebrated in the sacred writings. It is an evergreen. The winter comes; but "its leaf does not wither." Fit emblem of the child of God! "He shall grow like a cedar in Lebanon." (Ps. xcii. 12.) The student of the Bible cannot look on the noble cedar without interesting associations. As I fixed my eyes on the stately grove, I thought of the beautiful imagery employed by the church, when describing her beloved — "His countenance is as Lebanon, excellent as the cedars." I remembered the prayer of Moses — "I beseech thee let me go over and see the good land that is beyond Jordan, and that goodly mountain, Lebanon."

The ascent was arduous and long. At length, however, I found myself in the bosom of the venerable grove. The spot was lovely beyond description. At the foot of a rock, gray with years, bubbled a little fountain, whose stream, skirted with green, rippled along in search of the valley below. The evening breeze had just strength enough to whisper among the branches, which acknowledged its presence by their gentle and graceful undulations. On every hand, the prospect was wide as the eye could reach. Meanwhile the sun sank behind the distant blue horizon; but scarcely had Night begun to spread her dark mantle over the earth, when, ascending in the east, a broad, bright moon appeared, to cheer the world her Creator made. I felt the inspiration of the scene and the hour. "Surely," I exclaimed, in a transport of enthusiasm — "surely, when ministering spirits take their flight from the throne of God on errands of love to our guilty world, it is here they first alight; and from this eminence they take a joyful survey of the magnificent works of the Almighty, before their sight is offended with a view of the vileness and impiety of man."

It was an hour for devotion. After praising the name of Him whose "kingdom ruleth over all," and commending myself to his mercy through the merits of the divine Redeemer, I fell into a train of reflections concerning the church of God. The strength of early impressions is wonderful. Through every period of our life, when we begin to meditate on divine things, how will the scenes of early youth, the period of our first strong religious excitement, present themselves before us in all their freshness and force, until sometimes we can scarcely realize that they belong to "the days of other years"! How often in the book of Psalms do we find David celebrating the loving-kindness of the Lord which visited him when young! and how sweet are the lines in which Addison commemorates the goodness and mercy which crowned the morning of his life!

The scenes which now recurred to my mind were those of the first great western revival, which transpired when I was but a child. Those ministers whom we now see entering the pulpit old and gray-headed, were then vigorous and young; and many others were then active who now "rest from their labors, and their works follow them." I remembered the preaching of Ramsay, and Lapsley, and Witherspoon. Departed brethren, we have not forgotten you. While your souls rejoice in glory, your names and your memory are affectionately cherished among your brethren on earth. Yes, I remembered the day when Joseph B. Lapsley stood, in the name of his Redeemer, before the immense congregation, while with one hand he pointed to Mount Sinai, wrapped in smoke, and flashing out the terrors of a violated law, and with the other to Calvary, bathed in tears, drenched with blood, and echoing the groans of the dying Savior. How deep and awful was the religious solemnity of that period throughout the western country! Individuals, and even whole families, would travel thirty, forty, and fifty miles, to attend a sacramental occasion. No house could contain the multitudes that convened; but the people took their seats on the ground, or on logs of wood, in the open air; and the minister stood before them, having the earth for his pulpit, and the heaven for his sounding-board, praying sinners, in "Christ's stead, to be reconciled to God."

This extraordinary religious awakening gave rise to the camp-meetings of the west. The vast crowds that assembled found it impracticable to obtain accommodations in the neighborhood of the places of worship; and as sacramental meetings were continued for four, five, and six days, it was found best for families at a distance, who wished to attend, to come in their wagons, bringing with them provisions and bedding, and camp on the ground. Thus the worship was continued day and night, except during the hours necessary for repose. The strong religious impression of the time imparted its influence to all the exercises of public and private devotion. Ministers preached for eternity! Christians prayed as if indeed they were entreating the Lord to redeem their souls from hell, and to fill the whole earth with his glory; and when the congregation took up one of the songs of Zion, they sung as if in truth they were praising the everlasting God for sending his Son to redeem them from the second death, — as if in truth they were attuning their voices for the employments of heaven. While musing on this pleasing and affecting subject, the long-departed scene came up distinctly in the view of my mind, — the extended encampment, the mighty congregation assembled for evening worship. Night was around them; but the darkness was dissipated by quantities of rich pine, piled on elevated hearths, which, from all sides of the encampment, sent its broad, bright flame on high. And I seemed once more to hear a thousand glad voices, animated by the hope of glory, chanting that delightful hymn which my childhood so ardently admired: —

"Now, 'Glory to God in the highest' is given;
Now, 'Glory to God' is reëchoed through heaven;
Around the whole earth let us tell the glad story,
And sing of his love, his salvation, and glory.

Hallelujah to the Lamb, who has purchased our pardon!
We'll praise him again when we pass over Jordan.

"O Jesus, ride on! thy kingdom is glorious;
O'er sin, death, and hell thou wilt make us victorious;
Thy name shall be praised in the great congregation,
And the saints shall delight in ascribing salvation.
Hallelujah to the Lamb, who has purchased our pardon!
We'll praise him again when we pass over Jordan.

"Enraptured I burn with delight and desire;
Such love, so divine, sets my soul all on fire;
Around the bright throne loud hosannas are ringing:
O, when shall I join them, and be ever singing,
Hallelujah to the Lamb, who has purchased our pardon!
We'll praise him again when we pass over Jordan?

"When on Zion we stand, having gained the blest shore,
With our harps in our hand, we will praise evermore;
We'll range the blest fields on the banks of the river,
And sing hallelujah forever and ever.
Hallelujah to the Lamb, who has purchased our pardon!
We'll praise him again when we pass over Jordan."

Scarcely could I refrain from attempting to join my voice with that of the congregation of other years, as these charming verses passed through my mind; so strong, and so enchanting, is that power of the soul by which it calls up from the grave departed days of delight.

At length, sleep, which refreshes our weary bodies and our care-worn minds, came down with its balmy influence; but its dominion was soon overcome by notes of the most surprising and heavenly melody. "Shepherds of Bethlehem," thought I, "surely these are the delicious and ravishing strains that fell upon your ears when angels came down and sang the advent of the blessed Redeemer!" The music ceased; but instantly I perceived, at a little distance, a splendid circle of light, so brilliant and dazzling as almost to overcome the powers of vision. For a moment, the eye could discern nothing distinctly within the luminous space; but presently it was easy to perceive

"Forms, clad in peerless majesty,
Move with unutterable grace."

It would be vain to attempt description; for there is no language understood among mortals capable of describing them. The heavenly lustre in which they are arrayed can only be told in the dialect of that world where they dwell. As I gazed on these celestial beings, I thought of the epithets applied to them by prophets and apostles — "Angels that excel in strength," "strong angels," "angels of God," "mighty angels," "angels of glory," "an angel having power over fire," "an angel standing in the sun." I remembered, also, that the beloved disciple was so affected with the resplendent glory of that heavenly visitant that came to him in the Isle of Patmos, that he was once and again in danger of paying him divine adoration. "When I had heard and seen, I fell down to worship before the feet of the angel which showed me these things. Then said he unto me, See thou do it not; for I am thy fellow-servant, and of thy brethren the prophets, and of them which keep the sayings of this book. Worship God."

In a little time they were seated, and the accents of familiar conversation were distinctly audible. On drawing near to hear the subject of discourse, it was easy to distinguish the well-known names of Raphael, Uriel, Abdiel, &c., &c.

"Raphael," said a voice of the most seraphic sweetness and harmony, "though we are all 'ministering spirits, sent forth to minister for them who shall be the heirs of salvation,' yet as 'there is one glory of the sun, and another glory of the moon, and another glory of the stars, and one star differeth from another in glory,' so among angelic minds there is a like variety of capacity and powers. God has said that when he 'created all things by Jesus Christ,' it was his intention to make his 'manifold wisdom known to principalities and powers in heavenly places by the church.' Now, though we have all been employed in the service of the church, where God is unfolding his uncreated attributes, yet as our capacities are various, as our errands and fields of labor have often been different, it will be profitable and delightful should we spend a portion of this fine evening in familiar converse, each detailing what he has seen of the dealings of God with man."

"With all my heart," said Raphael, while his deep, melodious tones caused me to think of

"David's harp, of solemn sound"—

"with all my heart; for not only have our employments and fields of action been various, but created minds being limited in their observation, no one, at first, sees a fact in all its bearings and relations. Even the holy apostles, when recording the sufferings and death of the Son of God, do not dwell invariably on the same circumstances. One instructive view of the great transaction is taken by Matthew, another by John, another by Luke, and another by Mark. It is by taking the united testimony of these inspired witnesses, that the broad, full view of that stupendous miracle of redeeming mercy is placed before the world."

Seraph. Thy ministry, Raphael, has usually been about those saints, and in those sections, of the church where the light of revelation shone most clearly. Rehearse, then, in our hearing, what thou hast seen of the wonderful works of God, as displayed in the history of man.

Raphael. I was often commissioned to visit the earthly paradise while man was innocent and holy. He was the admiration of angels; for he was created in the image of God. Divinely constituted lord of this lower world, his condition was truly blessed. He walked abroad in immortal vigor, his beautiful partner by his side, arrayed in the perfection of terrestrial loveliness, beholding the impress of their Maker in every object, and holding uninterrupted fellowship and communion with the Fountain of love and joy. Smoothly and sweetly these hours rolled on, while their evening and morning anthems of praise went up as pure incense to heaven. I had been abroad on an appointed service, and returned immediately after the first transgression. O, it was enough to make angels weep, to behold how the scene was changed! Deep gloom hung over the bowers of Eden. The tokens of Jehovah's presence were there; but they were tokens of wrath and offended majesty. I looked for the parents of the human race; but they were not to be found. At length, stained with guilt, pale, and trembling with terror, I discovered them hid among the trees of the garden. At that moment, they were startled with the awful question, "Adam, where art thou?" The beasts shrunk to the ground, the birds of paradise screamed and fled, the trees shook, and the earth trembled at the voice of the Almighty. But — praise the Lord, ye heavens of heavens, and thou, eternity, be filled with his praise — mercy was mingled with righteousness in the sentence pronounced on man. The great Redeemer was promised, who, in the fulness of time, should bring life and immortality to the ruined race. The sentence, however, included the death and dissolution of the body, and their expulsion from the garden the Lord had given them. Never shall I forget the speechless anguish that appeared in the countenance of the mother of the human family, when first told she must leave forever her happy home. She cast one troubled, despairing look over the beautiful walks, bright flowers, and fruits of the garden, while fast, fast, the bitter tears streamed over her cheeks; then convulsively clinging to the arm of her husband, they were driven out from Eden. The cherubim took possession of the gate, and a flaming sword, which turned every way, prohibited all return.

As redemption was promised to man, through the mediation of the Son of God, I took a lively interest in the destiny of Adam after his banishment from paradise. Little was then known by man or angels concerning the plan of redeeming love. God designed that light on the moral world should arise in a manner somewhat analogous to that of the natural day — first the solitary beam, struggling through the darkness; then the distinctly visible dawn; then the rising sun; then his upward march, "shining more and more unto the perfect day." But the little of revealed truth then made known was embraced by the parents of mankind. Their faith in the promised Messiah was strong, though they did not fully understand the manner in which he would atone for sin. Though they had obtained pardon of God, yet they could never forgive themselves for having introduced sin and death into the world. Like Peter, in after ages, who never could hear a cock crow without bursting into tears at the remembrance of having denied his Master, so they, throughout their long life, when they saw among their descendants any case of aggravated crime, — and they lived to see many, — or any affecting instance of death, perpetually recurred to their first apostasy, and reproached and humbled themselves before God, for having brought rebellion and ruin among their children. Earth was to them a "vale of tears;" but their sufferings were sanctified, and as they advanced in age, they ripened for heaven.

There was a circumstance in the history of Adam that I will mention. The infirmities and frailties of old age are the fruits of sin. Jehovah chose that these should be exhibited to his children, in their fullest extent, in the experience of the first man. None have ever travelled so far down into the valley of old age as he; in no other individual have the feebleness and frailties of exhausted strength, and worn-out powers, been so mournfully and so strikingly portrayed.

Seraph. But did not Jared, Methuselah, and Noah live to a greater age than Adam?

Raphael. Counting from their birth till their death, they saw more years than Adam; but, observe, in that day the seasons of infancy, childhood, and youth were long. Human beings did not arrive at full maturity until they were from sixty to a hundred years of age. Take from the life of Jared, Methuselah, or Noah, the years that passed by before they came to maturity, and you will find that, after the age of manhood, none of them remained so long on earth as did their great progenitor. Adam had no infancy. His life began with manhood; and, measuring from that point, his stay on earth was protracted many years beyond that of any of his sons. His death was deeply deplored by all his pious offspring. Long had he been their instructor in heavenly wisdom. Much had he told them of his converse with God, and with angels, before his fall; but chiefly he had encouraged and urged them to hope for redeeming mercy, through the mediation of that mighty Savior Jehovah had promised to send into the world. When their great father expired, his pious descendants felt themselves a family of orphans. None now remained who had seen humanity in its first estate of holiness and bliss. All now alive upon the earth had commenced their existence after the world was involved in sin and ruin.

Seraph. You observed, Raphael, that, in that early day, knowledge was very limited among the saints on earth, and the light they had on divine subjects was feeble and dim. When and how was this light increased for the greater edification and comfort of the people of God?

Raphael. About fifty years after the death of Adam, by the translation of Enoch. "By faith Enoch was translated, that he should not see death." This took place in a public manner, in the view of many of his brethren, as that of Elijah, afterwards, in the view of Elisha, and the ascension of Christ, in the view of his disciples. Thus the righteous of that age were assured of existence after their removal from the earth, — a doctrine which, before this event, was not so satisfactorily established, — and thus, also, they were assured of the final deliverance of their bodies from Death. Before this event, many had sunk under his awful influence; many in infancy, many in youth and middle age; and, at last, Adam himself had gone down to the grave. Till now, Death had sternly stretched his cold sceptre over the body of every human being that had entered eternity. "Shall he reign forever over our bodies? Shall they never be delivered from his tremendous sway?" were questions of amazing interest among the saints; but there was none to answer. Enoch is translated. At once, the righteous lift their heads. They see for the body, as well as the soul, victory over death; that it is the design of God that the body, made mortal by sin, shall put on immortality; and that soul and body, united in glory, shall dwell forever with the Lord.

Uriel. There was another grand purpose which the high and holy One designed to answer by the conveyance of this eminent saint, at that early day, in this extraordinary manner, to heaven. The angels were appointed "ministering spirits for the heirs of salvation." They all felt an eager desire to know as much as their Lord was pleased to reveal concerning the result of these long and diversified labors to which they were appointed. By the introduction of Enoch into heaven in a glorified state, body and soul united, the blessed One placed before all his angels a perfect sample of that ransomed multitude with which he designed to people heaven, that each might be fired to delightful activity in the holy employment assigned them.

I remember the morning well. We had been told God would that day bring one of Adam's children, in a new form, to associate with the sons of glory. I went to the portal of the heavenly city, and looked down towards the earth, when, far as angel's eye can see, I discovered the glorified saint. He was rising past the intervening worlds, as a radiant pillar of light, while the ministering angels around him appeared a bright rainbow of glory. Soon their hosannas were heard, and soon they rolled far and wide over the plains of eternity. The exulting spirit of Abel rushed forward to hail a brother redeemed from great tribulation. Cherubim and seraphim bent from their thrones to gaze on the wondrous specimen of glorified humanity. It was a triumphant day in heaven. "The morning stars sang together, and all the sons of God shouted Amen! Blessing, and honor, and glory, and power be unto Him that sitteth on the throne, and to the Lamb, forever and ever!"

Raphael. As in this age, the same gospel which proves a "savor of life unto life" to the penitent believer, is a "savor of death unto death" to the incorrigible sinner, so in that day, those notable acts of divine Providence which deeply affected the saints with a sense of their obligations to duty and devotion were by the ungodly grossly perverted, and used as the occasion of more exorbitant license to sin.

The venerable example and patriarchal authority of Adam long exerted a powerful restraining influence on mankind. This was corroborated by the faithful warnings, the eloquent and fervent public exhortations, of Enoch. But when the one was removed by death, and the other by translation, the ungodly world, freed from these checks, yielded to the strong impulse of every unholy passion, and, in the emphatic language of inspiration, "the wickedness of man was great in the earth." At first, a general spirit of worldliness pervaded all ranks of society. Men,

> "With impious hands,
> Rifled the bowels of their mother earth
> For treasures hid, and digged out ribs of gold."

With the increase of wealth grew Pride, and Fashion, with all her train of frivolous and contemptible follies, and Envy, and deadly Hate.

To this succeeded a political mania; and many a brain was goaded to frenzy in attempts to invent new methods for the organization and management of civil society. Many, whose names have long since perished from the earth, were then "men of renown," figured high in the political hemisphere, were greatly admired by themselves, and imagined they were by others. The political institutions of the first great patriarchal governor of the human race were, a few years after his death, indignantly cast aside. It was contended that they were unfriendly to civil liberty, because they contained an acknowledgment of the existence and perfections of God, the claims of his holy law, and the sacredness of the Sabbath, which God gave to man the first day after his creation.

Seraph. As Adam, the first patriarchal governor of men, acknowledged these divine truths, did no one charge him with aiming to obtain a religious establishment, and insist that the acknowledgment of these truths was but "the entering wedge" to some perfidious and horrible scheme against the welfare of the community?

Raphael. No such allegation was made; for, in that age, the minds as well as the bodies of men were very vigorous. Satan was under the necessity of reserving this folly, as materials for clamor and calumny in a more feeble-minded and stupid generation. However, the principles of those politicians of whom I spoke were founded in atheism. They acted on the doctrine which, at a later day, the devil had the impudence to advance in the presence of the Son of God, viz., that all the kingdoms of the world belong to him. The existence of Jehovah was denied, his law rejected, and the Sabbath insolently trampled under foot. A rage for idolatry ensued; for God, whose existence they had denied, and whose institutions they had insultingly spurned, "gave them up to strong delusions." They soon became the scourge and tormentors of each other. Loathsome debauchery and prostitution became general. Green-eyed Jealousy infested the family circle; cloven-tongued Slander, daughter of hell, shed her "noisome pestilence" through each neighborhood; red-handed Murder, in broad day, walked the streets; Theft and Rapine lurked in each dark lane and alley; foul-mouthed Blasphemy was heard at every corner; while villanous War, covered with ghastly wounds and scars, stalked frightfully through the land.

> "Before the palace door
> The beggar rotted, starving in his rags;
> And on the threshold of luxurious domes
> The orphan child laid down his head, and died."

"The world was filled with violence," till insulted Heaven prepared to wash the guilty generation from the polluted face of the earth. Yet even here the wonderful forbearance of God was strongly manifested. During the long period in which the ark was preparing, Noah, a preacher of righteousness, was commissioned to warn the rebels of their approaching ruin, and entreat them to repent and humble themselves before the Lord, if peradventure his anger might be turned away, and their dreadful doom averted; but his warnings by some were treated with the coldest neglect, while by others they were answered with scoffs, and taunts, and the bitterest ridicule; yet, like infidels in every age, they all had their fears lest the word of God should prove true at last, and the scornful smile often covered a trembling and an aching heart. But they had the multitude on their side. Noah was denounced throughout all the country as a fanatic, a hypocrite, an enthusiast, a madman. His name was the jest and by-word of the witty, and the song of the drunkard.

I was deeply affected with an occurrence that took place the evening before the deluge began. The ark was finished. Provisions for its destined inmates, also, had been laid up in store. The numerous band of workmen so long in Noah's employ were now dismissed. As this remarkable vessel had been constructed on the confines of a large commercial city, the wealthy, the gay, and the pleasure-loving citizens resolved, as the strongest proof they could devise of their contempt and defiance of Noah's God, and their fearlessness of the threatened judgment, to treat, on that night, all the workmen who had been employed about the ark to a splendid ball, in a spacious temple near the centre of their city, dedicated to the worship of Belus, an idol afterwards known among the Chaldeans. Every effort was made to have the entertainment of the most brilliant character, and to collect the beauty and wit of all the surrounding country. To show the grossness of insult to which they were capable of descending, they sent tickets of invitation to the younger members of Noah's family. On that evening, the angels of God were engaged in bringing to the ark the beasts and fowls designed to be preserved alive. As their angelic attendants were invisible, these creatures seemed to the eye of man to come of their own accord to take shelter in the ark. A young woman, of amiable countenance, who had buried her mother but the day before, having been on a visit to an elder sister in the city, was now returning home. Her name was Tyresah. She had excused herself from attending the ball, on account of her late bereavement. She passed by the ark about the going down of the sun. It was then the dumb animals, of all classes, were crowding in to obtain their stations. She was shocked with amazement. She knew that many of them were wild by nature, and that this strange movement was perfectly miraculous. Noah was near. She called on him, from the window of her coach, for an explanation. He told her the cry of man's wickedness had gone up to heaven before God, and that the end of all flesh was at hand. "To-morrow," said he, "God will sweep this guilty generation to eternity. Humble yourself before him; pray for mercy to your immortal soul; for as the Lord liveth, there is but a step between you and death." Tyresah was greatly affected, and wept bitterly. She urged the driver to hasten home. Her father yet retained great bodily vigor, though his locks were grizzled with age. She fell on her knees before him, told him what she had seen, and entreated him to pray that God's anger might be turned away. He was in a transport of fury as soon as the subject was mentioned, uttered a volley of oaths, demanded if she had become a fanatic — had lost her reason — had run mad. "Why went you not to the party?" She answered, she "could not go." He fiercely swore she should, called the servant to bring the carriage instantly, told her that what had alarmed her was all idle nonsense; that she must go to the ball, to drive away melancholy, and cheer her spirits: he would go with her. She saw remonstrance was vain. The carriage came. He handed her in, then lifted a little son of five years old, and entered himself, bidding the servant to drive with all speed to the place of amusement. I followed them, to witness the result. A gay multitude were assembled to spend in sinful revelry the night ordained to be their last. As they quaffed the wine, they "praised the gods of gold, of silver, of brass, of iron, of wood, and of stone." For some time, a pensive and serious air sat on the brow of the young and beautiful Tyresah; but she was surrounded by a crowd of admirers, and Noah, and his ark, and the threatened deluge were the subjects of perpetual jest and merriment. At length, her seriousness gave way. It was only the effect of alarm; for the Spirit of God had already forsaken the earth. Gradually she became gay, excessively gay, laughed at her former fears, and joined the infatuated company in scoffing at the warnings of God. I returned to the ark; but often, through the night, the sounds of wild extravagant mirth and frolic were heard. They continued even till the break of day.

The morning arose brilliant and beautiful. The sun appeared, and smiled upon the green earth from an unclouded sky. No token of wrath was visible ; but as the report of the wild beasts and fowls entering the ark on the preceding evening had by this time spread through the city, a numerous throng, impelled by eager curiosity, hurried early to the place, to see this strange sight. At this juncture, a large and merry marriage party from the country drove up. They were in haste to reach the temple of Belus, and share in the festive mirth ere its close. Before the "eastern blooming bride" moved a superb band of lively and enchanting music. Surprised at finding so many of the jolly revellers collected here, they halted, and the music ceased. Noah's family were just entering the ark as these multitudes met before it. He himself, strongly impelled by compassion, paused at the door, and turned to give them a last address. The day of wrath, he assured them, was come, and would presently array around them all its terrors. It was now too late to secure their earthly lives. The death of the body was inevitable. "But who," said he, "can fathom the mercy of God? Prostrate yourselves before him, and entreat that he will not destroy your souls and bodies in hell forever." With awful solemnity, he appealed to gray-headed fathers of the assembly, his acquaintances and neighbors from early youth ; but they hurled upon him their horrible imprecations, and madly cursed his God. He then turned, and began to speak to a crowd of children and youth that stood near. At this, the father of Tyresah caught up his little son, sprang forward, and, holding him up before the righteous man, bade him "curse the abominable old hypocrite—curse his God!" The child attempted to stammer forth the hideous execrations his father dictated; others cried, "Stone him with stones!" but ere their fury could find weapons, I pushed him into the ark, and, according to my commission from above, "shut him in." When they saw the door closed, their madness was uncontrollable; and, as if possessed by the same hellish demon, all, with one voice, exclaimed, "Set fire to his pitchy den; and let him have a conflagration, instead of a flood." Some ran to bring fire, and others to collect the fagots; but at that moment a dense, dark fragment of cloud eclipsed the sun,* and every star of heaven looked down with unwonted brightness upon the earth. Another moment, and the angel of destruction, a tall, terrible form, appeared standing on the tower of the temple of Belus. Shuddering horror seized all who saw him. Thrice he glared frightfully around, and thrice he flapped his sable wings over the quaking city. Then, with a mighty voice, such as earth, since her creation, had never heard, he called to the great deep to come forth from her storehouses. He called to the clouds of heaven to muster all their armies, and execute the vengeance of the great God. At his word, all the storms of the north and south awoke, and prepared to discharge their magazines of wrath upon the earth. Instantly all heaven was wrapped in blackness. But who may speak of the terror of sinners in that hour? Some fled, they knew not where, in search of refuge; others stretched their hands towards heaven for help, and cried to the God they had despised. But the day of mercy was past.

* Fearful sights and appalling prodigies preceded the destruction of Jerusalem. See the accounts given by St. Luke, and by Josephus.

He answered their prayers in awful peals of thunder, and the shriek of despair was lost in the fury of contending tempests. Amidst the confusion and wild uproar of the convulsed and distracted elements, I could mark the mighty angel of destruction putting forth all his tremendous energies to drive the ruin on. He uprooted the hills, burst the rocks, and rent the earth, till from her deep centre the troubled waters spouted up, "ten thousand fathoms wide, ten thousand fathoms high." Nor did he wait for the heavens to distil their showers in the usual form, but rushed fiercely up, and tore the thick cloud asunder, till its contents were precipitated in foaming cataracts, while through the tortured air I perceived a ghastly cloud of guilty ghosts going up, blaspheming, to their last dread account at the bar of God.

Innumerable buildings were prostrated, and immense destruction of human life effected, by the breaking up of the "fountains of the great deep," and the opening of the "windows of heaven;" yet here and there a strong house still resisted the shock of the tempest, and braved the violence of the current, which now rushed with singular vehemence over the plain. From these issued deep groans and unavailing prayers, mingled with distracted screams and bitter lamentation. Fragments of houses, furniture, garments, and dead bodies of beasts and men, were every moment drifting by, with, now and then, a "strong swimmer" still buffeting the waves and struggling for life. At length, the ark itself rose from its resting-place, and began to move with the waters. On perceiving this, the pious family within united their voices in a solemn hymn of praise and adoration to God, their Preserver. The direction it took was along the great street of the now ruined city. A huge stone building of strongest masonry was still standing, and from within came the voice of wailing, lamentation, and woe; the waves, already near the top of the walls, were rapidly rising higher and higher, as if still hungry for their prey. I looked till the roof was burst open from within, and several miserable wretches came forth and stood upon it, silent and shivering in the extremities of horror. Among these I marked the unhappy Tyresah. Her reason was totally dethroned; her cheek was sunken and ghastly pale; the wild, irregular glare of insanity shot from her eyes; her gray-headed father held her by the arm, while with the other hand he sustained the little favorite son. The swelling waters now dashed quite over the roof, and rippled among their feet; another surge rose to their knees; another came and swept the child from the hand of the affrighted father. Tyresah saw him sink among the waves, and answered his last cry with a frenzied and fiendish laugh; then turned her maniac visage, and looked full in her father's face, as she pointed to the ark, now passing near them, furiously exclaiming, "Father! curse the abominable old hypocrite! — Curse his God!" He spoke not, but

> "Lively bright horror and amazing anguish
> Stared through his eyelids."

At that instant, the strong building gave way; the raging billows flashed and boiled over them, while the shrill tempest went howling by, his voice no longer interrupted by the shrieks, and wailings, and blasphemy of man.

A few there were whose destruction was more protracted. They attained a point of land of a great elevation, from whence they looked down on the resolute advance of the raging waters. Finding that prayers addressed to Heaven were unheeded and fruitless, they turned their supplication to the waves, and wept, and wrung their hands, and besought the waters to stop the pursuit, and spare their lives. The waters were deaf and inexorable; the angry upward march was continued, till the fugitives, driven to their last retreat, were overcome and washed into eternity.

The dominion of Ocean was now complete. Earth was buried. The vast billows of the shoreless deep, as if flushed with victory, and proud of the wide range and unlimited ascendency they had obtained, wheeled, and tossed, and foamed, and practised their huge, unwieldy gambols, above the tops of the tallest mountains.

Raphael paused, when all the splendid assembly raised an anthem of praise to the Most High. The sentiments were exceedingly elevated and grand. In the language of mortals, their song might be rendered thus: —

"Loud hallelujahs to the Lord,
From distant worlds, where creatures dwell;
Let heaven begin the solemn word,
And sound it dreadful down to hell.

"The Lord, how absolute he reigns!
Let every angel bend the knee;
Sing of his love in heavenly strains,
And speak how fierce his terrors be.

"The world's foundation by his hand
Is poised, and shall forever stand;

He binds the ocean in his chain,
Lest it should drown the earth again.

"When earth was covered with a flood,
Which high above the mountains stood,
He thundered, and the ocean fled,
And sought its own appointed bed.

"Let clouds, and winds, and waves agree
To join their praise with blazing fire;
Let the firm earth and rolling sea
In this eternal song conspire.

"Speak of the wonders of that love
Which Gabriel plays on every chord;
From all below, and all above,
Loud hallelujahs to the Lord."

ANECDOTE OF REV. E. F. HATFIELD.

In the month of June, 1848, I labored for some weeks in Calloway county, Missouri. Many of the early settlers in that county were religious people; and the ordinances of the gospel have now been sustained among them, with little interruption, for quite a number of years. About the year 1833 or '34, brother Hatfield, now of New York, labored among this people with very great success. He was with them at a sacramental meeting of five or six days' continuance. He preached every day. The gospel was accompanied with the Holy Ghost sent down from heaven. Christians were revived, backsliders were reclaimed, and many souls were brought from the bondage of sin into the liberty of the children of God. During my visit, in 1848, I was delighted to find, that after the lapse of so many years, the memory of that brother, who had been so much blessed as the messenger of God among them, was still affectionately embalmed in their hearts. Knowing that I had been much associated with brother Hatfield since he left Missouri, they called on me for such portions of his subsequent history as were in my possession. Among many other facts, I gave them the following anecdote, which, as it was favorably received, I now lay before the reader.

In the winter of 1836, the Lord poured out his

Spirit, in a remarkable manner, on the Seventh Presbyterian Church in the city of New York, of which brother Hatfield was then the pastor, and, indeed, of which he is the pastor now. The awakening was extensive and powerful. The number of serious inquirers was great, and soon there were many cases of hopeful conversion. As is usual in such an attitude of affairs, the tidings went abroad that the Lord had visited his people of the Seventh Presbyterian Church, and the friends of Zion in neighboring churches would occasionally come to weep and to rejoice with them.

Brother John —— —— was pastor of a church not far distant. That church had been blessed, in years gone by, with precious revivals. Many of its most efficient members had been born to God in those interesting seasons. Such individuals, of course, when they could find opportunity, that is, on Sabbath afternoon or evening, when they felt at liberty to leave their own place of worship, would go to brother Hatfield's church, and share in the blessings of the revival. With brother John —— —— my acquaintance has been very limited. I have never had the opportunity to hear him "define his position" in relation to revivals. But it seems that his zeal did not carry him so far as to approve of members going from his own church in order to witness the progress of a revival in another. And yet, from Sabbath to Sabbath, as he appeared in the pulpit to address his people, empty pews, with alarming frequency, were yawning in every quarter of the church, and the evil was evidently on the increase. Brother John determined that the offenders should meet with speedy rebuke. Accordingly, one Sabbath morning, when they were mostly in their pews, at their own church, brother John arose in the pulpit. Perhaps it could scarcely be said, as in the case of Goldsmith's village schoolmaster,

"Well had the boding tremblers learned to trace
The day's disasters in his morning face."

But when he announced his text, they began to look one upon another. His text was Matt. xi. 8: "What went ye out for to see?" This text he repeated, looking earnestly, now on one part of the congregation, and now on another. As he fixed his eyes on those on the right hand of the pulpit,—and a number of the delinquents were there,—he demanded, "What went ye out for to see?" Then turning to those on the left hand, he repeated, "What went ye out for to see?" And then the assembly in front were addressed, "What went ye out for to see?" The preacher, (I pretend not to give his identical words, but the substance, merely,) according to the good old custom, raised from the text an important *doctrine,* to wit: That when he preached in that pulpit, there was no propriety in those who ought to attend his church, going to hear or see what might be transacting in other churches. "What went ye out for to see?"

Brother John maintained that any departure from the above doctrine was unauthorized: 1. By Scripture; 2. By the confession of faith; and 3. By the Catechisms, both the Larger and the Shorter. And to many of his hearers the sermon abounded in "striking" remarks. It was not long, however, until there came one that had "escaped," and told brother Hatfield. On the Sabbath afternoon, therefore, when many of the same persons were present, of whom it had been demanded, "What went ye out for to see?" brother Hatfield arose in his pulpit, and announced his text: "Go and show *John* again those things which ye do hear and see: the blind receive their sight, and the lame walk, the lepers are cleansed, and the deaf hear, the dead are raised up, and the poor have the gospel preached to them. And blessed is *he* whosoever shall not be offended in me." (Matt. xi. 5, 6.)

A friend desires to be informed of the difference between Calvinism and the Fatalism maintained by Mahometans. I answer, Fatalism teaches that all things are governed by blind, *undesigning* fate—atheism asserts that all things are the sport of blind chance and contingency. The Bible teaches that "all things are of God." On this holy ground Calvinism plants her standard, distant alike from the two extremes of blind fate and blind contingence, (Truth lies in the middle,) and rejoices, with joy unspeakable, that an infinitely INTELLIGENT and BENEVOLENT BEING, for his own glory and the greatest good, "works all things after the counsel of his own will."

THE MISSISSIPPI JUDGE.

In the month of February, 1839, I was riding, in company with a Mississippi judge, along the bank of the great river which gives its name to the state in which he resided. Said he, " There are some portions of the Bible that are very difficult to be understood, and require, I should think, a great deal of explanation."

" Mention, if you please, some of the passages to which you refer."

" Well," said the judge, " one of them is found in the writings of Solomon, where he says, ' Cast thy bread upon the waters; for thou shalt find it after many days.' Now, suppose a man should cast his bread on the Mississippi River, — would he ever find it again ? "

" The text you have quoted, judge, is the first verse of the eleventh chapter of the book of Ecclesiastes. It is a beautiful text, and teaches a great lesson. You must observe, that in the sacred Scriptures that is often called bread out of which bread is made, — bread-corn, for example ; because out of it bread is manufactured. Thus we read, that in the days of Joseph ' the dearth was in all lands ; but in all the land of Egypt there was bread.' That is, there was bread-corn there, out of which bread could be made. Now, Egypt was the most famous of all the ancient countries for the production of bread. Very soon after Abraham came first into Canaan, 'there was a famine in the land; and Abram went down into Egypt, to sojourn there.' (Gen. xii. 10.) Again, in the days of Isaac, 'there was a famine in the land; and the Lord appeared unto him, and said, Go down into Egypt.' (Gen. xxvi. 1, 2.) In like manner, Jacob was driven by famine into Egypt. Egypt was the storehouse of bread to the ancient world, and continued so, in fact, until the time of the Roman empire. The ship in which Paul sailed to Rome was bound from Alexandria, in Egypt, to Rome, loaded with bread-corn; for when the storm came upon them, you read that 'they lightened the ship, and cast out the wheat into the sea.' Now, Egypt being thus famous for the production of bread, and Israel having sojourned there during so many years, it is not strange that Egyptian scenery should mingle with the Bible language on this subject. The unparalleled fertility of Egypt was owing to the annual overflowing of the Nile. At a certain season, every year, immense tracts of the level country were entirely inundated. When the water was about receding, the husbandman would take his seed-corn, and sow it over these wide fields. The grain would fall on the face of the water, and sink down into the soft loam that was just below. Presently the water was gone; and that grain, cast thus upon the waters, would spring up, and yield an abundant harvest.

"Now, the command is, To you who have wealth, disperse it abroad among the poor and needy. Do not aim to consume it all yourself, but appropriate a portion of it, as the wise husbandman appropriates a portion of his bread-corn when he uses it for seed, and you, also, in due time, shall enjoy an abundant harvest. 'Cast thy bread upon the waters; for thou shalt find it after many days.'"

"That is, indeed, an instructive and valuable lesson," said the judge, "and beautifully inculcated. And now I am encouraged to mention another text which I have not been able satisfactorily to understand."

"I shall be gratified to hear you."

"The text to which I now refer," continued the judge, "is found in Rev. xiv. 13: 'And I heard a voice from heaven, saying unto me, Write, Blessed are the dead which die in the Lord from henceforth: yea, saith the Spirit, that they may rest from their labors; and their works do follow them.' The difficulty in my mind is with the words, 'from henceforth' — 'Blessed are the dead that die in the Lord from henceforth.' Have not the dead, in every age, who have died in the Lord, been blessed? Were not those blessed who died in the Lord in the time of Abel and of Noah? Were not those who died in the Lord blessed in the days of Abraham, and Joseph, and Moses? In short, has there ever been a period when those were not blessed who have died in the Lord? What, then, can be the meaning of the words 'from henceforth'?"

"You must observe, judge, that the book of Revelation contains a prophetic history of the church, from the apostolic age until the end of the world. The Scriptures clearly teach, that while we are justified before God only for the sake of Christ, and our own obedience is entitled to nothing on the score of merit, yet the Lord graciously rewards his people according to their works; and this is held up before the church as a motive why we should 'always abound in the work of the Lord.' Now, in the present day, the plain Christian has an opportunity of accomplishing much more in the vineyard of Christ than could have been accomplished with the same means five hundred years ago. Suppose your lot had been cast in the world as early as the thirteenth century, and that you had then set your heart on doing good to men by circulating the word of God. At that period, the art of printing was unknown; and one copy of the Bible in England cost the sum of thirty pounds sterling, — that is, about one hundred and forty-five dollars of our money. Now, for the cost of one Bible at that time, you can at this day put in circulation more than five hundred copies. The same principle will apply to other good books, and to religious tracts. How great, then, are the facilities for doing good which have come up in divine providence, and are within the reach of those who live in the present age! These facilities extend to other departments of Christian enterprise, as Sabbath schools, missions, &c. It may be affirmed that additional value is given to time, and additional value is given to health, and to influence, when such precious opportunities of 'abounding in the work of the Lord' are brought even to our door. We live in an age which

'Prophets and kings desired to see,
But died without the sight.'

"Now, the book of Revelation contains a prophetic view of the progress of the church, from the apostolic day until the end of time. 'The Lamb in the midst of the throne' has taken the book of God's eternal counsels, and as he opens seal after seal, the future condition of the church rises to view. Age after age of trial, perplexity, and persecution passes by — periods in which the church, like Noah surrounded by the wreck and desolations of the deluge, finds that the utmost that she can do is to 'remain alive.' (Gen. vii. 23.) But the opening of the seals goes on. Page after page of futurity rises in sight; when, behold, a day appears, in which the iron rod of persecution is broken, and the church is free. The light of divine truth shines clearly, and Zion's King 'walks in the midst of the golden candlesticks.' The minister of the gospel is blessed in his labors. His preaching is accompanied with the Holy Ghost sent down from heaven. The members of the church find that the vineyard of God furnishes to each the opportunity of becoming a successful and honored laborer. One can circulate Bibles by the thousand; another rejoices in the Sabbath school enterprise, and sees how he can benefit immortal souls, and lay up treasure in heaven; another beholds the missionary field opening to him a prospect full of immortality. Every child of God discovers that 'the time to favor Zion, yea, the set time, is come,' and that now he has before him an open door for the wise and happy employment of health, time, influence, wealth, every talent that he possesses, for the glory of God and the everlasting good of his kingdom. Is it strange that at the dawn of such a day of salvation in the apostle's vision, he should record the passage under consideration? — 'And I heard a voice from heaven, saying unto me, Write, Blessed *are* the dead which die in the Lord from henceforth: yea, saith the Spirit, that they may rest from their labors; and their works do follow them.' "

"Very satisfactory," said the judge. "And what

rich and delightful meaning the text possesses when viewed in that light! But as you speak of the unprecedented circulation of the Bible among all people at this day, allow me to ask, is this great movement of the church noticed in any of the predictions of the ancient prophets?"

"Certainly, judge; it is noticed very particularly by the prophet Isaiah, in the third verse of the second chapter of his book: 'Out of Zion shall go forth the law and the word of the Lord from Jerusalem.' Zion and Jerusalem are well-known titles of the visible church. The word of the Lord, his law, and his gospel shall go forth, and a glorious moral revolution shall ensue. Hear the prophet specify the particulars: 'The Lord's house shall be established in the top of the mountains, and exalted above the hills.' That is, the worship and the service of God shall stand higher in the estimation of men than every earthly interest. Higher than politics, higher than commerce, higher than agriculture, the Lord's house shall be established in the top of the mountains, and exalted above the hills, and all nations shall flow unto it. 'And many people shall go and say, Come ye, and let us go up to the mountain of the Lord, to the house of the God of Jacob; and he will teach us of his ways, and we will walk in his paths. And he shall judge among the nations, and shall rebuke many people; and they shall beat their swords into ploughshares, and their spears into pruning-hooks: nation shall not lift up sword against nation, neither shall they learn war any more.'"

"That is, indeed," answered the judge, "a very notable prediction of the universal circulation of the Bible in the latter day, and of the happy results that shall follow. I have one question more. Perhaps you will smile when I mention it. Is there any prediction of railroad travelling and steam cars, in the Bible ?"

"Prophecy was not given merely to entertain or gratify our curiosity. 'All Scripture is given by inspiration of God, and is profitable for doctrine, for reproof, for correction, for instruction in righteousness.' And yet, in answer to your question, the student of the Bible, when he beholds the long trains of railroad cars, each bearing six or eight hundred passengers, darting by each other with the speed of birds on the wing, is forcibly reminded of the prophecy of Daniel xii. 4: 'Many shall run to and fro, and knowledge shall be increased.' In the book of Nahum, chap. ii. verse 4, there is this remarkable passage: 'The chariots shall rage in the streets, they shall *justle* one against another in the broad ways: they shall seem like *torches*, they shall *run like the lightnings*.' Who that has travelled in these conveyances has not felt them 'justle one against another in the broad ways'? and who that has looked on the fiery horses, speeding on their way in the night, could not say, 'they seem like torches, they run like lightning'?

"Well," said the judge, "the word of God is now to me a source of great delight. But O, I lived many years in sin. I am astonished when I review the stupidity and blindness of my former life. I lived more than forty years anxious for the world, and careful about my reputation. But in all that forty years, I had not spent one half hour in trying to please God. My Creator, my Redeemer, were wholly forgotten and neglected. When my mind was roused to look at the awful fact, I could scarcely live under the thought. I went directly to our minister, and asked him to give me the earliest opportunity of coming before the church and the congregation, and confessing my shame and sorrow that I had so long denied Christ before men, and neglected the great salvation."

RECOLLECTIONS OF GIDEON BLACKBURN.

Gideon Blackburn was in the prime of life at that period when the great revival of 1800 visited the population of the western country. He had been preaching, it is true, quite a number of years — how many I do not exactly know — before the commencement of that extraordinary visitation from on high; but the portion of time embraced between the years 1800 and 1830 may be put down as the meridian of his ministry. Most of the great events of his life appear to have occurred between those dates; while it should be borne in mind, that both the morning and the evening of his days were crowned with varied and extensive usefulness. A full and faithful record of the great and good results of his long and laborious life would fill the pages of a very voluminous work. A mere sketch of a few important facts is all that will here be attempted.

1. His Creator had bestowed upon him an exceedingly fine person. He was rather above the middle size, and well proportioned. His form was that which unites strength and activity in a very high degree. Thus it was that the "Lord of the harvest" had evidently fitted him for the important part he was designed to act in the great field where his lot was cast. The

exposure he was called to endure, together with the arduous and multiplied labors that devolved upon him, must have soon crushed a man of ordinary constitution. But to him the promise was made good, "As thy days, so shall thy strength be." While as yet the country was very new, no regular roads established, and the rivers in general without ferries, he traversed almost every part of the great west where settlements had been formed. He penetrated the canebrakes, he travelled through the wilderness, he swam the rivers, "always abounding in the work of the Lord." In very many of the newly-formed neighborhoods, he was the first to set up the standard of his divine Master. Should you now visit Knoxville, Nashville, Gallatin, Huntsville, Cincinnati, Louisville, or almost any of the prominent cities of the west, and inquire of the aged people concerning the state of the church at the period of their first recollections, you will hear the name of Gideon Blackburn pronounced, with a frequency and a fervor of enthusiasm which show how intimately his life and labors are interwoven with the early religious history of those sections of our country.

2. He had a singularly captivating countenance, in which benignity and authority were delightfully blended. When he arose in the house of God, and cast over the assembly that benevolent and commanding *look*, every human being in the congregation felt the power of his presence. His voice was musical and attractive to an extent that enabled him at once to seize the attention of any company or crowd which he undertook to address. In the court-yard, or in the market-house, on the public square, or on the crowded wharf, wherever the tones of his remarkable voice reached the

ear, and his graceful and impressive attitude caught the eye, the multitude was instantly reduced to silence and attention.

The venerable Dr. Griffin has remarked, that in attempting to promote religion among the careless and the ungodly, the first great object at which we should aim is, to secure "attention" to the gospel. There is no doubt that a leading instrumentality in that immense success which attended the preaching of Gideon Blackburn, is to be found in that extraordinary power, with which he was endowed by his Creator, for arresting the attention of men. Sinners would press near to him in crowds, and while they were melted into tears, they wished those overwhelming addresses to continue. They were reluctant to have the meeting close, and the opportunity pass away: even children would designedly throw themselves in his way, that he might say a word to them concerning the salvation of their souls. I remember, distinctly, when he had spent a night at my father's house, and was about to depart in the morning, that I, though then very young, went out and took his horse by the bridle, and stood there till he came. There was no need for me there at the horse's bridle; but it was my wish to throw myself in the good man's way, that he might speak to me of the great salvation. He did speak; and not only the substance of what he then said, but the very words in which it was expressed, are indelibly engraven on the tablet of my heart.

There was something in Blackburn's manner of preaching, that fastened his text, for life, on the memory of his hearers. You will mark this peculiarity whenever you hear the old people, at this day, speak of his

30

preaching ; and one will say, "I heard Blackburn preach at Knoxville, in the year 1805, on this text, (Ex. xii. 30:) 'And there was a great cry in Egypt: for there was not a house where there was not one dead.'" Another will say, "I shall never forget the sermon which he preached at Maryville, in 1807, on the text, (Ex. xiv. 15,) 'Speak to the children of Israel, that they go forward.'" A third will speak up, "I heard him at Nashville, in 1810, and his text was, (John i. 14,) 'And the word was made flesh, and dwelt among us, and we beheld his glory, the glory of the only begotten of the Father, full of grace and truth.'" On my arrival in Boston, May, 1849, I found venerable old deacons who spoke with the warmest interest of the preaching of Blackburn in Boston, as early as the year 1802 or 3, when evangelical religion in Boston was very low. And I was delighted to find that these old men could yet repeat the texts on which those discourses were founded, that so much encouraged and revived the people of God. At Ipswich, in Massachusetts, I was addressed thus by a man advanced in years: —

"You are from the west?"

"Yes, sir."

"Well, I heard a man from your country preach, many years ago. His name was Blackburn. I shall never forget that sermon. His text was, 'The tree of life, that bare twelve manner of fruits, and yielded her fruit every month: and the leaves of the tree were for the healing of the nations.'" (Rev. xxii. 2.)

I know no reason for the texts on which he preached being so accurately and so long remembered, except that his preaching abounded in *exposition* of the sacred text. His aim was, to place the truth, the beauty, the grandeur of God's word in a clear and forcible light before his audience; and this he accomplished so successfully, that an impression was made on the minds of his hearers, which could never be effaced.

3. A strong and unwavering confidence in God was another characteristic of Gideon Blackburn. For this he was remarkable when young, and this he retained through all the multiplied vicissitudes of his checkered and eventful life. He had the care of a large family, when the west was a wilderness, and when provision for the support of a minister's family was a thing scarcely known; yet, by his remarkable industry, and his firm reliance on the promises of a covenant-keeping God, he was enabled to bring up and educate that family, so that its members became a blessing to the church, and a blessing to the world. All his children who attained maturity made an early consecration of themselves to God in the gospel. Two of his sons became useful ministers. They are now gone from earth. All the surviving members of the family are adorning the gospel which their father preached, by an irreproachable and consistent walk and conversation. How should our hearts rise in gratitude to God, when he sets the seal of his divine approbation to the life and labors of a self-denying minister, by crowning with blessings from above his children, and his children's children! I have repeatedly visited the family of Gideon Blackburn since he has been called to "go up higher" in the temple of God. I have looked upon his aged widow. I have looked upon his surviving children and grandchildren; and I have been pleasingly reminded of that precious promise which the "God of glory" gave to Abraham, "the father of the

faithful," — "I will bless thee, and thou shalt be a blessing."

The venerable Dr. Clelland, of Kentucky, gave me this anecdote of a little grandchild of Gideon Blackburn. At a sacramental meeting in Woodford county, Kentucky, when the elders of the church had met to converse with those who were desirous of uniting with the body of professed Christians, among other candidates was a very small girl. She was a granddaughter of Blackburn. Her apparent age was not more than six or seven years. Blackburn was moderator of the session, and conducted the examination. When the turn of this little girl came, her answers were most satisfactory. Her profession of repentance for sin was distinct and clear; and her love to Christ, and her trust in him for pardon and salvation, were expressed in the most appropriate and decided terms. But she was so little: that was all the difficulty. Others were received into the communion of the church; but she was advised to wait longer. After some five or six months, another communion season came round. The session met. Blackburn again was moderator. A number of applicants appeared, and among them this same little girl — clear, decided, firm in her attachment to Christ and his cause, but still very small. Again she was advised to wait. Some months afterwards, when she had made her third application, with a similar result, she lifted up her little eyes, swimming with tears, and said, "Grandfather, how old must I be before I can love the Savior?"

It should here be remarked, that Blackburn's views of early piety were scriptural and unwavering; but there is often unbelief in the church, that cramps the minister; and this being his own grandchild, he thought it not best to take that stand which he would have taken in the case of another. The early history of this little girl is an instance of the blessing which crowned this good man's family.

4. Gideon Blackburn was distinguished by zeal for the advancement of the gospel, and for the salvation of men. In the early part of his ministry, there was little or no support provided by the church for the family of a minister. Like the apostle Paul, Blackburn labored with his own hands for the supply of the temporal wants of his family, while he kept the banner of the Redeemer constantly unfurled. I have heard his neighbors tell how he would maul two hundred rails in the fore part of the day, and then mount his horse, and ride twelve or fifteen miles, and preach the gospel to some little assembly of plain people in the evening. Sometimes he labored on a farm, sometimes he taught school, to sustain a dependent family; but the fire of divine love burned continually on the altar of his heart, and the "trumpet of the gospel" was ever at his mouth; and verily, when blown by him, it gave no "uncertain sound." When, at the age of eight or nine years, I sat under his ministry, and felt the impressiveness and power of his awful appeals, repeatedly was I reminded of the record that is given of the preaching of his divine Master — "The people were astonished at his doctrine; for he taught them as one having authority, and not as the scribes." (Matt. vii. 28, 29.) I distinctly remember a conversation among some intelligent Virginians, after they had attended one of Blackburn's overwhelming discourses. They spoke of the preaching of the celebrated William

Graham, so long and so extensively a blessing to the churches in Virginia. They spoke of the preaching of James Waddell, the noted blind preacher. Some of their number had sat under the ministry of both of these distinguished men; and after commending these favored servants of God in very exalted terms, their conversation was directed to Blackburn, to whose discourse they had just been attending; and one then made an observation which I shall remember to the close of life. Speaking of Blackburn, he said, "Indeed, he is the great Elijah of our day."

Beyond a doubt, if future generations receive an accurate history of our country, Gideon Blackburn will be regarded as the early "apostle of the west." I have no hesitation in pronouncing, that Isaac Anderson, John McCampbell, David Nelson, and many others who have risen to great usefulness and distinction in the church of God, were much aided and blessed, in the commencement of their ministry, by the beams that streamed forth from that "burning and shining light" which a gracious God had kindled up in the heart of the west, in the very morning of its Christian history. And, with ample justice to all the excellent men that have since appeared, — the Joshuas, the Samuels, and the Nathans that have blessed the western church at a later day, — I may apply to this subject the words of inspiration — "There arose not a prophet since in Israel like unto Moses, whom the Lord knew face to face."

In conclusion, I must record two notable illustrations of the zeal of Blackburn in his Master's service. The first is the case of John Glocester, a colored man, and a slave. In the revival of 1800, John was a convert.

Pious slaves often took part in the prayer meetings of those days. John was very able and edifying in his prayers. Blackburn heard John offer up a prayer in more instances than one. He also heard some of his attempts at exhortation; and he concluded that if John had his liberty, and were properly educated, he might be useful as a preacher of the gospel, especially among his own people. "Immediately he conferred not with flesh and blood." His maxim was, "Whatever ought to be done can be done." Soon John Glocester had his liberty. In due time, he received a respectable education, and became an ordained minister. His career was one of eminent usefulness. In a few years, he settled in the city of Philadelphia, and collected a church of colored people. In the year 1819, when I first attended the General Assembly of the Presbyterian church, I found John Glocester in Philadelphia, at the head of a large and respectable African church. I attended a communion season with them. The communicants were in number about two hundred and fifty; and, on the same day, eleven well-dressed colored infants were brought before the congregation, and solemnly dedicated to God in the ordinance of baptism. I was deeply affected by this tender and impressive scene. There was much of the venerable and the apostolic about John Glocester. He possessed in the pulpit extraordinary eloquence and power. He has long since gone to his reward.

The other example of enlightened zeal to which I referred, is found in the efforts of Blackburn in the cause of foreign missions. Long before the American Board, or the General Assembly's Board, was formed, or thought of, this man of prodigious, heaven-born enterprise had planted Christian schools at a number of important points among the Indians on the south side of the Tennessee River. Although the cry for his labors came up from every quarter of the American settlements that were then forming in the west, yet, in the ardor of his flaming zeal, he would cross the great river, and, by the aid of an interpreter, tell to listening and weeping multitudes of copper-colored savages the story of God's wondrous love to sinful man, and how the beloved Son of God agonized in Gethsemane, and suffered on the cross, that our souls might be redeemed from death. These early missionary efforts were warmly sanctioned by Return J. Meigs, Indian agent of the general government at that period. The schools were afterwards patronized by the general assembly of the Presbyterian church. It is believed that much good was accomplished; but the entire results can only be known when the books are opened in the great day.

Rev. Charles Coffin, D. D., who was a disciple of Dr. Samuel Spring, of Newburyport, Mass., gave me the following anecdote of Blackburn: When quite a young man, he was travelling in one of the Atlantic states. He had been desired by some of the people of a certain village or town to preach them a sermon. He consented, and when he was able to fix on the time, he sent an appointment to the place, never dreaming but that it would be acceptable to the resident minister, should there be one, that the people should hear the gospel from the lips of another witness of Jesus, as well as from himself. Blackburn himself had much of the spirit manifested by Moses, when Eldad and Medad prophesied in the camp, and a young man came and said, "My lord Moses, forbid them." And Moses said,

"Enviest thou for my sake? Would God that all the Lord's people were prophets, and that the Lord would put his spirit upon them." (Num. xi. 29.) Such was the spirit of Moses; but not so was it with the presiding genius of the village above mentioned. He seemed rather to be animated by the spirit of Daniel's ram, which the prophet so graphically describes, (Dan. viii. 4:) "I saw the ram pushing westward, and northward, and southward, so that no beast might stand before him." This man received Blackburn's note, but refused to make the appointment. Blackburn came at the specified time, and learning that the minister had refused to give publicity to his appointment, he went to his house and inquired for the facts of the case. The minister attempted to be very dry, distant, dignified, and told him that he was not willing that he should preach to the people at that place, and therefore he had refused to make any appointment. It must be borne in mind that Blackburn's person was remarkable for elegance and gracefulness, and that he had a presence of peculiar solemnity and power. As soon as he was told how his proposal to preach had been rejected, he arose and stood for several seconds in the most solemn attitude, right in front of the now fluttered and agitated man of dignity. "Sir," said he, "I have a very painful duty to perform, but it is imperatively enjoined by my Lord and Master. When he sent forth his disciples to preach the everlasting gospel to dying men, he laid upon them this command: 'Whosoever will not receive you, nor hear your words, shake off the dust of your feet for a testimony against them.' Sir, as a rejected minister of the Lord Jesus Christ, I shake off the dust of my feet for a testimony against you!" As he thus spoke, he extended, in his own impressive manner, the right foot, and shook it with a deliberate solemnity that was awful. He then extended the left foot, and shook it in like manner; then turning entirely away, he left the important "place man" to his own meditations. This minister's name was Flint. "Sir," said Dr. Coffin, when he told me the story, "Flint as he was, the performance of this awful duty by Gideon Blackburn made him turn as white as ashes."

CAMP MEETINGS.

The origin of camp meetings in the United States was among the members of the Presbyterian church. They were first held in Logan county, Kentucky, during the revival of 1800. The multitudes which came together were so great, that accommodations could not be found in the neighborhood of the place of worship. Many of these people had recently removed to the west from Virginia, North Carolina, or Pennsylvania. On the road, while they were removing, they had *camped out*, and cooked their own provisions, and provided their own lodgings. The idea originated among them, during the great revival, that they could camp out near the place of worship, and take care of themselves, as well as they had done on the road, while on their journey. The experiment succeeded admirably. The country being new, this mode of holding large meetings seemed peculiarly adapted to their circumstances. Indeed, it was believed to possess a striking resemblance to the "feast of tabernacles" in the Old Testament church. Moreover, these meetings were crowned with precious divine blessings. Among the Presbyterians of the west and south, also the Methodists, the Baptists, the Cumberland Presbyterians, and other denominations, such meetings have been held, with great and good results. In many parts of the west and south, they have now worshipped in this manner, occasionally, for the space of fifty years. During that extensive and powerful revival in the state of Ohio, from 1828 till 1831, quite a number of camp meetings were held, at which many thousands assembled to worship God. One of the ministers engaged in these meetings spoke on the subject thus : —

"The camp meetings in Ohio were not undertaken without much serious and prayerful deliberation. The ministers of Jesus Christ in that country saw, with much concern, an immense population spreading over the land, while the regular preaching of the gospel was neglected by at least two thirds of this living multitude. They also saw a deep, dark, blaspheming infidelity, rolling far and wide through the country, scoffing at the Bible, cursing religious tracts, trampling on the Sabbath, and breathing out bitterness against all that is sacred. They saw that if the deadly pestilence was suffered to spread and extend its pernicious influence a few years longer, not only would our religious institutions be destroyed, but our civil liberties would be jeopardized ; the monster would break down our churches, set up the guillotine, and dip its hands in the blood of the innocent, as deep as did the infidels of France during the 'Reign of Terror.' They felt that something must be done to arrest the conquests of the enemy, who was 'coming in like a flood ;' and the only weapon with which they could successfully oppose him, was 'the sword of the Spirit, which is the word of God.' And as the multitudes, among whom the plague was raging, could not be assembled in the regular houses of worship, the 'soldiers of the cross' resolved to *take the field* 'in the name of the Lord of hosts, the God of the armies of Israel.' Preparations were made, seats in a shady grove sufficient to accommodate a vast assembly, and a 'pulpit of wood,' erected. The day appointed arrived, 'and all the people came out by hundreds and by thousands.' It was a season 'of the right hand of the Most High.' The tide of war was rolled back from the gates of Zion, and trembling was in the camp of the enemy. The infidel renounced his blasphemy; the Universalist fled from his refuge of lies; the gray-headed sinner cast himself at the feet of the Savior; and infant voices were heard proclaiming, 'Hosanna to the Son of David! Blessed is the King that cometh in the name of the Lord!'

"Meeting after meeting of this description was held. The everlasting gospel was preached, the blessing of God sent down, sinners converted, the church made glad, and heaven filled with rejoicing."

"Look at the example of our blessed Savior. He might have preached every Sabbath in the Jewish synagogue, if he had chosen; but he did not. On one Sabbath, he preached in the temple; on another, he preached on a mountain; at another time, he entered a boat, and thrust out a little from the shore, and taught the people from thence; at times, we find him in the wilderness, or in the grove, surrounded by many thousands, who had nothing better to sit on than the green grass. Nor did these crowds come out in the morning from their homes, and return the same evening; but they continued together day after day, to hear the Savior's words. At one time, we learn that they continued with him three days, where they had nothing to eat; and how much longer they continued

31

on other occasions, when they had made better preparations, we are not told. I have no doubt, that while the Savior designed the miracles that he wrought to confirm his divine mission in the view of all inquirers, he, at the same time, designed those miracles to wake up the public mind, and excite attention, that the people might come together, that he might have an opportunity of preaching to them the word of God. Accordingly, we find, when he began his wonderful works, that 'his fame went throughout all Syria. And there followed him great multitudes of people from Galilee, and from Decapolis, and from Jerusalem, and from Judea, and from beyond Jordan.' The immense results of the Savior's ministry to these vast congregations are amongst the things that 'are not written' in the New Testament; but, doubtless, the disclosures of the great day will show that they were worthy of the time and labor thus devoted.

"Now, if we wish all the inhabitants of our land to feel the blessed influences of the gospel, we must be willing, after the example of our Savior, to bring vast multitudes together, and let them remain together day after day, and preach to them the word of life. This must be done, this will be done, before all flesh sees the salvation of God.

"In this age of benevolent effort, Christians and Christian ministers are doing much to push forward the tract cause, the Bible cause, the Sunday school cause, &c.; but we have not made corresponding efforts to push forward the preaching cause, and yet it is by the foolishness of preaching that God is pleased to save them that believe. While we have been solicitous to prepare the way for the salvation of the rising generation by Sabbath schools, and the education of suitable young men for the ministry, have we done as much for the present generation as we ought? Have we employed the ministers now in the field to the best advantage? Without slacking the hand in any other good work, can we not make a more vigorous effort to save the present generation, who are past the period for Sabbath schools, and who must die, many of them, before the young men now in a course of education can enter the field? Yes, let a great effort be made to save the present generation."

CAMP MEETING ANECDOTE.

Great care was taken to preserve good order among the thousands that came together at our camp meetings. This was essential to the accomplishment of good. It was also of great importance because of the enemy; for there were many watching, eager to find fault, and raise the cry that our meetings were scenes of confusion and disorder. I would just here quote the remark of the venerable "skeleton preacher," that fault-finding is an easy business. It can be set up with a very small capital. It requires neither genius nor talent, neither education nor goodness, to fit out a fault-finder in business. I have seen men of little or no valuable endowments, — men who were scarcely worth a straw for any useful undertaking, or any effort at doing good, — who were, nevertheless, capital fault-finders, and could make themselves noisy and conspicuous in opposing the labors of others. Fault-finding — I repeat it — is a business that can be set up on "very small capital." Our plan was, to have seats prepared for all who might attend, and then, from the commencement of the public worship, require all the congregation to be seated. There is little difficulty in preserving good order during worship in the largest assembly, if they are comfortably seated ; but if they are compelled to stand up, there is danger that they may begin to whisper and talk among themselves, and thus become disorderly.

I had been called by the brethren to preside over the camp meeting at Sharon, in 1831. It had been in progress from Thursday noon until Saturday night. The whole scene had been solemn and delightful. The preaching was enlightened, captivating, and powerful. The seasons of prayer and praise were edifying and precious. The Holy Spirit brooded over the assembly. The awakened sinner exclaimed, " Surely God is in this place, and I knew it not ! " and the young convert answered, " This is none other but the house of God, and this is the gate of heaven."

Saturday night had come. The lamps were lighted, and suspended to the trees that stood here and there through the camp ground, and the seats before the pulpit were occupied by perhaps about two thousand people. But the congregation was not yet complete. New accessions were pouring in continually, and our custom was to occupy those who first collected with short addresses, and seasons of praise and prayer, until the assembly was full, and then we would have a regular sermon. During these preliminary services, a number of young men clustered around a tall sugar-tree that stood some twenty steps from the pulpit, and commenced a low-toned conversation. There was no palpable proof that they meant to be rude ; but still their position, right by the congregation of worshippers, and the hum of their continued conversation, was quite an annoyance. A statement was now made aloud from the pulpit, that the rules of our meeting required that all who met with us should be seated during the hours of public worship, and the hope was expressed, that with this regulation all would cheerfully comply; but the cluster around the tree remained unmoved, and the hum of their conversation seemed rather to rise than fall. It was now quite a disturbance, and had all the appearance of being the result of a preconcerted plan to give us trouble. Yet I wished, if possible, to get them seated and silenced without the necessity of a public rebuke. Rev. Mr. Stafford, of North Carolina, was there. I requested him to make an address to the assembly, of about ten minutes' length; for the people were still collecting, and the hour for the sermon had not yet come. Mr. Stafford's address was appropriate and powerful. The congregation were interested, but not a man in the circle round that tree moved or sat down, and the vexatious hum evidently increased. Mr. Cressey, of Salem, Indiana, was then requested to make a short address. Brother Cressey is now in glory. His address was admirable. The congregation hung on his lips with rapture and astonishment. He sat down; but around that tree the ring was unbroken, and their disorderly conversation was still kept up. A hymn was sung at the close of Mr. Cressey's exhortation, and during the hymn, I left the pulpit and took a seat in the crowd, half way from the pulpit to the circle around the tree. At the close of the hymn, I arose and said, "I have long endeavored to avoid giving any public rebuke for the improper conduct of an individual at a place of public worship. I believe the practice generally does more harm than good, and therefore I have shunned it. But now I am about to depart, for once, from my long-established practice. There was an individual here this morning that came for no good. Indeed, I understand that he came with the preconcerted design to do mischief, and make all the trouble he can. He was on the ground this afternoon. He is a very bad character, and I learn that he is here to-night. I am not speaking at random. I have documents in my possession to establish every word that I say. And as this matter of exposing an individual is somewhat trying, I mean to make thorough work now, as I have undertaken it, and I will tell you his name before I have done. Now, I wish you all to sit down," waving my hand to those around the tree. Instantly the tree was deserted; every man was seated and profoundly silent. During a pause here of some seconds, the interest was intense. Father Thomson and the ministers in the pulpit thought I was acting most rashly. They thought it likely that the individual alluded to, as soon as he should be named, would reply, and try to raise a party in his own defence, and that most likely a row would ensue. They seemed to catch their breath in the thrilling anxiety of the moment. I then proceeded: —

"The individual to whom I allude is a liar, a most notorious liar, and I am able to prove it on him by testimony that none of you will dispute: further, he is a thief!"

"O! O! O!" said low voices in the crowd.

"Yes, he is a thief; and more than all this, he is a murderer!"

"O, that is too bad!" said low voices in the crowd.

"No, it's not too bad. I tell you he is a murderer. I have the proof at hand. He is a murderer from the beginning. The proof to which I refer you is contained in the New Testament, and the name of this disorderly and troublesome individual is the Devil." Rarely has the name of the devil brought relief to so many anxious minds as on this occasion. The deep, long respiration, denoting that the burden was gone, could be distinctly heard from the pulpit, and from many in the crowd. I then, in few words, told them that the Scriptures warned them to beware of their adversary, the devil — that he is exceedingly malignant; the great foe of God and man — that he is very powerful, having no less than the tremendous energies of "archangel ruined" — that he goeth about as a roaring lion, seeking whom he may devour. Thus this address was speedily wound up; and then we had a sermon from another minister, to a very silent and attentive congregation, all seated in the most orderly manner.

I had almost forgotten the above incident, and perhaps it would have faded entirely from the pages of memory; but, some eight or nine years afterward, Dr. McKinney, now of Southern Missouri, came to my house at St. Charles. "Do you remember," said he, "the company of men at the Sharon camp meeting, in Ohio, who gathered around the sugar-tree, and kept talking after the commencement of worship, and refused to sit down when requested?"

"You remind me of the circumstance," said I.

"Well," said the doctor, "I was one of that company. I was not then a professor of religion; indeed, I was very far from it. A number of us had come down from Oxford. Gay, thoughtless young men, we had high notions of our consequence and independence and thought we were entitled to do very much as we pleased. We had been somewhat stiff, stubborn, and unruly through the day, though no public notice had been taken of us. I aspired to be something of a leader among those associates; and we had formed a mutual league, that we would stand shoulder to shoulder. When you commenced speaking of the individual that had come there for no good, but with the purpose of being troublesome, I began strongly to suspect that the reference was to me. The further the description advanced, the more exactly it appeared to fit my case. I became greatly alarmed, insomuch that even when those severe charges were made, 'the liar,' 'the thief,' 'the murderer,' conscience told me I was guilty of all. I had been *false* to God. I had vowed, and basely broken my vows. As a sinner, I had *robbed* God; and I deserved the charge. I had indulged *hatred* against my brother; and God calls such a murderer in the heart. I was awfully agitated; and when you said that you would tell the *name* of the offender, I fully calculated that my name would presently be called out before the whole assembly. When you requested the company to be seated, I was down in a moment; and never was I more relieved than when told that the offender was the devil; and never was I better pleased than when I found nothing more required of me than to keep my seat, and keep quiet, and listen to a good sermon."

Such was the narrative of Dr. McKinney; and the reader should know that he was now a Christian minister, preaching "that faith which once he destroyed."

RECOLLECTIONS OF DR. DAVID NELSON.

LETTER TO A FRIEND IN THE EAST.

"Dear Brother,—

"You inform me that you have been greatly interested in perusing the volume entitled 'The Cause and Cure of Infidelity,' by Dr. Nelson. You desire to know whether he has left any other writings than those contained in the book already named; and you further wish to be informed of the state of religious society at the west, in which such a man arose, lived, and labored. Dr. Nelson has left other theological writings, of great value, which have been in my possession since the period of his death. I design soon to give them to the public. It shall now be my aim in this letter, and the articles connected with it, to give you some such sketches of his life and times as may be for general edification. Having been born and educated in the same neighborhood with Dr. Nelson, graduated at the same college, licensed and ordained to the gospel ministry by the same presbytery, and for many years associated with him as co-editor of the Calvinistic Magazine, and fellow-laborer in preaching the gospel in the great and growing west, I gladly avail myself of this opportunity to 'speak that which I know, and testify that which I have seen.'

"The parents of Dr. Nelson settled in Washington county, East Tennessee, at a very early day in the history of that country. His father, Henry Nelson, was, for many of the later years of his life, a ruling elder in the Presbyterian church. His mother's maiden name was Kelsey. Her family stood high for intelligence and respectability. Dr. David Nelson was born in the year 1793 — in which month of that year I have not the means of knowing.

"Although the Indians were hostile at this period, a number of pious families had associated together, and formed a Christian church. Their preacher was Rev. Samuel Doak, a graduate of Princeton College, during the presidency of Dr. Witherspoon. This worthy and venerable man had emigrated to East Tennessee from the valley of Virginia, soon after the close of the revolutionary war; and he had collected some two or three little churches, in contiguous neighborhoods. Among these he labored as a minister of the gospel, while, at the same time, he devoted a portion of his attention to the instruction of youth. He founded, at this early day, a literary institution, known, at first, as Martin Academy, but ultimately as Washington College, which proved a source of rich and lasting blessing to the church, and to civil society. And now, since this worthy old patriarch has entered into his rest, we contemplate with amazement the immense results of his life and labors. Without support as a minister, without patronage as a teacher, he toiled on, amidst difficulties and discouragements, through a period of more than fifty years. He cultivated a farm, and kept a boarding-house, for the support of his family, while as a preacher and teacher he labored abundantly. As a herald of the gospel, he was remarkably efficient. The great Head of the church set many seals to his ministry, in 'souls renewed and sins forgiven,' through all the surrounding country, while many eminent lawyers, physicians, and statesmen were trained under his instructions; and the ministers of the gospel educated by him have proved a rich blessing to the church, in, perhaps, every one of the Western and Southern States. Faithful servant of Zion's God! though gone to thy reward in glory, thou art not forgotten in the church below; and while we embalm thy memory in our hearts, we will tell to generations following of that divine goodness which crowned thy abundant labors with such triumphant success.

"The early days of the west are gone. No future generation can arise, and witness what their fathers have seen. Now, the steamboat, with its travelling multitude, is on the bosom of our long rivers. Now, the hand of cultivation is stretched out over our broad and fertile plains. Now, cities, with their fifty thousand, and their hundred thousand inhabitants, are springing up here and there amongst us. But I remember the day when, in the older states of the west, the rivers and smaller streams were lined with the dense and almost impenetrable canebrake; when the plains and hills were covered with the rank, luxuriant peavine, so that you could follow the trail of the elk, the deer, or the buffalo, for hours together. I remember the period when, at nightfall, the wolf howled on the hill, and was answered by the scream of the panther; and the wild and warlike Indian, with his scalping-knife and tomahawk, was the terror of old and young. In those days, the habitation of the best families, even the most thrifty and enterprising, was the primitive log cabin, with its clapboard roof, its puncheon floor, and its wooden chimney, well daubed with clay; and often was the farmer called from his labors in the day, or roused from his slumbers in the night, to drive the bear from his hogs, the wolves from his cattle, or the thievish Indian from about his horse stable.

"In those days, every man, when he left his home, carried with him his rifle, and his weapons of defence. Farmers went in companies of six, eight, and ten, to plant and cultivate their fields: two or three would stand as sentinels, at different points, while the others performed the necessary work. Thus they went from field to field, till each man's land was tilled. When they met for public worship, it was in the same style. Each man came with his rifle in his hand; and a sufficient number were stationed to guard against surprise from the Indians, while the others listened to the tidings of the everlasting gospel. And just among the trials and distractions which I have mentioned, the precious gospel of the blessed God proved the bread of life, and the water of life, to many a hungry soul.

"Such was the state of society in which the early days of Dr. Nelson were passed, while it must be borne in mind that his parents were *reading Christians*, and the 'family book-desk,' as the doctor used to style it, was supplied with a respectable number of substantial volumes of Scotch divinity. Early in life, he memorized the Westminster Catechism. Not long before his death, he wrote an article on the subject of the benefit he received, when young, from Willison's work on the Catechism. He was deeply impressed during the great revival, though I know not that he entertained any hope of conversion at that period. When about seventeen years of age, he went to Kentucky, where his elder brother resided. There he engaged in the study of medicine, and afterwards went to Philadelphia, to attend the medical lectures. When the war with England was declared, he went into the army as a physician. There he became associated with a number of sceptical men; and, finally, he imbibed their dangerous and destructive views. He was now desperately wicked. His constitutional courage, of which he had much, now put on an aspect that might be termed savage. The first time that I remember to have seen him, after his return from the army, he was hurrying along the streets of Jonesborough, with a naked dirk in his hand, the very image of a reckless desperado. There had been a street fight in the village, and Nelson was in the midst of it, apparently highly entertained, and ready to act his part.

"At this period, his mother was much engaged in prayer in his behalf. She was a woman of deep piety. Her earnestness in prayer for him was remarkable. I saw and conversed with her often, about that time. She had, in her heart, set aside this son, from his childhood, for the service of God in the ministry. She had hoped much while he was serious in early youth; but now those hopes seemed blighted, and appearances were fearfully unfavorable. In prayer, she was importunate and persevering. Her importunity seemed to verge on agony. But she lived to receive an answer of peace; and her heart was glad. Her son regarded himself, while he lived, as a brand plucked from the burning, in answer to the prayers of a mother.

"In this brief sketch, I can notice but few particulars. I must not, however, neglect to mention that, after his conversion, he was, for a time, strongly inclined to Arminianism, and tried hard to reconcile it with the Bible. His own account of this portion of his history is contained in the following article, which he wrote soon after he commenced preaching: —

AN INEFFECTUAL STRUGGLE.

There was a young professor of religion, in the Presbyterian church, who felt very frequently a rising repugnance to the doctrines generally denominated Calvinistic. The secret workings of his heart, unknown to himself, (if they had been plainly translated,) ran nearly thus: "It were a pity those doctrines should be true: it is, in short, out of the question. I hope God will act more in accordance with my ideas of propriety. I must, if possible, find some passage of Scripture to overset them," &c. But to all the texts he could produce, proclaiming the general offer, the unlimited efficacy of the Savior's death, his having no pleasure in the death of the sinner, &c., &c., he received from his brethren one short and simple reply: "God offers salvation freely to all, through a Redeemer's blood. All as freely and with one accord reject it. Shall he let them all take their own road to death? or save all? We see he does neither, but makes as many willing in the day of his power as he chooses." And no matter what the number or variety of passages he cited, this answer (or the substance of it better expressed) was always ready, and seemed to fit the whole of them. His next undertaking was, to try and have those passages which seemed to declare God's eternal purposes explained so as to get them, if possible, out of his way. He was intimate with several pious and worthy men who did not believe the views of his church on those points, but thought them false and hurtful. To them, then, he would go with such a passage from the Bible as the following: "And they that dwell upon the earth shall wonder (whose names were not written in the book of life from the foundation of the world.)" (Rev. xvii. 8.) He would receive an explanation which would satisfy him for the time; but when he next opened his Bible, he would perhaps stumble upon Acts xiii. 48: "And as many as were ordained to eternal life believed." Here he would find that the former explanation would not fit this; for to say they were ordained to eternal life before they believed, would be election; and to say they were ordained after they believed, would prove the final perseverance; and yet it would appear that some time or other they were ordained. Again, he would go for an explanation to this and many other dark passages. Sometimes he would receive an explanation which appeared very satisfactory, and at others not so much so. But the greatest dilemma was, that almost every verse required a different road to get round it. And again, the task was endless; for it appeared that at least one half of the New Testament required him to have not only ingenuity and skill, but absolute *cunning*, to escape from the incessant bearing it had towards God's unqualified sovereignty. He could scarcely commence a chapter of the epistles in peace. Even the introduction was, "Paul called to be an apostle," (and he remembered that verily the call on the Damascus road was a cogent one,) — "to the church at Corinth," —

"called to be saints." Thought he, "Are not all called to be saints?" But perhaps he would next stumble upon 1 Cor. i. 26: "For ye see your calling, brethren, how that not many wise men after the flesh, not many mighty, not many noble, are called." Not only whole verses, but whole chapters, seemed to demand a dexterous transmutation. He had to suppose that an apostle of God, and a preacher of the everlasting gospel, not only did not speak of himself when he said *I*, but that when he said *I myself*, he meant an unconverted Jew!

In short, the labor of explanation thickened upon him so fast, that no versatility of talent, and no storehouse of memory, seemed sufficient to invent and retain the various shifts and expedients necessary to fortify him against the continual recurrence and multiplied and inexhaustible variety of expressions. "According as he hath chosen us in him before the foundation of the world, that we should be holy," &c.; "Having predestinated us unto the adoption of children," &c.; "Being predestinated according to the purpose of him who worketh all things after the counsel of his own will." (Eph. i. 4, 5, 11.) "Therefore hath he mercy on whom he will have mercy, and whom he will he hardeneth." (Rom. ix. 18.)

The conclusion he was finally forced into was,—

"Must I never open God's Holy Book without having to summon my ingenuity of evasion?

"Dare I resort to artifice in expounding so large a portion of the written will of my awful Creator?

"I may new translate his Testament; but will he acknowledge the edition?

"I may appear before his bar with my hundred nice-wrought expositions, and say they were all made to protect his character from the imputation of partiality; but will he thank me for the trouble I have taken? Or will he say, 'Who hath required this at your hands? Can I not defend my own character? Thoughtest thou that I was altogether such a one as thyself?'

"I might write folios by way of commentary, and, with indefatigable zeal, paint with a thin coloring the whole of the Sacred Oracles; 'but in the glare of the judgment day, it would all vanish like smoke.'"

"THE LEARNED SCHOOLMASTER.

"Dr. Nelson delighted much in the preaching of the gospel. This he regarded as God's appointed instrument for renovating and saving men. His aim was to obey the apostolic injunction, 'Be instant in season, out of season, reprove, rebuke, exhort with all long-suffering and doctrine.' He took a peculiar pleasure in preaching the gospel in destitute places, where few opportunities had been enjoyed. Like his divine Master, he had compassion on the multitude, who were wandering like sheep without a shepherd, and he would seize on any occasion by which the word of life might be proclaimed in their ears. The wayside, the mountain-top, the field, the grove, no place came amiss to such a preacher.

"In the year 1829, he was travelling among the mountains that divide Kentucky from the state of Tennessee. As the day was wearing to a close, he approached a little village, in which he determined to spend the night. It is well known that almost every neighborhood in the great west has its presiding genius, its literati, its great man. You will rarely find, even in the mountainous districts, a little community but its master spirit is there, an object of as much regard and veneration as John C. Calhoun at Charleston, Henry Clay at Lexington, or Daniel Webster at the city of Boston. Thus it was at the little village where Nelson had stopped for the night. There were two small houses of entertainment, on opposite sides of the street, each having its sign hung out, with appropriate inscriptions. Near one of these was a schoolmaster, surrounded with a delighted circle of listening admirers, while he expatiated on the unparalleled march of mind within the period of his own remembrance. Difficult and hitherto inaccessible heights of science had recently, he alleged, been scaled by learned men, like himself, while the philosophical world had gazed at the achievement in mute amazement. He was, in short, the exact duplicate of Goldsmith's country schoolmaster.

'His words of learned length and thundering sound
Amazed the gazing rustics ranged around;
And still they gazed, and still the wonder grew,
That one small head could carry all he knew.'

This illustrious genius had his literary harangue arrested in mid volley, by the halting of a stranger before the door of the tavern on the opposite side of the street. All eyes were at once turned in that direction.

"'There!' exclaimed the schoolmaster, "we'll go over and ask that man. I know that he is a scholar, by the looks of him.' So the whole party, lifting their feet with high expectation, came stalking over the street.

"'Stranger, can you tell me which is the greatest of all the sciences?' said the schoolmaster.

"'I can tell you which is the most important,' answered Nelson.

"'Well, let us hear, stranger.'

"'To fear and honor our Creator,' said Nelson.

"'Ah!' exclaimed the schoolmaster, raising both his hands, and stepping backward — 'ah, that kills me!'

"The company, whose admiration had been so highly excited by the exhibition of such rare endowment by this son of science, and who, while listening to his rhetorical flourishes, really regarded him as perhaps the most marvellous man within the circle of the literary world, were now perfectly stumbled and astounded on beholding their champion throw down his arms, call for quarter, and surrender at discretion, when the stranger had merely thrown himself into an attitude of defence. Here the modern schoolmaster fell far short of Goldsmith's hero, of whom he testifies,

'In arguing, too, the parson owned his skill;
For, e'en though vanquished, he could argue still.'

"All eyes were now, of course, turned to the newly-arrived gentleman, who was still on horseback. After staring for a few moments in silence, one, more bold than the rest, started forward.

"'Are you a preacher, sir?'

"'Yes,' said Nelson.

"'Suppose you preach for us to-night.'

"'Agreed,' said Nelson.

"'Well, I'll alarm the town.'

"'Start!' said Nelson.

"Away went this self-constituted towncrier, announcing to the people that a 'high-learned' man would preach at the court house at early candlelight.

"At the appointed hour, quite a congregation of plain, serious-looking people assembled. Dr. Nelson took his position among them, and commenced the services by singing his favorite hymn, —

'Lord, when I read the traitor's doom,' &c.

Many of those who have heard Nelson preach, will long remember that hymn. On the occasion of which I am now speaking, he proceeded, in his earnest and faithful manner, to preach to them 'the glorious gospel of the blessed God.' The fruit of his labors will appear 'at the resurrection of the just.' Such seasons were exceedingly precious in the estimation of Dr. Nelson. It was sowing the good seed where, with the blessing of God, it might spring up and bring forth fruit unto eternal life. It was the joy and rejoicing of his heart to be employed in such humble labors. He would often quote the apostle's language, (Eph. iii. 8,) 'Unto me, who am less than the least of all saints, is this grace given, that I should preach among the Gentiles the unsearchable riches of Christ.'

"THE STARTLED LANDLORD.

"Some critic has remarked of the Iliad of Homer, that it is a picture rather than a poem; that is, the scenes there appear to stand out before the eye, and the impression left upon the reader is, that he has beheld those scenes, rather than heard them described. Such was the preaching of Nelson. When he addressed an assembly, you were a spectator rather than a hearer. You *saw* the facts and scenes with which he wished to impress the mind. This characteristic also entered largely into his conversation. He had a peculiar power of throwing before the mind a vivid picture of that which he wished you to understand and feel. I will mention an example. Many of the plain country people, remote from large cities, have heard strange stories of dissecting-rooms, how dead bodies are dug up and brought from their graves into these places, and then cut to pieces by the doctors as ruthlessly as the butcher carves up his pork and his beef. Rumors of what is done in these dark dens have found their way into remote country districts, and have been rehearsed in circles of awe-stricken hearers, while the hair of their heads stood up, and their eyes seemed ready to start from their sockets.

"About the year 1830, Dr. Nelson spent a night at a public house among the mountains of Virginia. The landlord was a strong-built, jovial, merry-hearted man, who evidently was in the habit of using freely what the New England people call 'rum.' Early in the morning, Nelson was up, making arrangements for proceeding on his journey. The landlord, polite and attentive, was bestirring himself for the accommodation of his guest.

"'Come, stranger,' said he, setting out a bottle of spirits, 'help yourself to a morning dram.'

"'I don't drink spirits.'

"'Let me, however, recommend a little of this. The morning is chilly, and this is good as an "anti-fogmatic."'

"'Excuse me,' said Nelson, 'I know it to be injurious, and I would advise you to quit it.'

" 'Well,' said the landlord, with a horizontal shake of the head, and a self-satisfied strut across the room, 'if it is a poison, it is a very slow one. I've been trying it a great while, and I always find that a little does a man good.'

" 'Sir,' said Nelson, turning and looking him full in the face — 'sir, let me tell you that I'm a doctor; and I've cut open dead people. I've seen what frightful havoc this liquid fire that you are drinking makes on the inside of a man. You think that you are now in firm health; but I can tell by your looks that the work of destruction within you is far advanced. Could you have a view of your entrails at this moment, you would see them all dappled, streaked, and discolored by this deadly poison which you are drinking. Yes, you would now see great bloody knots there, dark and gory, as big as the end of my thumb.'

" Scarcely did Daniel's interpretation of the handwriting on the palace wall produce a more visible change in the countenance of the Babylonian king, than was made in the looks of our stout, jocular, but now *startled* landlord, by this account of the frightful inscriptions of King Alcohol on his inner man. In a moment his haughty airs were dropped, his proud strut abandoned; even his round, joyous face seemed to lengthen, and his short, chubby neck looked, for the time, surprisingly slim.

Nelson mounted his horse and resumed his journey. Whether his remarks produced on the landlord any thing beyond a mere temporary effect, he had never afterwards an opportunity to learn.

"A SCEPTIC IN TROUBLE.

"Dr. Nelson having been, for many years, a professed infidel, and intimately associated with that class of men, he ever appeared, after his conversion, to have a special concern for them. Where he could discover but the dim dawning of honest inquiry, and willingness to know the truth, his sympathies seemed inexhaustible. With untiring assiduity, he would labor night and day for the recovery of one such victim from the meshes of scepticism; but when, as was often the case, he encountered the *pride of ignorance*, — some little soul, who thought to render himself conspicuous by strutting against the ordinances of the Most High; some Tom Thumb, in the boots of the giant Incredulity, thinking to stride from hill to hill, over all that is sacred and venerable in society, — in such cases, he took high and peculiar delight in demolishing, at a single blow, the imaginary greatness of the self-deceiver. Like Abishai, the son of Zeruiah, his first blow was perfectly decisive. There was no need why he should 'smite a second time.' (1 Sam. xxvi. 8.) Many an anecdote is told in the west of inflated, towering, cloud-capped Infidelity, that was shivered to the ground by one flash of his terrible genius. An instance of this kind occurred in 1831. A fine steamboat, crowded with passengers, had left the wharf at Louisville for Cincinnati. The cabin was thronged with travellers, of genteel appearance, cheerful countenances, and engaging manners. An ignorant, conceited sceptic on board concluded that this was a favorable opportunity for making an advantageous display. To some who were near him he remarked, in a louder tone than others had thought proper to assume, 'The literary eminence of the age in which we live is matter of congratulation to all the real friends of man. The superstitions and prejudices of former generations are dissolving and disappearing before the full-orbed glory of modern science. The researches of learned men have, at length, ascertained, conclusively, that the Bible is false; and that the religion it teaches is without the shadow of foundation in truth.'

"'How's that?' said a passenger at a little distance. 'Do you say the Bible is false?'

"'I do, sir. The discoveries of modern science have established that fact beyond a doubt. The Bible is false, its history is fiction, its doctrines a delusion, its hopes a dream.'

"These 'great, swelling words of vanity' attracted considerable attention among those who were not otherwise occupied; yet no one attempted to contradict the sceptic, who, delighted to find himself an object of so much notoriety, went on to expatiate, for some time, as he fondly imagined, in a very learned strain, evidently supposing that, like certain committees of Congress, he was 'reporting progress,' in fine style. Dr. Nelson was sitting near, but judged it best, for a time, to 'give rope' to the boaster. When he thought matters had gone far enough, he turned to the sceptic — 'Have you made yourself acquainted with these subjects, sir?'

"'Yes, sir, I have,' was the confident reply.

"'You have examined, then, the discussion of learned men on these points, have you?'

"'Well — why — yes, I suppose I have.'

"'Can you tell me, sir, at what period it was that Cecrops founded the city of Athens?'

"'Cecrops?' demanded the sceptic, looking rather blank.

"'Yes, sir, Cecrops. At what period, or about what year, did he found the city of Athens?'

"'Well, sir, I believe, really, that I can't remember.'

"'Can you tell me, then, at what time it was that Cadmus introduced letters into Greece?'

"'Cadmus?' said the sceptic, with a look yet more woe-begone.

"'Yes, Cadmus, the founder of Grecian literature, as all the world knows. I asked you at what period he flourished.'

"'Why, I — I don't think I am acquainted with his history.'

"'Well, sir, at what time lived that notable individual named Phaëton, whose singular exploits are so largely celebrated by ancient poets?'

"'Phaëton?' said the sceptic, with lengthened visage, and an attitude that seemed to implore commiseration.

"'Yes, sir, Phaëton.'

"'I believe, sir, I don't know.'

"'My dear sir,' said Nelson, 'you should inform yourself before you presume to talk so confidently on these subjects.' Then casting on him, for a few seconds, a dry, withering look, the power of which none could know but those who felt it, the doctor turned entirely away, and engaged in conversation with those who sat near him. The crest-fallen sceptic presently shot for his state-room, and displayed himself no more during the remainder of the voyage. The style of his retreat resembled that of the prairie fox, whom the scorching flames have unexpectedly surrounded. He felt that he was sadly singed, and that all the company beheld him suddenly and surprisingly curtailed of his flowing honors.

"SACRED POETRY.

"In reference to sacred poetry, the mind of Dr. Nelson was endowed with peculiarly accurate and delicate perception. He possessed, in a very high degree, that exquisite intellectual relish, that nice discernment, which we denominate *taste*. Indeed, before his conversion, he delighted to revel amidst the gorgeous beauties of the English classics. Shakspeare, Milton, Dryden, Pope, Montgomery, Byron, and Walter Scott were his chosen companions; but after his mind and heart were turned to the Lord, Dr. Watts became his favorite author. Among English sacred poets, Dr. Watts stood, in his estimation, without a rival, while he valued highly some of the best productions of Cowper, Steele, Kirke White, and others.

"His extensive practice as a physician had led him to an intimate acquaintance with the mass of the common people. He found, by mingling familiarly among them, that a large proportion of the theological knowledge which they possess is embodied in the standard hymns of the church, which they have learned by memory. That individual, or that family, who have memorized eight or ten standard hymns, such as Dr. Watts's 2d and 7th hymns of Book I., and 9th, 30th, 66th, 69th, and 107th, Book II., and 1st and 13th of

Book III., — those, I repeat it, who have these hymns well fixed in their minds, are possessed of much important gospel knowledge. In no other form, where the English language is spoken, has divine truth, during the last hundred years, reached so many immortal souls, as through these and similar standard hymns. On this account, they were greatly valued by Dr. Nelson. These standard hymns were also very highly valued by him for the purpose of *admonition*. He regarded the exhortation of the apostle, when he enjoined on the church the duty of 'teaching and admonishing one another in psalms, and hymns, and spiritual songs.' Dr. Nelson would often sing one of those instructive and impressive hymns alone, at the commencement or at the close of a sermon, without reading it, or first repeating the lines. He believed that the divine truth embodied in one of these sacred songs, when it is sung 'with the spirit, and with the understanding,' is often blessed in arresting the attention and awakening the conscience of the hearer, when a solemn sermon may have entirely failed. Thus he often used singing as a species of sacred rhetoric, for the purpose of extending the knowledge and the impression of gospel truths among the children of men.

"He also commended the standard hymns of the church, because they were such effective sources of consolation to the afflicted. Often, while as a physician he was among the sick and the dying, he found the sufferer sustained and cheered by the precious, divine truth contained in some rich stanza, such as the following: —

'O, if my Lord would come and meet,
My soul should stretch her wings in haste,

Fly fearless through death's iron gate,
Nor feel the terrors as she passed.

'Jesus can make a dying bed
Feel soft as downy pillows are;
While on his breast I lean my head,
And breathe my life out sweetly there.'

"In the social circle, he delighted to take Dr. Watts's Psalms and Hymns, and read, and point out the beauties of favorite passages. I have heard him expatiate, in such circumstances, on the 3d stanza of the 2d hymn, Book I.: —

'Ere Sin was born, or Satan fell,
He led the host of morning stars:
Thy generation who can tell,
Or count the number of thy years?'

In the two former stanzas of this hymn, the poet has been dwelling on the divine grandeur of Christ. He pursues the same theme through the first two lines of this stanza; then his soul is suddenly so overwhelmed with the ineffable glory of Immanuel, that he breaks off abruptly from description, and bursts forth into adoration, closing the stanza with a sublime reference to the eternity of the Son of God. The 69th hymn of Book II., on the subject of God's faithfulness in fulfilling his promises, and the firmness of his word, was a great favorite with Dr. Nelson. I have heard him dwell on the 6th and 7th stanzas of that hymn with an enthusiasm that bordered on rapture: —

'His every word of grace is strong
As that which built the skies;
The voice that rolls the stars along
Speaks all the promises.

'He said, *Let the wide heavens be spread,*
And heaven was stretched abroad;
Abra'am, I'll be thy God, he said,
And he was Abra'am's God.'

"It is much to be regretted, that, in so many of the American editions of Watts, the corruption 'very,' instead of 'every,' should have crept into the first line of the above quotation. The stanza, as Watts wrote it, is one of the finest in the English language; but when 'very' is suffered to usurp the place of 'every,' a sad eclipse is thrown over the whole stanza.

"Dr. Nelson's poetical powers, which were of a high order, and his exquisite and carefully-cultivated taste for compositions of that kind, prepared him to place a proper estimate on that wretched mania for mutilating standard hymns, which has been the vexation and scourge of the church for a number of the past years. He regarded the cutting to pieces, or, as he sometimes expressed it, the 'scalping and tomahawking' of a beautiful hymn, which the judgment and good taste of the church has sanctioned for, perhaps, a hundred years, as a grievous outrage, which the perpetrator has no right to expect the Christian public to endure. His views are, in substance, the following: —

"1. It is flagrant injustice to the *author* whose name is used. Hymns are now circulated over the name of 'Watts,' that Watts never saw. Not only entire lines, but whole stanzas, of miserable doggerel, that had no existence till long since Watts left the world, are now published over the name of that 'sweet singer of Israel;' and the public are told that the author is 'Watts.' This is falsehood and injustice. You would not allow a worthy man to be slandered, merely because he had crossed the ocean, and is now in Europe. He is in existence still, and still has his rights. And will you allow that the worthy man who has crossed the 'narrow sea' that divides earth from heaven, has no claim to be treated with truth and justice? Is it not as wrong to misrepresent the dead as the absent? And because the name of Watts, attached to a hymn, will induce the public to buy the book containing that hymn, is that a reason why the great poet should be made to father wretched doggerel, scribbled by some mutilator, whose brain never was capable of producing even the abortion of a poetical idea? How indignantly did John Wesley protest against the conduct of those who attempted to introduce lean, poverty-stricken hymns into public notice, by attaching to them his name, and the name of his brother Charles! Shall the dead be slandered, and the church sanction it? Jesus Christ maintained that Abraham, and Isaac, and Jacob are yet living, (Matt. xxii. 32,) and yet retain their relation to the God of the living. Shall Abraham be represented as saying what he never said? as teaching what he never taught? And why should this injurious violation of truth be allowed in the case of a modern saint, — Watts, or Cowper, or Steele?

"2. The mutilation of standard hymns is a great annoyance to the church. Many of those who delight in the praises of God have committed to memory quite a number of the choice hymns which the church has been using for a long series of years. These have become very dear to them, not only because of their intrinsic value, but by reason of many interesting and precious associations in Christian history and experience.

But, lo! suddenly up starts an inflated, fidgety mutilator, and protests that the hymn which the church has sanctioned and enjoyed for a hundred years is 'wrong end up, wrong side out, and wrong foot foremost,' and that there is a clear call in providence for him to *revise* and *improve* it. So at it he goes; and, by the time he is done, lackaday! you may apply to it the description given by the Scotch poet of one of his heroes: —

'Poor wretch! the mother that him bare,
If she had been in presence there,
In his wan cheek, and sunburnt hair,
She had not known her son.'

The fact is notorious, that, since the irruption of the hordes of hymn-mutilators into the church, *congregations* have, to a mournful extent, given up the singing of God's praises in his sanctuary. How can it be otherwise, when reckless pretenders are suffered to tamper with and mar the songs of Zion, until they retain scarcely the ghost of resemblance to their former beauty and perfection?

"3. Dr. Nelson regarded the conduct of the mutilator as insufferably presumptuous. Who is this that, without the shadow of claim to poetical talent, rashly presumes to tear to tatters the sublime productions of exalted genius? Shall the friends and admirers of Watts, Cowper, and Henry Kirke White look on this wanton havoc, and be silent?

"4. He maintained, further, that it was a plain violation of the ninth commandment. He who writes a string of wretched doggerel himself, and then proclaims to the public that Watts wrote it, bears false witness against his neighbor.

"5. And, moreover, it is altogether a question whether the mutilator is not guilty in the eye of the sixth commandment. There is certainly 'hymn-slaughter' in the case; for the crippled hymn, or, as Nelson expressed it, the hymn that has been 'scalped and tomahawked,' invariably dies. Its lot is more melancholy than that of the poor man who 'went down from Jerusalem to Jericho,' and was 'stripped of his raiment, and wounded, and left *half dead;*' for the wounded hymn dies out and out. It dies in the esteem and affection of the church. It is not sung in *its mutilated form* in the prayer meeting, or in the social circle. It is dead, and, if remembered at all, with interest, it is as you remember a murdered friend: the interest is in the memory of what it once was, and not in the mangled remains now before you.

"Dr. Nelson would sometimes talk familiarly of scenes that he believed would take place in the next world. He believed, with Milton, that there may be more likeness between things in heaven and things on earth than is often imagined. He would sometimes entertain his friends with an account of Watts, Cowper, and Steele meeting the hymn mutilator in a future state. The scales that prevented him from seeing the beauty of their productions will then have fallen from his eyes, and he will be heartily ashamed of what he has done; and should he, when walking along the streets of the New Jerusalem, discover Dr. Watts coming towards him, how eagerly will he look round for a by-lane or alley, that he may speedily turn a corner, and escape from the eye of one on whose works he had perpetrated such outrageous mischief!"

ARMINIANISM *vs.* THE MILLENNIUM.

No impartial man can examine the subject carefully, without being fully convinced, that if the peculiar doctrines of Arminianism be true, there never will be a millennium; and, on the other hand, that if it be true that a millennial day is approaching, then the peculiar doctrines of Arminianism are unquestionably groundless; and when that bright day of Zion's glory arrives, all nations of the earth will look upon those peculiar sentiments for which our Arminian friends now contend so zealously, as nothing better than "wind and confusion."

No Arminian can avoid seeing, that if he admits that God designs to convert the whole world at a "set time," (Ps. cii. 13,) he admits, broadly and fully, what Calvinists have always meant by the "purpose of God according to election;" for the most remarkable instance of God's *electing love*, is his determination to convert and save all nations in the millennial day.

No Arminian can avoid seeing, that if he admits that the Lord will "make bare his arm" in the latter day, and turn all families of the earth from Satan to God, then he admits the very doctrine of *effectual calling*, against which Arminians have so long and so violently contended.

No Arminian can avoid seeing, that if he admits

that in the latter day Zion's King will "take to him his great power," and subdue all hearts to the obedience of the gospel, then he admits the doctrine of divine sovereignty; for all acknowledge that God did not subdue the hearts of all men in the days of Sodom and Gomorrah, or in any age that has yet passed.

No Arminian can avoid seeing, that if he admits there will be a long millennial day, a thousand prophetic years, in which there shall be "none to hurt or destroy in all God's holy mountain," then away goes his favorite doctrine of "falling from grace;" for the inhabitants of the earth will not only be converted at first, but they will *remain* converted. They will persevere in holiness till the end of life.

Thus it is evident, that when the light of the millennial morning bursts upon our world, the mists and clouds which now obscure the vision of many professing Christians will be rolled away, and divine truth will stand out with "sevenfold" brightness in the view of all nations.

The question may now arise, What will our Arminian friends do, in view of the conclusive evidence which God's promise of a millennium furnishes against their peculiar sentiments? I answer, some of them, when they look at this subject candidly, and see how absolutely inconsistent their doctrines are with the promise of God, that the whole earth shall be converted in the latter day, will doubtless renounce their errors, and embrace the truth. Of this I am persuaded, for, —

1. All Christians love truth when it is clearly perceived by the mind; and, although there are many ways in which their minds may be prejudiced, and led

to take a perverted view of certain Scripture doctrines, yet error is not the native element of the renovated heart. And we are assured that, when all hearts are renewed, and all prejudice is put down, and all misrepresentation is done away, then all the inhabitants of the earth shall see eye to eye.

2. We see that, as the Scriptures are examined more and more, many are coming over from error to the side of truth. In the county where I live, I calculate there are now many stanch advocates for the doctrines of sovereign grace, where there was one twenty years ago. Knowledge increases, and truth advances, as the day of the Lord draws nigh.

3. All Christians admit that, in the millennium, the church will be much more enlightened than at the present time. Show any denomination that the peculiarities for which they contend will certainly be rejected by the whole church during the millennium, and at once their faith in those peculiarities is shaken. No good man is willing to make efforts for the propagation of sentiments which he clearly sees the whole church will reject as soon as God's glory fills the earth. For these reasons, I doubt not that many who have hitherto stood up for the peculiarities of Arminianism will give up the contest, and admit they had been mistaken, as soon as they perceive the absolute inconsistency of those doctrines with the promise of God that all nations shall be converted "in his time." But will all renounce these errors? Not immediately. Error will not quit the field without a violent struggle. And although I cannot attempt to point out all the arts that will be employed to prop a tottering cause, yet the principal one will be, to deny absolutely that God will

ever grant to the church a millennium, in which, for many ages, "all shall know the Lord, from the least to the greatest." I have no doubt that, so soon as those Arminians who are determined to yield to no array of argument, discover how totally irreconcilable the hope of a millennium is with the leading features of their scheme, they will come out and broadly deny that there will ever be a day of millennial glory enjoyed by the church on earth. Nor let this be thought incredible. We find that the advocates of error have, on former occasions, acted a part altogether as strange, and have denied doctrines as plainly taught in the Scriptures as the doctrine of a millennium is or can be. I will mention one instance. In the days of President Edwards, Arminians in Europe and America had breathed out much complaint against the doctrine of God's decrees, pronouncing it absurd, ridiculous, inconsistent, &c. &c. Edwards took up his pen and showed them, that the doctrine was not only most clearly taught in the Bible, which they professed to believe, but that it was also necessarily connected with the doctrine of God's foreknowledge, which they all maintained; for, said Edwards, if God foreknows all events with absolute certainty, before they take place, then they must be fixed and certain before they take place; for it is absurd to suppose that God knows that to be certain which is uncertain. And if God has foreknown all events from eternity, then they must have been fixed and certain from eternity. But if so, some being must have fixed them, or made them certain; but no being existed from eternity but God. He therefore must have fixed them, in his eternal purpose. Such was Edwards's argument from the admitted doctrine of foreknowledge — an argument too plain to be misunderstood, and too powerful to be encountered. The champions of error were not a little perplexed with this view of the subject. "And one spake after this manner, and another after that manner," all feeling that something must be done to save their favorite sentiments, yet each at a loss to know what that something was. At length it seems to have been agreed that the plain, unvarnished doctrine of God's foreknowledge is inconsistent with many of the Arminian peculiarities. And consequently, singular methods have been resorted to, either to put down that doctrine entirely, or so to "darken counsel by words without knowledge," that the force of Edwards's argument might not be felt.

One class allege, that the actions of free agents are contingencies in themselves, until they take place; and therefore it is not dishonoring God to say, that he cannot foreknow them with certainty; for how can that be certain in the view of God, which is uncertain in itself? This subterfuge, however plausible in the eyes of those who use it, is unfortunately directly in the teeth of those Scripture passages where the Lord foretells the actions of free agents. He foretold that Solomon should build the temple, that Cyrus should take Babylon, that Herod would slay the children in Bethlehem, and that Peter would deny his master. These, and a thousand other instances, show that the future actions of men are not uncertain in the view of God, for he can foretell them, and of course does foreknow them with absolute certainty.

Another class, conscious that the above scheme of escaping from Edwards's argument would not do, have alleged that, in the view of the Almighty, no events are past, and none are to come; that all things are present with him from everlasting to everlasting; and therefore it is not proper to speak of God's *foreknowledge*, for in his view one event does not take place before another, as in ours, but all events stand equally present with him from the beginning to the end of time. On this scheme I would remark, —

1. It is an improvement in theology that has been discovered since the days of the apostles. Neither Peter nor Paul was aware that it is improper to speak of God's foreknowledge. One says to the Jews, "Him being delivered by the determinate counsel and foreknowledge of God, ye have taken," &c. The other says to the Romans, "Whom he did foreknow he also did predestinate." Mistaken apostles! Had they only penetrated into the subject far enough to discover that with the Lord there is, properly speaking, no foreknowledge, and that, in his view, one event does not take place before another, they might have avoided such gross blunders.

2. If Arminians are correct when they say that, in the view of the Lord, one event does not take place before another, but all events have in his view the same present existence, whether, with respect to us, they are present, or a thousand years past, or a thousand years to come, then it will follow that, in the view of the Almighty, a man is not born before he dies, for he does not view one event as taking place before another. In the view of the Almighty, Noah's flood did not take place before the American revolution. In the view of the Almighty, Isaiah did not preach in Jerusalem before Wesley preached in England; the Bible was not written before the Almanac for A. D. 1850; the

law was not given by Moses before the coming of Christ; the world was not created before the judgment day.

3. If it be true, that with the Almighty there is no foreknowledge,—that those events which in our view are future, are present in his, so that he does not foresee them, or look upon them as things yet to come, but views them as now in actual existence,—then it will follow, that all the saints now on earth are now, in the view of the Almighty, as holy and as happy as they will ever be. There will never come a period when God will view them in heaven any more than he does now; and all the wicked are now, in the view of the Lord, as absolutely in hell as they will ever be; and not only so, but it has been thus from the foundation of the world—there is no foreknowledge with God. On the morning of creation, he did not look forward and see that, in after ages, some of Adam's race would rise to heaven, and others be cast down to hell. But in his view, it was all then present; it had actually taken place as really as it ever will! This throws Calvinism into the shade! Arminians have long exclaimed against the Calvinistic doctrines, because they represent God as having determined, before the foundation of the world, to take a part of mankind—the righteous—to heaven, and to send another part—the wicked—to hell. But according to their own scheme, which we have been noticing, the Lord not only determined to do this, but in his view it was actually done,

> "Ere sin was born, or Adam's dust
> Was fashioned into man."

The saints were placed in heaven, and the sinners were

sent to hell, as really as they will ever be. Such are the monstrous absurdities into which men will run, in order to support a favorite scheme. And now you may calculate that the doctrine of a millennium will be denied, as certainly as the doctrine of foreknowledge has been. For every one must see that the promise of the millennium is as totally irreconcilable with the peculiar doctrines of Arminianism, as the doctrine of foreknowledge is with their scheme in relation to divine decrees.

They will come out and broadly deny that the whole earth will be converted, and remain converted for a thousand prophetic years.

REVIVAL MEASURES.

To us, short-sighted mortals, it seems matter of regret that a controversy about *revival measures* should ever have sprung up in the Christian church. As this world perishes by *neglecting* the great salvation, it is impossible for one man to legislate for another, how he may most successfully, in all cases, call up public attention to the great truths of the gospel. Let the right thing be attempted at the right time, in the right spirit, and by the right man, with judgment and good taste, and the results will be admirable. But let the ass attempt to put on the lion's hide, or the crow undertake to emulate the eagle, and you will have a dolorous account of the indiscreetness and the unhappy character of the *measure*. The agitation of this subject has often reminded me of the notable lines of Pope: —

> "For forms of government let fools contest;
> That which is best administered is best."

Dr. Anderson, of Maryville, Tennessee, came forward during a sacramental meeting to receive into the communion of the church a large company of young converts. The assembly was crowded, the solemnity intense, and the stillness awful, while every eye was fixed on the affecting scene. In that congregation were a number of professed infidels. Some of them avowed Deism, some Atheism; but they were men of genteel manners, who, in a Christian assembly, would deport themselves with the utmost propriety.

The solemn profession of the religion of Jesus Christ was now made, the young converts took the vows of God upon them, and then all who had not received baptism in infancy came forward one by one, and kneeling down on a little platform in front of the pulpit, were baptized "in the name of the Father, and of the Son, and of the Holy Ghost." At the close of this deeply interesting service, Dr. Anderson made a brief address to the young converts, exhorting them to "walk worthy" of the high and holy "vocation wherewith they were called."

"A wicked world," he exclaimed, "will watch for your halting. It has crucified your Lord and Master, and with malicious eagerness and hellish skill it will spread its snares for you. With flattering vanities, with deceitful smiles, with bewitching arts, it will labor to turn your feet aside, that religion may be dishonored, that the Savior may be wounded in the house of his friends, and sadness, sorrow, and despair, brought into your own souls. O, watch and pray. Spurn temptation. Resist all the artifices of sin, of Satan, and of hell. O, follow the Lord fully. Serve him with all your heart. Lay aside every weight, and the sin that does so easily beset you, and run with patience the race that is set before you, looking unto Jesus, the Author and Finisher of faith. Never faint or tire, until you have gained the mark of the prize of the high calling of God in Christ Jesus our Lord. So shall your Redeemer be honored, the name of your God exalted, your own souls divinely blessed, and others shall see your good works and glorify your Father who is in heaven. And now I turn to the ungodly part of this assembly. Ye candidates for the second death, I turn to you. You have witnessed this solemn transaction. You have witnessed the consecration of these immortal souls to God. You have heard their vows of eternal allegiance to King Jesus. Now, though you have rejected the gospel for your own souls, though you have judged yourselves unworthy of eternal life, yet, in behalf of these who have named the name of the Lord Jesus, I appeal to you. Does not conscience tell you that, though you have chosen the downward road, yet it is best for them that they should prove faithful unto death? that they should be firm in the service of their God? Unto you, O men, I call! You, whose backs are turned on heaven; you, whose faces are set for dungeons of hell; you, who are hastening headlong towards the worm that never dies, and the fire that never shall be quenched, — I appeal to you. Will not you pledge yourselves to-day, that you will throw no stumbling-blocks in the way of these souls? that you will not attempt to entangle them in the net of perdition, and drag them down with you to the agonies and the darkness of hell? And now let every man that, before earth and heaven, is willing to enter into this solemn pledge, signify it by holding up his right hand." The solemnity was overwhelming. The burning zeal of the minister kindled a flame through the entire audience; right hands arose, and were held up over the whole congregation. The sinner's heart trembled because of the presence of the God of the whole earth; the Christian bowed his head, and worshipped, saying, with the venerable patriarch of old, "This is the gate of heaven." The first right hand that was lifted up, in this memorable scene, was that of Dr. McGee. He had professed, for many years, to be a confirmed atheist. He was a scholar, a gentleman, and possessed many amiable endowments, but had long been settled down in absolute atheism. Argument had been tried with him by many strong men, but he seemed immovable as the cliffs of the Alleghany. This atheistical Dr. McGee was the first man to hold up his right hand in the above-described scene. Within a short time, he came before the congregation, and publicly renounced his atheism, and solemnly professed his repentance and his faith in the Lord Jesus. Long will the church at Maryville remember the day when Dr. McGee, with tears of penitence for the follies of his past life, asked to be received into their communion, and they gave him the right hand of fellowship in the service of their God. The doctor soon became a preacher of that faith which once he destroyed, and lived many years to adorn the gospel profession by a holy life, and proclaim the riches of a Savior's love to dying men.

Such is a brief history of one of the boldest, strongest, and *newest* measures that I ever saw attempted in a revival of religion; and yet, perhaps not one of the vast assembly present ever dreamed of calling in question its propriety or its usefulness. Why? Because it was done with judgment and good taste. It was done in the right spirit, at the right time, in the right circumstances, and by the right man. But now let the wrong man, without judgment or good taste, attempt such a measure, and he will soon be in a condition to deliver lectures or publish letters on the "evils of revivals."

TEMPERANCE SONG.

THE following ode was composed at the request of Governor Boggs, of Missouri, and sung in the presence of the members of the legislature, in the hall of the House of Representatives, February, in the year 1843: —

WHEN the dark cloud of war threw its gloom round our land,
And the rod of the tyrant was o'er us suspended,
Our fathers aroused, "put their life in their hand,"
And bravely and nobly their country defended.
Then Victory's bright crown encircled their head;
The haughty invader was routed, and fled;
And the "star-spangled banner in triumph did wave
O'er the land of the free and the home of the brave."

But a deadlier foe still was lurking around —
A foe more insidious, and deeply annoying,
Inflicting on health an incurable wound,
And the life of the soul and the body destroying.
We've roused, like our sires, our country to free;
Already is dawning the glad jubilee;
And the temperance "banner in triumph shall wave
O'er the land of the free and the home of the brave."

'Twas an empire of woe, with a despot enthroned;
The tears of the mother and widow were streaming,
While around them, in rags, and starving for bread,
Neglected and fatherless children were screaming.
But loud notes of joy on the breezes now swell;
Our country 's all rising, the foe to expel;
And the temperance "banner in triumph shall wave
O'er the land of the free and the home of the brave."

'Twas a long, dreary night, fraught with danger and death;
  Diseases and vices around us were prowling;
O, the "darkness was thick!" 'twas a night of despair,
  And the voice of a terrible tempest was howling.
    But the star of the morn now rises in sight,
    And a new, lovely day is diffusing its light;
    And the temperance "banner in triumph shall wave
    O'er the land of the free and the home of the brave."

'Twas a deluge of fire that invaded our land,
  And mingled hot poison in life's sweetest fountains;
O, it flooded our fields, and swelled o'er the hills,
  And rolled its huge billows above the tall mountains!
    But the dove now returns, with the "olive leaf" green;
    Lo! spanning the heav'ns a bright rainbow is seen;
    And the temperance "banner in triumph shall wave
    O'er the land of the free and the home of the brave."

O, how blest is our cause, where friends all unite, —
  The son and the father, the husband and brother, —
While beauty looks on, and cheers us with smiles, —
  The sister, the daughter, the wife, and the mother!
    Come, enlist in this cause; let all hearts agree;
    Come, *down with your name*, and the land shall be free;
    And the temperance "banner in triumph shall wave
    O'er the land of the free and the home of the brave."

O, how happy our land, where the bounty of God
  Flows freely and richly, and broad as a river,
While the gospel appears in robes of pure white,
  And points us to blessings forever and ever!
    Hail! dear native land, in loveliness dressed,
    Through ages on ages, thy children be blessed;
    And the temperance banner — O, "long may it wave
    O'er the land of the free and the home of the brave!"

PATRIOTIC SONG OF THE TENNESSEEAN.

Why wander from our early home,
  Impelled by hope or fear,
Since bounteous Heaven hath richly shed
  Its choicest blessings here?
Our homes are sweet, our friends are kind,
  Our children hale and free;
"And the best of land, we understand,
  Is'n the bend of the Tennessee."

We envy not the frozen north,
  Its fields of ice and snow;
We envy not the torrid south,
  Its sun's o'erpowering glow.
From scorching heat, from piercing cold,
  Our happy clime is free;
"And the best of land, we understand,
  Is'n the bend of the Tennessee."

In days long past, our fathers came
  As pilgrims to the west,
And reared their rude and humble homes
  On thy fair, bounteous breast.
While panther, wolf, and Indian howled,
  They fixed their choice on thee.
"O, the best of land, we understand,
  Is'n the bend of the Tennessee!"

Like olive-plants, in blooming youth,
  Thy duteous daughters rise,

Adorned with charity and truth,
  Endowments from the skies.
How oft they've taught the child of woe
  To keep a jubilee!
"O, the best of land, we understand,
  Is'n the bend of the Tennessee!"

How promptly, at our country's call,
  Thy sons have sallied forth,
And in the bloody battle-field
  Have proved their matchless worth!
Before their arms the invading foe
  Was forced to turn and flee.
"O, the best of land, we understand,
  Is'n the bend of the Tennessee!"

Our sister states rehearse the deeds
  Of many a valiant son,
Of Taylor, Perry, Gaines, and Scott,
  And honored Harrison.
We love them all, but can't forget
  Our own tall HICKORY TREE.
"O, the best of land, we understand,
  Is'n the bend of the Tennessee!"

I've wandered long, and wandered far,
  Almost from pole to pole;
Yet still the thought of early friends
  Is precious to my soul.
Till life's last hour, my tongue shall speak
  In warmest terms of thee.
"O, the best of land, we understand,
  Is'n the bend of the Tennessee!"

END.

www.ingramcontent.com/pod-product-compliance
Lightning Source LLC
LaVergne TN
LVHW020107110826
845151LV00001B/90

* 9 7 8 1 4 2 5 5 4 4 3 4 8 *